CW00918936

1000 IDEAS BY 100 ARCHITECTS

SERGI COSTA DURAN
MARIANA R. EGUARAS

ROCKPORT PUBLISHERS
BEVERLY MASSACHUSETTS

First published in the United States of America by
Rockport Publishers, a member of
Quayside Publishing Group
100 Cummings Center, Suite 406L
Beverly, MA 01915
Telephone: (978) 282-9590
Fax: (978) 283-2742
www.rockpub.com

ISBN-13: 978-1-59253-573-6
ISBN-10: 1-59253-573-9

Editorial Coordinator: Simone K. Schleifer

Assistant Editorial Coordinator: Aitana Lleonart

Editorial Assistant: Cristina Paredes

Editor in chief: Sergi Costa Duran

Editor: Mariana R. Eguaras

Text: © by participating architects

Translation: Cillero & de Motta Traducción

Art Director: Mireia Casanovas Soley

Design and layout coordination: Claudia Martínez Alonso

Layout: Cristina Simó, Esperanza Escudero Pino

Editorial project:
2009 © LOFT Publications
Via Laietana, 32, 4th floor, Of. 92
08003 Barcelona, Spain
Tel.: +34 932 688 088
Fax: +34 932 687 073
loft@loftpublications.com
www.loftpublications.com

Printed in China

contents

Of concepts and realities: notes on the making of *1000 Ideas by 100 Architects*

The main aim of this book is to give a star role to the architects involved. Unlikely as it may seem, many other publications on architecture and interior design do not quite achieve this, since it is the editor who decides which projects should appear and what they should look like.

Before embarking upon this project, we envisaged a book that would be highly practical, and we conveyed this vision to the architects. We offered these pages as a platform for speaking, choosing, and writing about certain projects was the element that appealed to most of those who wanted to or were able to participate. Something similar to having given them the microphone and asked for a ten minute speech in front of a large convention of architects or architecture students—this is how we wanted the architect to feel. And we hope this has been the end result.

While drawing up the contents for this publication there were a series of anecdotes that are well worth a mention. First, were the numbers, always present in the world of architecture. For every three participation requests we sent out, we received one confirmation, thus re-shaping the idea that architecture is a demanding profession, and showing the difficulty of involving architects whose studios have greater consequence on the global stage.

Second, we used four main selection criteria when choosing participants: a) studios with more than ten years of practice; b) the widest possible geographical diversity; c) a broad representation of markets (residential, institutional, corporate buildings, etc.); d) that 80 per cent of projects were completed or were underway in order to give the book the desired practicality. Likewise, another important factor, although this was not a determining one, was that a large proportion of studios should have a line of sustainable architecture projects, as we believe this represents the design of today and tomorrow.

We wish to express our satisfaction with the line-up of participants, including specialists in green architecture (Kirkland Fraser Moor and Bruno Stagno), young talent in the field of green urbanism (Ecosistema Urbano), revered figures in spiritual architecture (Imre Makovecz), and well-established architects' studios, such as Ingenhoven Architects, Boora Architects, or Mario Botta Architetto. Not forgetting, of course, the participation of prestigious landscape architects, such as Paolo Bürgi and Latz & Partner. And, bearing in mind that the green revolution sweeping through architecture is reliant on knowledge of new materials and experimentation into them, we also thought that the participation of specialists from academic circles, such as Blaine Brownell or Field Office, was essential.

Europe and the United States generally receive a bias in architectural texts, although some efforts have been made—sometimes rather unsuccessfully—to give a slant toward the more traditionally ignored studios of North Africa, the Middle East and the Far East, where Japan is a real architectural hotspot. In this book, we believed the wider the geographical representation the better; this was another pivotal factor defining the contents of these pages.

We have always aimed to make this publication an important tool for its target readership, that is to say, architects and students. When assessing the overall results, we found some very interesting proposals, some of them recurrent, as can be seen in the different tips.

Some participants opted to give a short explanation of the architectural concept (we hope that some are not a little too abstract for the reader), while others seem to have been pushed for time to be able to fully express the details of the *raison d'être* of their designs. Nevertheless, for the editor, it has been a great pleasure to learn a little more of the thought processes of all the participants through their tips and the corresponding images. And we wish to thank the architects for bringing the end results closer to the reader.

Sergi Costa Duran

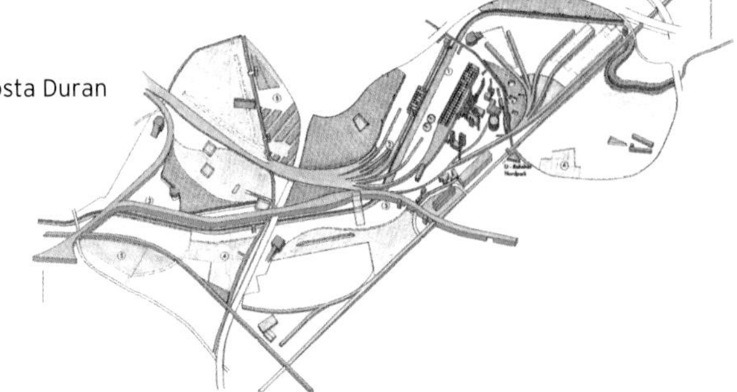

MITHUN
architects+designers+planners

Pier 56, 1201 Alaskan Way, Ste. 200
Seattle, WA 98101, USA
P.: (+1) 206-623-3344
www.mithun.com

0001

Do the Math

Equations underpin the relationship between a finished project and its component parts. Focusing on the math means goal setting with metrics, a consistent rigor in specifications, merging spirit with economics, and seizing every opportunity to push for new knowledge in science and design. At Yesler Community Center in Seattle (Washington), building aperture and ventilation strategies are interwoven to provide natural lighting and eliminate air conditioning.

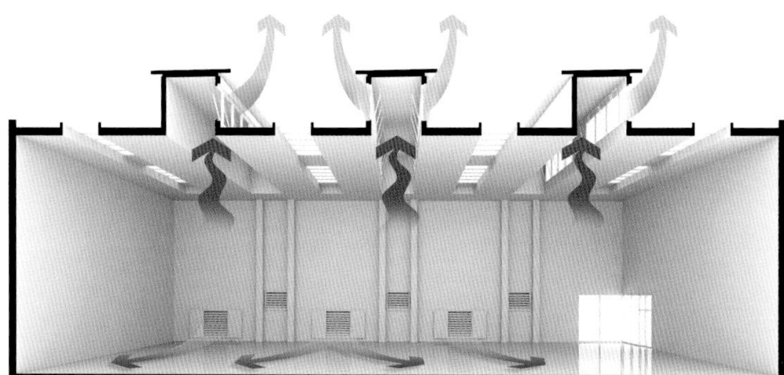

© JH

0002

Use Nature as a Guide

Without replicating nature exactly, you can still employ its characteristics and functions. Nature uses only what it needs and no more. Let this logic permeate your work so that designs operate like sailboats rather than powerboats.

From adobe brick and rammed earth walls to rooftop solar panels, the design of Miraval Resort and Spa, Tucson, takes every opportunity to conserve energy while enhancing access to the beautiful surroundings.

© Robert Reck

0003

Grow an Idea

Ideas require stewardship. Begin with a seed rather than a complete concept. It is important to learn from the program, place, and needs of the client: all the circumstances that inform a project and bring the concept to life.

In Novelty Hill Januik Winery, Woodinville, the orderliness of a vineyard translates the structure's modern feel and the fine art of winemaking into nature, and invites nature into the winery.

© Ben Benschneider

© Ben Benschneider

0004

Strengthen Community

Translate a community's hopes and dreams into designs that strengthen human activity, enhancing people's lives in meaningful ways. Community implies taking responsibility for ourselves, future generations and other species.

In High Point Community, Seattle, a natural drainage system enhances an entire community's ecosystem, supplying clean water for a nearby salmon stream, a habitat for birds, and parks for residents to enjoy.

© Mithun: Juan Fernández

0005

Bring Passion/Leave Ego

Increase the odds for discovery through a passion for learning, experience, and teamwork. See designers as students, partners, and mentors. The best new idea could come from anywhere. In IslandWood, Bainbridge Island, this learning center in the woods for urban students brought together architects, engineers, artists, founders, and children to find ways to reduce site impact and maximize experience.

0006▼

Public/Private Partnerships
Urban areas, as hubs of activity and consumption, offer the best opportunity for innovation, but everyone must participate in the solution to decrease energy demand, switch to green power and offset any remaining carbon footprint.

Puyallup City Hall, Puyallup: integrated strategies created this focal point for future sustainable development, initiating the city of Puyallup's transformation from a small agricultural community into a vibrant town center.

0007▲

Expand the Boundaries
The best projects question everything. For example, how might you help the urban and natural worlds support each other as integrated systems? In addition to the building, investigate broader issues about place and community.

In Stephen Epler Hall, Portland State University, this six-story university residence hall couples smart technology with climate-responsive design to take full advantage of rainwater, natural lighting and natural breezes to assist the building's operation.

© Eckert & Eckert

© Eckert & Eckert

0010

Create Beauty & Spirit

It is the perfect moment: the culmination of a sense of place, time, and movement. Beautiful design is sustainable, meaning inherently elegant, functional, dramatic, and enduring. Along with proportion and form, celebrate details that contribute to a greater whole.

The Teton Science School, Jackson Hole, is a living laboratory for students and teachers that creates environmentally intelligent spaces where learning goes hand-in-hand with research, and buildings integrate with their natural surroundings.

© Robert Pisano

0008

Walk the Talk

Reinforce your values with strategies to reduce operational energy consumption. Mithun enlisted the green potential of a defunct industrial pier for new offices in 2000. Innovative renovation created a beautiful, expansive and sustainable space, naturally lighted and ventilated and filled with views of Puget Sound.

0009

Green Economics

Take a holistic approach to economics, values and vision. Costs for a sustainable project are long-term investments involving the people who use the building, systems that maximize limited resources, and the company brand.

Mosler Lofts, Seattle, is a 150-unit residential loft tower that offers environmental quality as an urban lifestyle choice for downtown Seattle's growing live/work community. It was the fastest selling condominium in Seattle's highly competitive marketplace in 2006.

© Ben Benschneider

[ecosistema urbano]

Ten things we have learned from the city

Estanislao Figueras 6
28008 Madrid, Spain
P.: (+34) 915-59-16-01
www.ecosistemaurbano.org

0011

Take care of the public. We believe the city concept is inextricably linked with public space creation

For Acupuncture Public Spaces, a row of projects were designed to improve public spaces in central Madrid. Selected points were chosen as catalysts to initiate a broader reconfiguration of the city's public spaces. [review]

0012

Tackle issues the optimistic way: use constructive criticism in order to generate creative solutions

We approached an Ecoboulevard on the outskirts of Madrid as an operation of urban recycling in order to reconfigure the existing urban development. Three pavilions, or artificial trees, function like open structures to multiply resident-selected activities. The air tree is a light structure, easily dismantled and energetically self-sufficient. [recycle]

0013

Exploit low budgets to create big projects using less resources

For Matadero Umbrellas we suggested a shadow space of 27,000 sq ft (2,500 sq m) to host summer activities. The low budget is the basis to cover the whole space employing standard means. Citizen participation and the reuse of standard objects made this possible. [reuse]

0014

Bring about instant change through urban actions

We believe everything is architecture, that small actions provoke huge reactions, and that everything is connected. Through these public space actions we built a park in just five days that a mayor had been promising for the last fifteen years. We created a new artificial "municipal government" to denounce the real one that was planning crazy new Guggenheims for a small city, and we used technological interventions to promote social life and interaction. We tried to reactivate a huge region through a series of fast actions in order to enhance certain existing aspects, to show citizens that it really is possible to change the urban environment. [react]

0015

Involve citizens in the processes of changing their environment

The Philadelphia Ecological Reconfiguration project is a strategy based on placing a series of low cost interventions in the city's street network in order to create mechanisms that promote citizen participation: a launch pad for the self-regeneration of the urban fabric. [revitalize]

0016➤

Build networks to share knowledge and experiences

Our ecosistemaurbano.org blog is an Internet platform showing worldwide experiences of creative urban sustainability.

The portal euabierto.com is an open network allowing professionals to share experiences and knowledge on creative urban sustainability.

And ecosistemaurbano.tv is an interactive television channel for exchanging multimedia concepts related with urban sustainability.

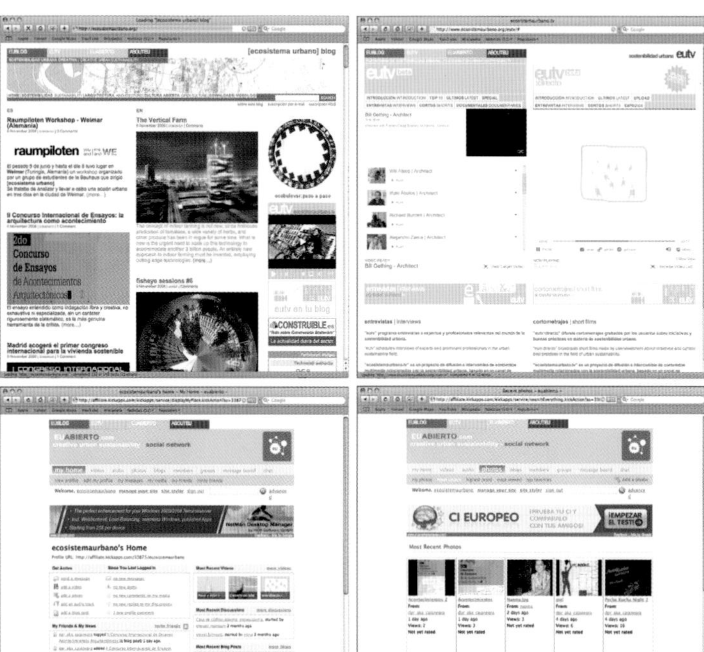

▲0017

Remember the intangible elements through using new technologies as a mechanism to create complex features

Architecture used to manage energy sources—water, wind, and sun—becomes the driving force for activity, forming the mutations of the landscape. A network of technological elements characterize the image of the Metropolitan Water Park in Zaragoza in order to demonstrate that natural systems can transform urban waste into new resources for the city. [regenerate]

◄0018

Create open systems to permit reality to evolve

On the outskirts of Maribor, Slovenia, a former municipal landfill site is now being ecologically recovered. We used this temporariness as a leitmotif throughout the project, understanding that temporary processes should be highly connected with architecture. [renaturalize]

0019

Reactivate 'the existing' as an alternative to uncontrolled expansion
The question we faced was how to improve the public space of Fuenlabrada, a neighborhood in the outskirts of Madrid. We wanted to demolish the limits separating different urban facilities and public spaces. This project reconnects activity points to reconfigure the whole network, viewing the city as a playground. [reprogram]

0020

Keep a positive mindset to be able to change reality
In contrast to traditional problem-solving methods for reactivating degraded public spaces in historical centers, we believe another form of intervention is possible whereby the citizen plays an active role in creating public spaces. This project *Beach on the Moon* demonstrates new notions of neighborhood connectivity, developed to positively affect the lifestyles through creating a new, temporary urban scene. [reactivate]

Germán del Sol

© Claudio Pérez

Camino las Flores 11441
7591295 Las Condes, Santiago, Chile
P.: (+56) 2214-1214
www.germandelsol.cl

© Germán del Sol, Guy Wenborne

><

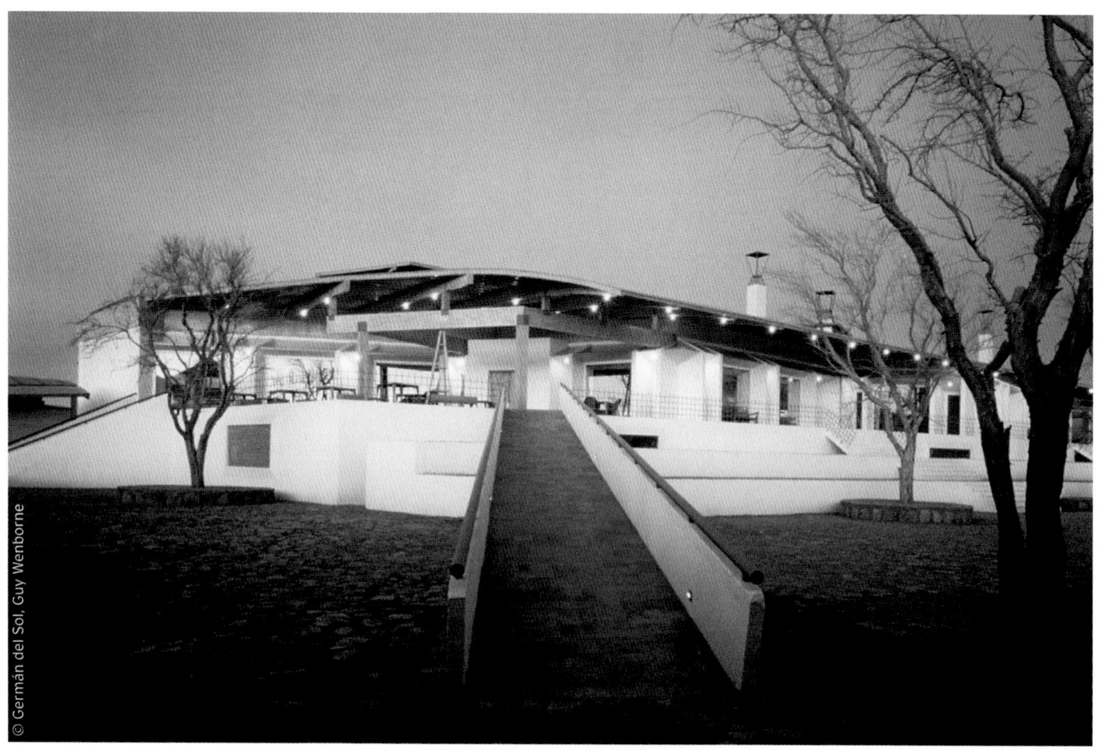
© Germán del Sol, Guy Wenborne

0021

Being contemporary, and heirs to the modern world, does not consist of the quest to innovate for the sake of innovation, but rather to return to the beginning, and try to make things a little better again.

© Germán del Sol, Guy Wenborne

><

© Germán del Sol, Guy Wenborne

0022

Good architecture is original when it is strongly connected to its origins. The most universal local traditions are the best inspiration for architecture. We must connect them with the world in order to break out of our splendid local isolation.

0023

Life in the city is enriched with the contributions from the culture and nature of its territory. Upon its own sustainable destiny, the territory becomes unique and unrepeatable. It gains value that protects it from being just another object of global trade, where 'the unique' no longer exists.

0024

We must make the most of the freedom that we have inherited from the modern world to ensure that the forms of architecture follow an order that is fertile for life, and not the product of intellectual abstractions.

0025

If you want to provide refuge with a floor or a roof, just like the route a shepherd takes when rounding up his sheep in the afternoon, you will most likely have to travel in many directions like the Nazca lines, or include all the steps possible in the clear square of a plaza. Order is the fruit of life, not its origin.

0026

For me, in a project or in a city, not everything should be good. It is the whole that should be good. We must use coarseness rather than fine tuning, and not get bogged down in anecdotal details, instead using our life experience that is the result of a whole. Use bold, imprecise lines, be firm but subtly insecure, accept errors, confirming and hesitating at the same time, about the certainties that architecture gives to human life.

© Germán del Sol, Guy Wenborne

© Germán del Sol, Guy Wenborne

© Germán del Sol, Guy Wenborne

© Germán del Sol, Guy Wenborne

0027

Work with greater confidence rather than control. Direct workers with enthusiasm, letting them make some decisions in their work, sometimes relying on their life experience, rather than on the details in the plans. Trust in the fact that architecture is cultural and that in the end they will all like the same things.

When a utilities worker says "I would like my bathroom to be like this," or the driver of the concrete truck says "these thermal springs are incredible," I know that we are on the right track. Beauty is common to all, although no one today dares to say its name . . .

© Germán del Sol, Guy Wenborne

0028

Don't ever confuse importance with urgency. It may be urgent to construct a house, but it is important that the house has dignity. Grace does not cost money. Is the fruit of poetry, which shows the assets that exist everywhere.

© Germán del Sol, Guy Wenborne

0030

Use saturated colors, because the world is neither white nor pure, and white reflects a far-away purity that seems dead.

0029

Movement must be contained in the eye that contemplates the architecture.

Estudio Arquitectura Campo Baeza

Almirante 9
28004 Madrid, Spain
P.: (+34) 917-01-06-95
www.campobaeza.com

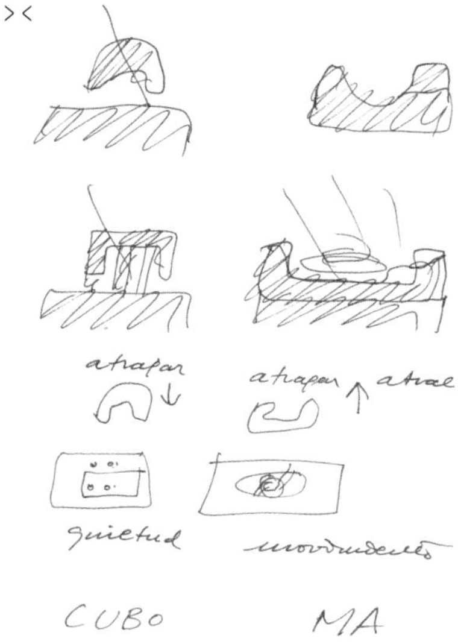

0031

This elliptical white patio has a bright white spiral ramp, connecting the earth with the heavens. These elements are all contained within a concrete box with a giant screen, connecting the structure to the world.

0032

A *hortus conclusus*: an enclosed cubic precinct filled with light, contained within a cylindrical box. Between these elements there are four patios containing the four pre-socratic elements of water, earth, fire and air.

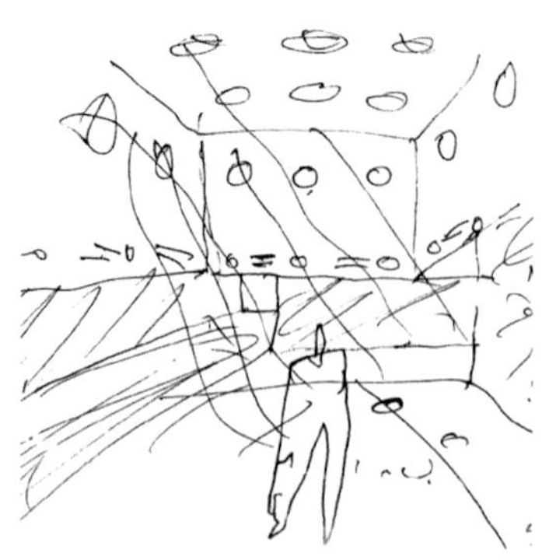

0034▲

The sun visits this *impluvium* of light every day, to calm the air and bathe it with new beauty and light. In Granada they call this *El Cubo*.

0033▼

A geode: a box open to the sky above, with exterior sandstone and interior Roman travertine walls enclosing a fragrant grove of orange trees.

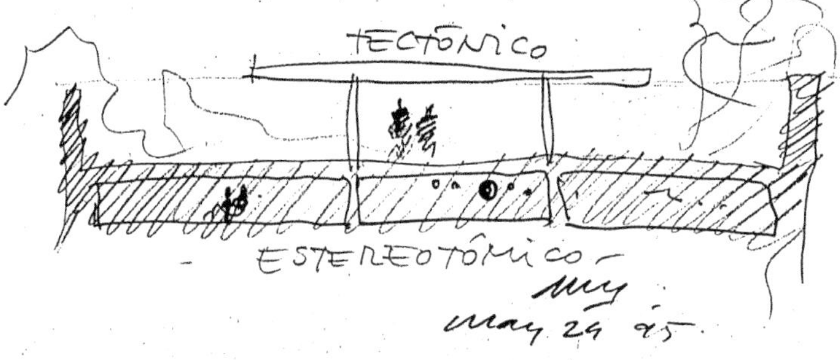

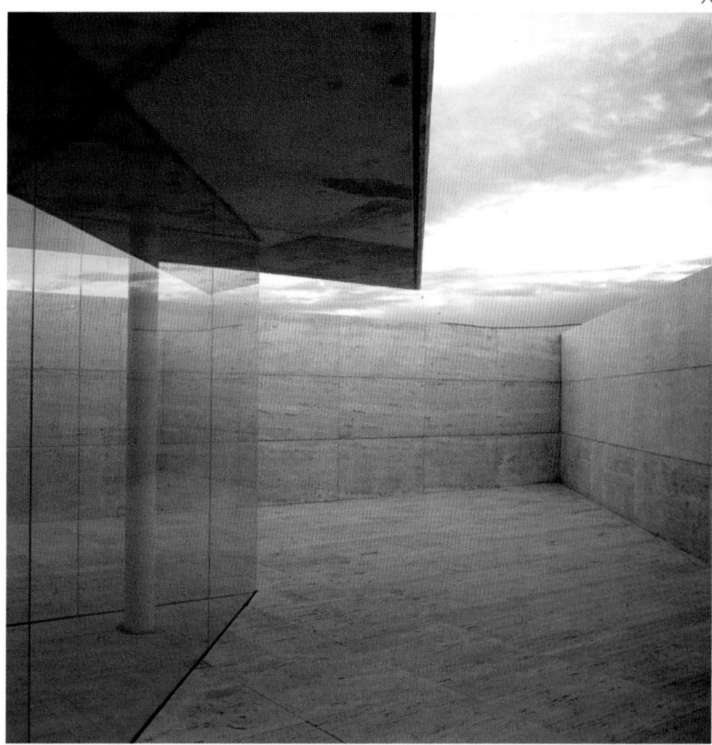

0035▼

This *hortus conclusus* is an open box containing four orange trees and a large pool. The inside areas are shaded and have high ceilings.

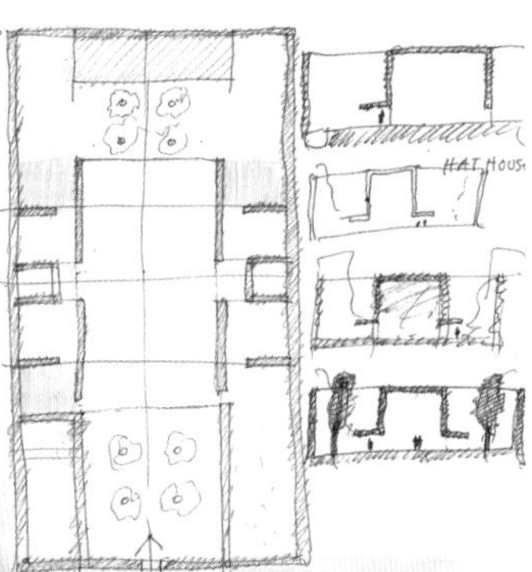

0036▲

This smooth white cube structure has a diagonal inner space that is stretched by diagonal light.

0037►

A belvedere: a glass box placed over a cave. Elementary.

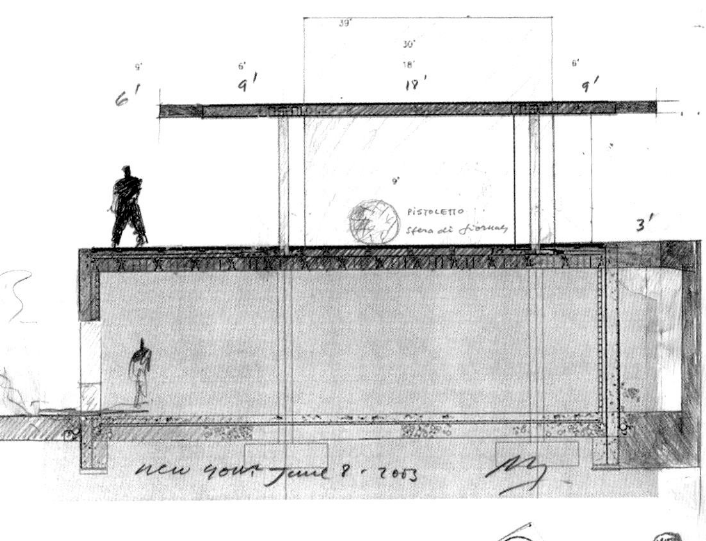

OLNICK-SPAN HOUSE
GARRISON

0038

This *hortus conclusus* contains four lemon trees and a water tower.

0039

Dream at the top, live in the middle, and die a little below.

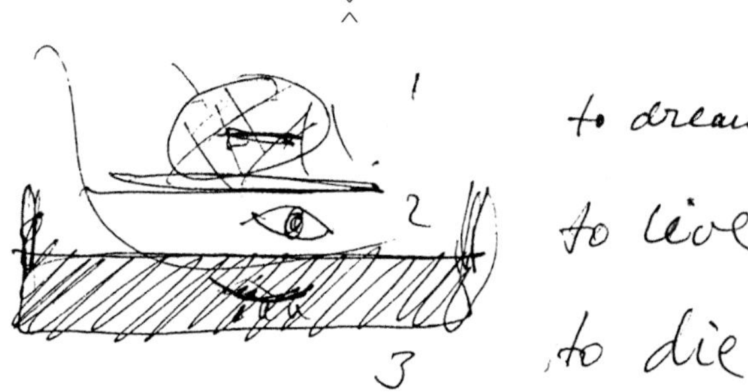

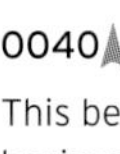

0040

This belvedere gazes out over the horizon, where the Hudson River meanders in the distance.

NIPpaysage

7468 rue Drolet
Montréal, Québec, H2R 2C4 Canada
P.: (+1) 514-272-6626
www.nippaysage.ca

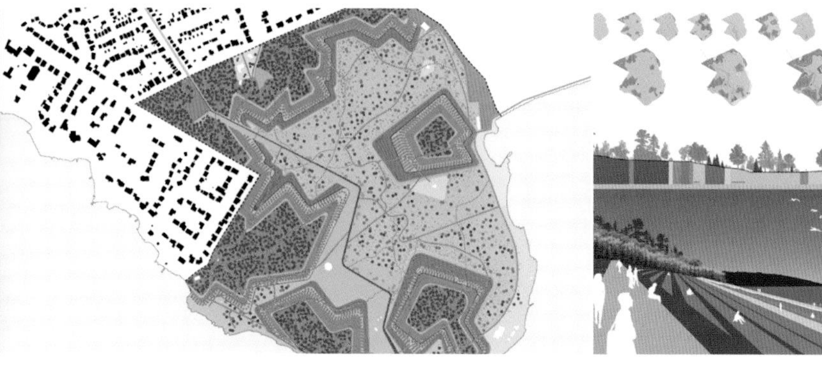

0041

Zoom out: focus on spaces, not objects
Create rich experiences where cohesion between elements is stronger than each component considered individually. For example, the multiplication of objects is a mechanism that creates strong spatial effects.

0042

Make nice stitches: express authenticity
Reveal the true character within various environments of intervention. Accept incidents, events, positives or negatives as pages of history that contribute to the richness of a place. For example, following a site disturbance choose interesting stitch marks over scar-free plastic surgery.

0043

Tell a story: use landscape as language
Juxtapose meanings. The addition of a narrative layer allows creating sites to go beyond functionality, enriching user experiences.

0044

Follow advice from a crystal ball: design for an uncertain future
Go beyond present needs and programs; transform places with evolving and shifting concerns. Allow for evolution and mutation.

0045

See landscape as a canvas: explore patterns

Explore the graphic aspects of design to clarify human actions on site transformation. Pure surfaces and clean lines fuel the creation of patterns; site work becomes the canvas for pictorial exploration.

© Jacques Bourdages

0046

Talk to nature: update representations of it

Actualize ideas of nature in a contemporary context where natural systems evolve and transform.

Updated representations are needed to counterbalance ever-present bucolic visions. The idea of nature must constantly be redefined.

0047

Wear thick glasses: rethink scale

Transform scale to voluntarily draw attention and provide unprecedented experiences to everyday items and spaces. Alterations of conventional scale transform the concepts of ergonomics, functionality, comfort, and security with relation to common components.

0048

Sculpt, cut and fill: use gradients for functional and aesthetic considerations

Consider topography and use earth as sculptural material. Encourage an ecological system approach by smartly reusing cut and fill, enhancing surface water management and merging site work into a 3D work of art.

0049 

Be eccentric: explore atypical materials and techniques

Question conventions and try to bring new materials and labor techniques to design projects. Seek opportunities to rethink standard assemblages and borrow methods from diverse and unexpected sources.

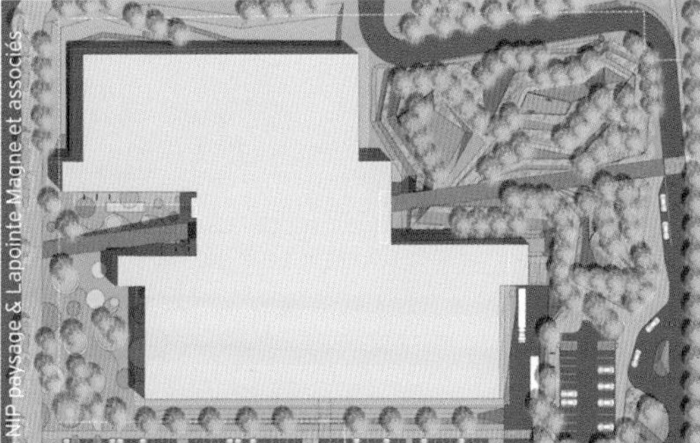

© NIP paysage & Lapointe Magne et associés

0050

Think positive: consider challenges as opportunities

Allow physical and programmatic constraints to initiate essential design reflexes, they are sources of inspiration and rich starting points from which to develop the foundations of projects. Transform limitative realities into positive and meaningful visions.

Artadi Arquitectos

Camino Real 111 Of. 701
San Isidro, Lima 27, Peru
P.: (+51) 1-222-6261/1-9924-1400
www.javierartadi.com

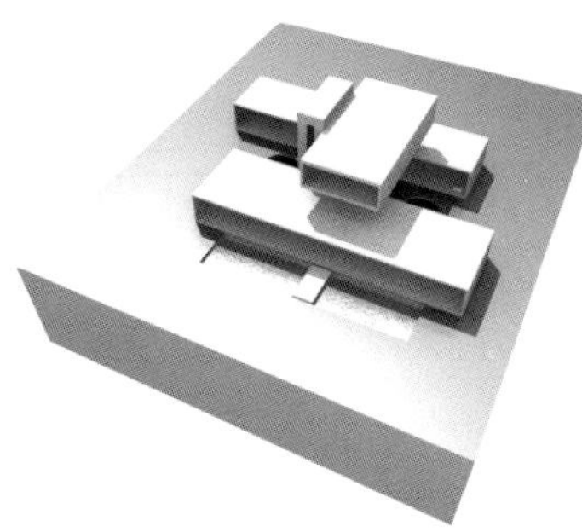

◄0051

Concept

Architecture is the consequence of conceptual reflection. The concept of a project is the vital gene that controls the development of the architectural design. I like to construct evolutionary outlines that explain the central concept of the project; these reveal the main components of the proposal and help to verify whether processes underway are correct or not.

© Alex Kornhuber

0052▲

Continuous material

I like the materiality of concrete or cement surfaces in that they are continuous. For an architect who is interested in creating a pure and simple conceptual architecture, a continuous material is the perfect ingredient to achieve this goal. Thus, a straight line is a straight line, a plane is a plane, and a cube is a cube.

0053►

Geometry

Working with basic, pure geometries enables me to architecturally explain the main principles of my projects. In the House in Las Casuarinas, the nexus of the three basic axes, X, Y, and Z, is clearly defined in an architectural solution whose geometrical force can be admired from afar in the city.

© Alex Kornhuber

0054

Nature as a background
Unique situations create the opportunity for unique natural settings as a background for architectural works. The majestic presence of Cerro Colorado hill, on the beach with the same name, helped me to envisage a club house project that would be utterly simple and have a geometry that would help to reveal the breathtaking location.

© Elsa Ramirez

0055 

Architecture as a background
For the Beach House in Las Arenas, the idea of a box opened up to the sky and the sea enhanced the design of the slices in the architectural solution in order to achieve spectacular views of the coastal landscape. In a way, the house is also a camera.

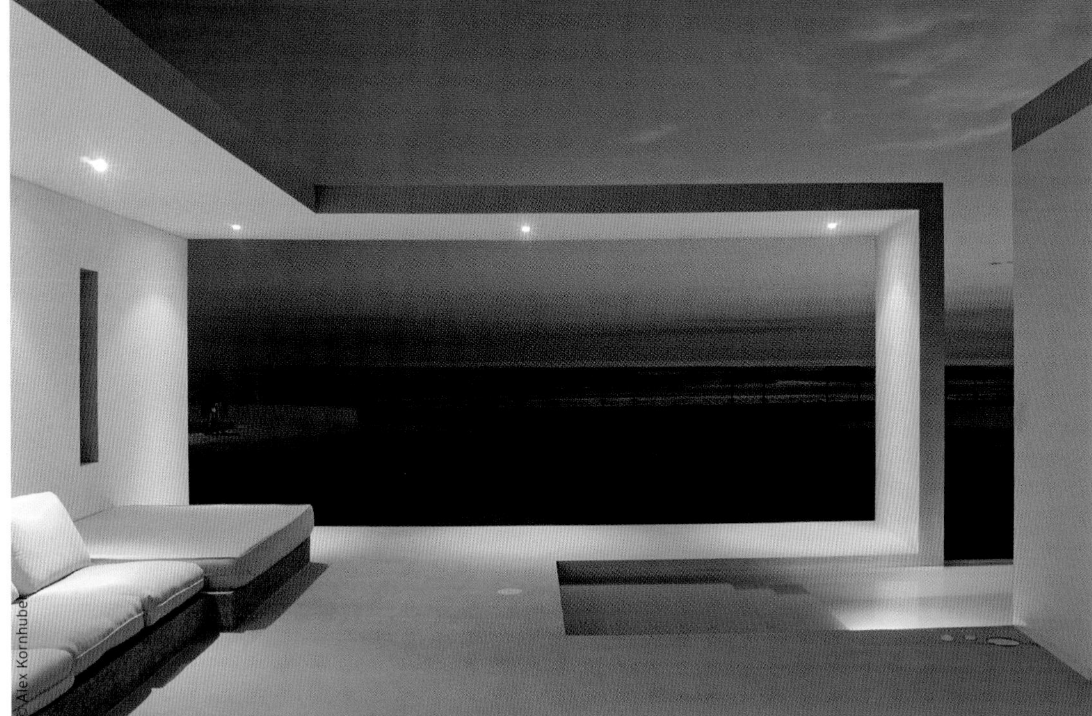
© Alex Kornhube

0056

Simple details
When a concept is powerful, executing the project is easy, and the process seems more like a game of taking away elements instead of adding them. Working with just a few materials and finishes helps to foreground a project's key concept.

© Elsa Ramirez

0057

Unforeseen uses

For years I have studied the behavior of people with relation to the uses they give to specific architectural solutions. Chabuca Granda Boulevard is a test bed to explore this topic. Here, a sequence of circular plazas is configured by basic geometric forms (cubes, spheres, etc.) that are utilized by visitors in unusual or non-conventional ways. Creating an architectural project that breaks us from the bonds of pre-defined uses for things, to encourage us to behave with greater freedom, is an important aim within our projects.

0058

Illuminating architecture

Architecture transforms by night. And this is when artificial lighting comes into its own as a defining concept in a project. In the Beach House in Las Arenas, the lighting design was envisaged not only to enhance the transparent or translucent planes of the project, but also to drive home the idea of the house as a floating box.

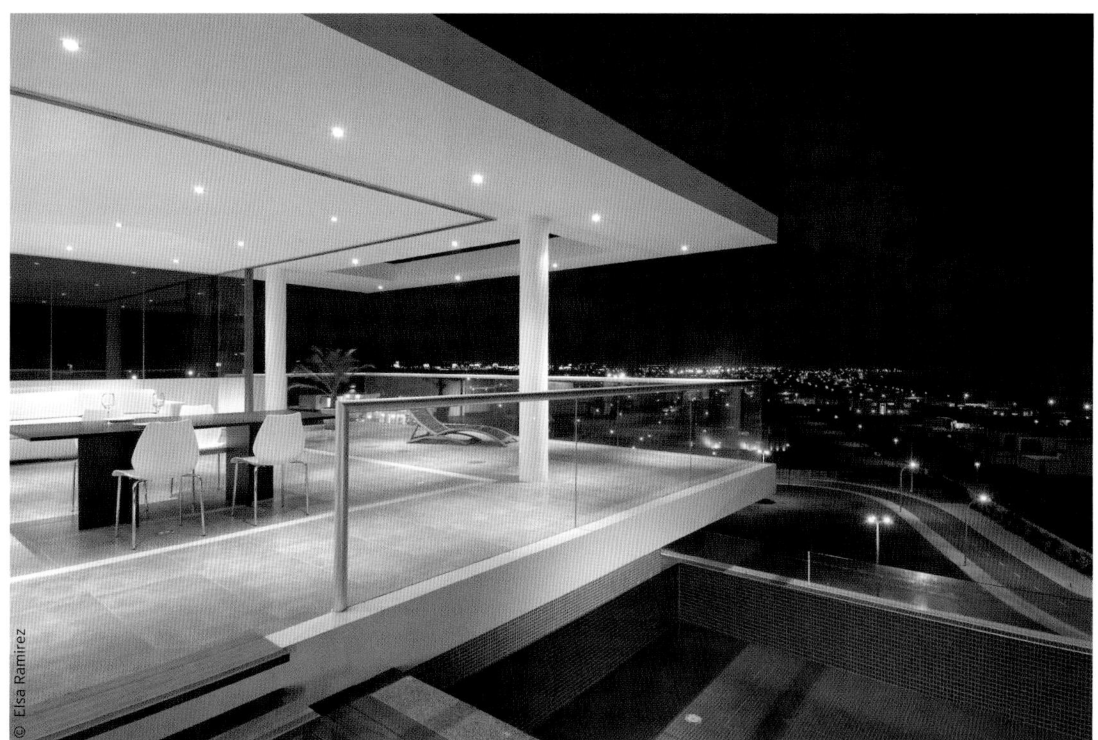
© Elsa Ramirez

◄0059

Weightlessness

I am fascinated by the way in which architecture manages to make a constructed mass seem to "lose weight" and start to "float." In the Beach House on a Hill, the aim was to push this concept to the limit by also bringing water into play. The result is that the house not only seems to float towards infinity, but also has a liquid frame that dramatizes this effect.

0060►

Environment

Architecture should help enhance the environment. For the Dasso Boulevard project, I designed a series of green vertical elements that, as well as acting as lighting columns, greatly increased the green spaces in the site, which hardly had garden areas. The result is a series of green plates that create a vertical garden, which is a reference point for the entire boulevard.

© Lorena Noblecilla

Fermín Vázquez/b720 arquitectos

Josep Tarradellas 123, 9ª
08029 Barcelona, Spain
P.: (+34) 93-363-79-79
www.b720.com

Juan Hurtado de Mendoza 19
28036 Madrid, Spain
P.: (+34) 91-376-82-14

0061

Cities with history have always been constructed using the new elements of the times. The Plaza del Torico project aims to insert a recognizable layer from our times into the city, while completely respecting its existing layers. Paradoxically the precise utilization of light helps the city reduce its excessive night lighting. This intervention uses a strictly contemporary language in order to reinforce the mysterious atmosphere of this historic setting.

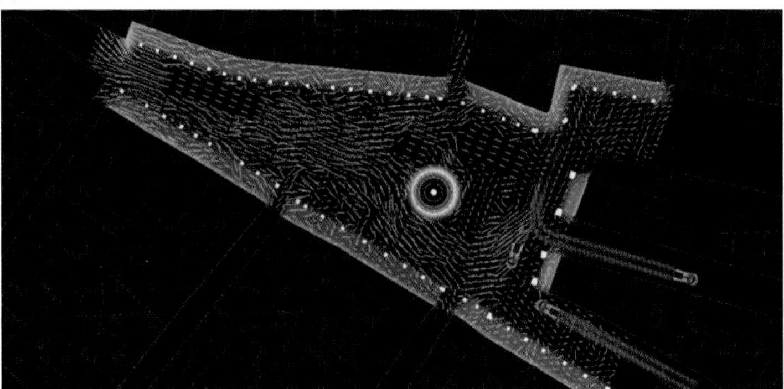

0062

This voluminous construction is located in a site hemmed in between a golf course and a forest. Three dispersed pavilions arranged on the hillside create a strictly rational, functional program that is not very open to interpretation. They are linked by a semi-buried structure with greater spatial liberty and which is protected from the sun by a trellis of foliage. The color becomes a contextualizing mechanism that, far from seeking to camouflage, provides a consciously artificial emulation of an unnatural medium in an intentional correlation with the nature of the forest and the artificial nature of golf. (La Mola Hotel and Conference Center)

0063

A small airport in Alguaire, Lleida, is located on a high plateau that stretches across a patchwork of farmland. The building's intention is to accompany the landscape. The image of the project is entrusted to a few bands floating on the ground, enhancing the flatness. The functional program is arranged below this colored mantle, mimicking the surrounding land. This mantle gently undulates to introduce natural light and a view of the sky from inside the building, which rises vertically to form the body of the control tower.

◄0064

This considerably sized building is inserted into the ground without being supported on it. It has two very distinct faces: on the one side, it has a unique corner façade with a huge cantilever and emphatic shapes, which is the public face of a casino and auditorium. The roof and walls fuse into total continuity, giving an almost geological appearance. To the rear, the building is nothing more than a continuity of the topography with a lush green space. No one would suspect from beneath the canopy of plants, hides a fierce animal. (Gran Casino Costa Brava)

0065►

This second-hand market, over one hundred years old, has been relocated from its original site. A large marquee protects the market from the sun, while maintaining its centennial outdoor market character. Its gentle slopes provide a sensation of continuity with the public transit areas. The elongated marquee allows shoppers to walk through the market as if it were part of the street. Its large roof, suspended at more than 66 ft (20 m) high, projects the reflection of the bustling activity below. (The New Encants Market)

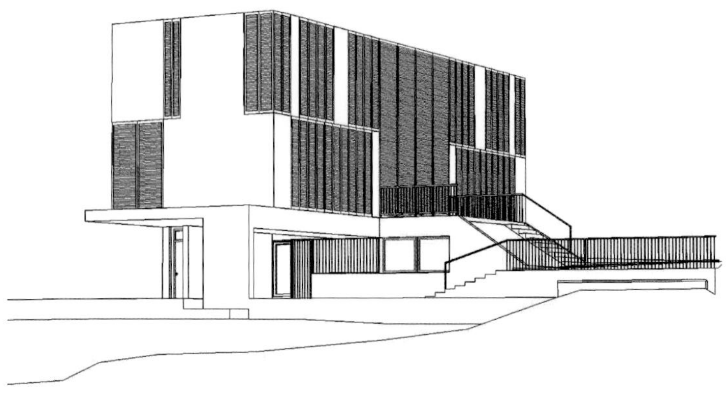

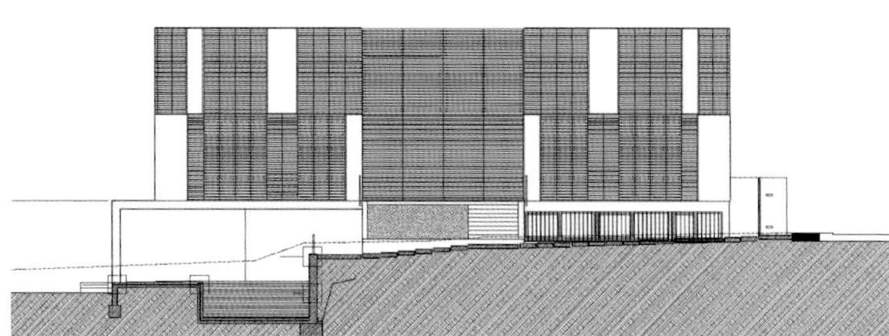

◀0066

This single building houses two virtually identical dwellings that were built for the families of two brothers who wanted to spend their summer vacations together. The Mediterranean sun is the raw material with which the project generates multiple degrees of shading. The two houses operate independently, but can combine their kitchens to function as one, and have a shared feature: a shaded terrace to share meals and family gatherings. (Casa Bovaira)

◀0067

A wire mesh shell has been designed to control solar radiation and to obtain a totally open and glazed office space. The spherical insets in this mesh break the severe abstraction of the continuous volume, giving it a motif alluding to the activity and the identity of the company that bases its head offices there. The subtle deformation of the metallic tissue causes changes to the building's appearance that vary according to the levels of sunlight during the day and across the seasons. (Indra Head Offices)

0068

Color is used as an instrument to integrate the project into a residential area filled with colored canopies over large balconies. Transparent colored glass slats form a floating layer with limits that blur into the walls. The building is gradually arranged in two directions: horizontally, the gradation of colors, ranging from yellow to orange, echo the tones in the canopies of the surrounding balconies and terraces; and vertically, the density of slats that relate to solar radiation and the size of the street, with the upper floors requiring higher levels of solar protection. (Offices building in Mestre Nicolau 19)

© Rafael Vargas Fotografía

0069

A 1960s office building has been transformed into deluxe apartments. The living spaces overlook the street through a sheet of adjustable slats. Meanwhile, a courtyard has been inserted into the heart of the building, crossing a single flight stairway with open sides in order to maintain the generous proportions of this void. With an exposed transit area in its central zone, the courtyard extends to the second floor entrance like a carpet of pebbles of different hues. The courtyard also provides a regulating function with slotted windows that increase in size as their positioning in the wall lowers. (Apartments in Rambla de Catalunya)

© Tomàs da Silva

0070

Restricted by strict regulations and a tight budget, this conventional program enables little experimentation in a lot between dividing walls, thus forming the basis for a sober façade.

Lightweight walls, constructed from prefabricated parts, play with the intentional restriction of elements and shades of coloring. (Diagonal Avenue, Housing residential building)

© Lluís Casals

GROSS. MAX.

6 Waterloo Place
Edinburgh EH1 3EG, Scotland, UK
P.: (+44) 131-556-9111
www.grossmax.com

0071

Big is beautiful
Landscapes are like a Russian doll; there is always a landscape in a landscape in a landscape. It is important to look across the boundaries of the site and study the wider context.

0072

Ecological taliban
How can we ambush the ecological Taliban? For our project for the new BMW plant in Leipzig we were only allowed to use native plants. But we wanted to use Italian Poplars. We only managed to convince the local authorities by showing an old gravure of the outskirts of Leipzig, which implied Italian Poplars had been part of the cultural landscape. We won the battle. Now Italian poplars have been planted by the hundred in ever-decreasing distances to visualize the rate of acceleration of the cars produced.

0073

Public realm of the senses
Landscape is the ultimate public realm of the senses. The art of landscape is to seduce. We often compare our attitude towards the landscape as an act of striptease; we like to reveal the landscape layer by layer. The image shows a glasshouse *Wunder-Garten* in Rotterdam which displays an organic orgy of orchids.

0074

Borrowed scenery
The oldest trick in the landscape trade is borrowing your scenery. Leap over the fence and see all nature is a garden, just as William Kent did. This image of North Korea's Great Leader Kim Yong Il overlooking one of our battlefield drawings was created for a competition in South Korea. It was never used as we censored it internally. Sometimes it is better to keep some cards up your sleeve. Our favorite book *The Art of Warfare* contains some excellent descriptors of varied terrain.

"Nature also creates monsters!"
Octave Mirbeau

0075

Beauty and the Beast
Who killed Bambi? Nature is the beauty and also the beast. Even flowers can be monstrous. Nature—that murky pool of genes—is not a shivering puppy that needs to be cuddled, but a force in its own right.

0076

Camouflage
Here camouflage netting is utilized as a shading device in an experimental glasshouse. If you put all the camouflage patterns of the Russian army together you can make a fantastic representation of the ecological diversity of the Russian landscape.

0077

Sparkle
Each scheme needs a highlight, a little piece of jewelry, a sparkle. It is better to concentrate the budget on one piece than to spread it evenly all across the site. Here is a stacked glass water feature that we designed as part of a the new Bullring mall in Birmingham

0078

Collaboration
New ideas always happen on the periphery of each profession, never at its centre. Collaboration is an important part of exploring one's own boundaries. Here is a vertical garden in London that we designed with the artist Mark Dion.

0079

GROSS. MAX.

The name of the office is a statement of intent. The office is a studio and should not be named after a person. Landscape is too soft and our name should sound more industrial; the name should not be linked to one specific country as we are a miniature multinational. The name GROSS. MAX. derives from the inscription on containers: "Maximum Content!" Above all, this means free publicity on all major freeways and shipping routes.

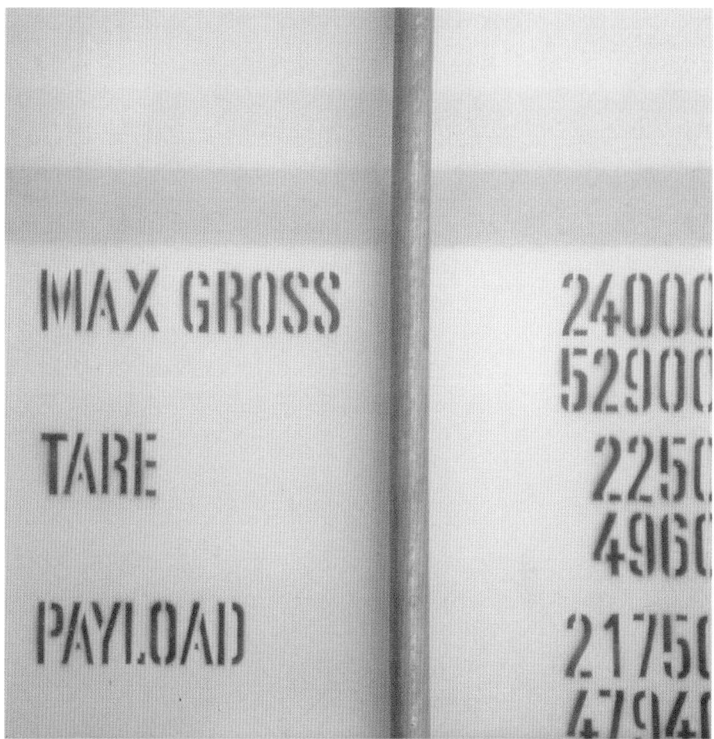

0080

A change of climate

The climate is changing. So what? In Dubai you will find the largest indoor ski slope, and in Berlin the largest indoor tropical beach. We all aspire for a change in climate; this is the most important factor in deciding our holiday destination. Here, we designed a project entitled *Global warming/Local freezing*; a nuclear powered iceberg to locally cool down the effect of global warming.

Atelier Tekuto

6-15-16-301 Honkomagome
Bunkyo-ku, Tokyo 113-0021, Japan
P.: (+81) 3-5940-2770
www.tekuto.com

◄0081

This is a dwelling on a narrow lot (due to rocketing land prices). The structure is a slender trapezoid with a property frontage of 10.6 ft (3.2 m) and a depth of 96 ft (29 m). The house was named *Lucky Drops* based on the Japanese proverb, "Sometimes the lees are better than the wine" (in other words, the final drop of the wine). As the proverb suggests, this property, which had been left unused, has been transformed into a comfortable living environment.

0082▲

As it was a living space occupied by a couple and a rabbit, surrounded by nature, we used "natural law" as a key phrase and contemplated the meaning of the word "rhythm," which is created by wavelengths derived from the cycles of the sun and moon, plant cycles, and human cycles.

0083 ►

The value of minerals is increased by cutting them, thus turning a negative factor into a positive one. We thought about this and drew on the keywords "mineral" and "reflection."

By entwining volume three-dimensionally in interior spaces and by using polyhedrons, optic reflections are produced, releasing us from the limitations of the space.

© Makoto Yoshida

© Makoto Yoshida

◄0084

The space in this dwelling is characterized by a curved ceiling covering the second floor. The gentle, cubic curve of the ceiling alters the height of the interior space, creating ambiguous sensory boundaries with the contrasting concepts of "oppression" and "openness." Such an approach based on changes in the ceiling plane may be difficult for the viewer to sense without a clear opportunity to do so, but it creates a richness in space, the likes of which have never been seen before.

0085 ►

In order to create a large living space, the post-and-beam concept was eliminated, and panels were created instead, combining 14.76-ft (4.5 m) iron sheets and 10.05 inch (25.5 cm) keystone plates. 2.4 x 12.6 inch (6 x 32 cm) flat bars were then inserted between two of these panels.

© Makoto Yoshida

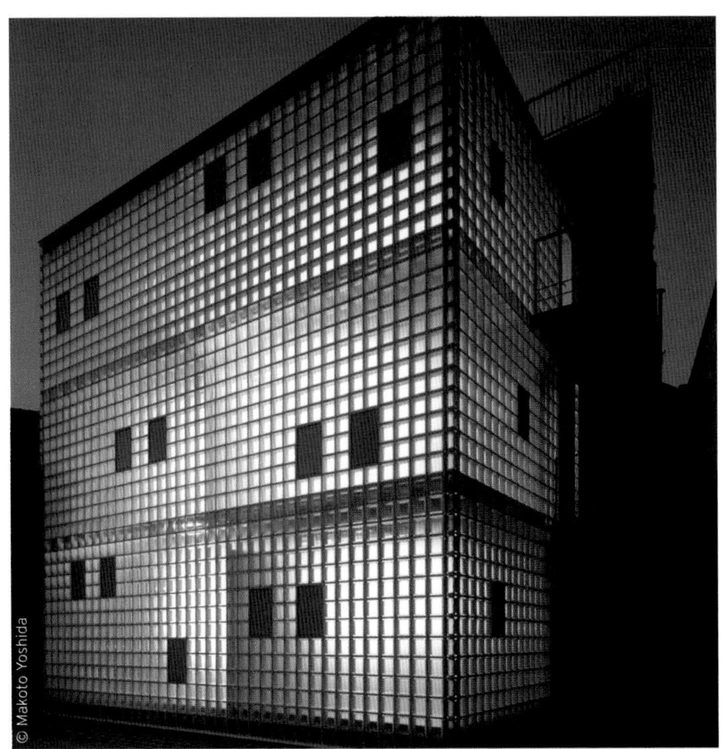

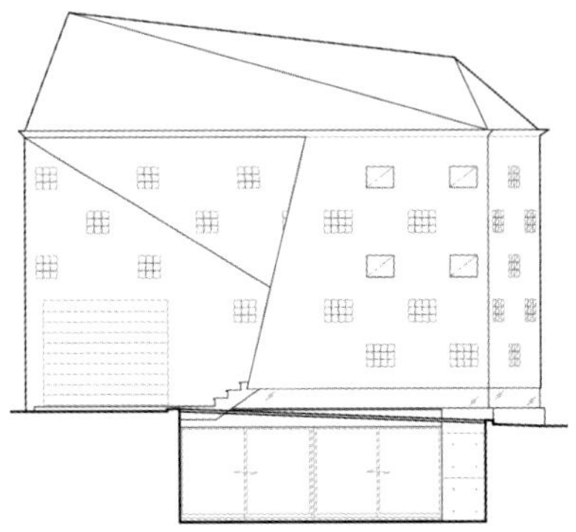

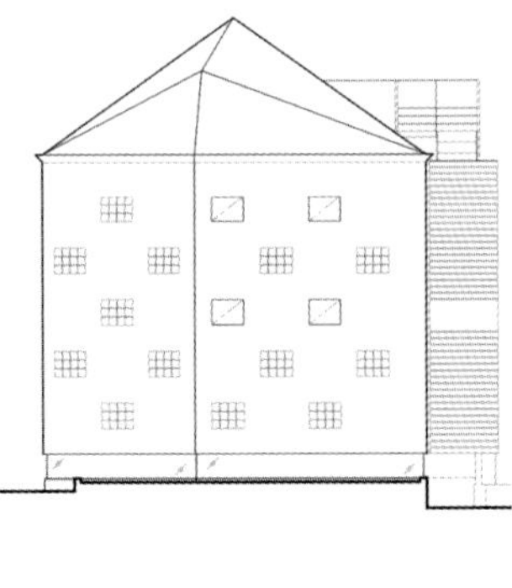

0086

Living in the middle of an urban setting increases the chances of selling your home, so this dwelling was designed to generate added value, based on the concept of resale value. Rather than a solid structure, the exterior wall is comprised of glass blocks and tiles. The light enters the dwelling through the glass blocks in patches and slanted walls create the interior spaces.

0087

In this dwelling, glass blocks are incorporated into the steel frame in a grid pattern, creating earthquake-resistant walls.

0088

This 14.75 x 39.5 x 10 ft (4.5 x 12 x 3 m) checkered dwelling consists of a storage box made of sheet iron. Problems relating to installation in small spaces were resolved by fusing together masonry and ideas on the Skin-House Project.

◄0089

We aspired to rediscover the value of both raw nature and the world we have created by allowing the viewer to simultaneously experience an architectural space and its magnificent natural surroundings.

0090►

This building is created primarily with timber, thus providing heat, illumination, and partitioning functions. Through repeated study, a space with a vague hierarchy was created in which the master-subordinate relationship is weak, as in branching coral. Round walls and a polyhedral outer shell give the rooms a curvy space, and aluminum rings create a sharp contrast in the space.

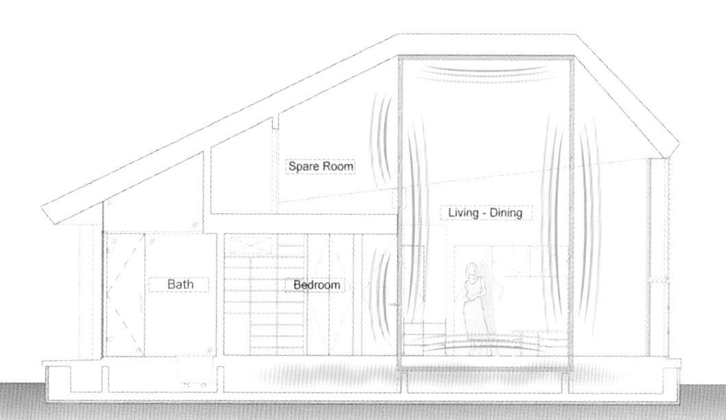

><

Kirkland Fraser Moor

Tips: David Kirkland

Hope House, 1 Stocks Barns, Stocks Road
Aldbury HP23 5RX, Herts, UK
P.: (+44) 144-285-1933
www.k-f-m.com

◄0091

Holistic concept planning
Before commencing a design, from the outset try to think of the project as less of an object and more of a system; one that positively contributes to promoting life on all levels: the client's business, the occupants' health, and the local community and environment. This will enable you to find better and more effective solutions to meeting sustainable design goals.

0092►

Local handmade clay bricks
Get everything on the table before making any design decisions. Issues like site climatology, and local material suppliers and skills will influence the built form and contribute to its ability to reflect its sense of place and belonging within a smaller carbon footprint. Local handmade bricks and tiles, and locally sourced timber assisted in creating this low energy contemporary house that blends in and extends the local vernacular traditions of the area without resorting to pastiche.

0093▼

Allow the building form to evolve in response to all the forces and constraints acting on the property
Wherever possible, allow passive energy opportunities to contribute to the process. The final built form will tend to be richer and more appropriate than if a more formal approach was adopted. This house was designed to fit seamlessly into a walled garden, within an important historically sensitive area. Its windows were oriented to optimize daylight and passive solar gain.

© Edmund Sumner

0094

A low carbon house made from local resources
Aim to effectively communicate these goals to all parties involved in order to bring them on board prior to starting the design process. A common vision can substantially increase the energy of a project's development and its ability to bring about benefits.

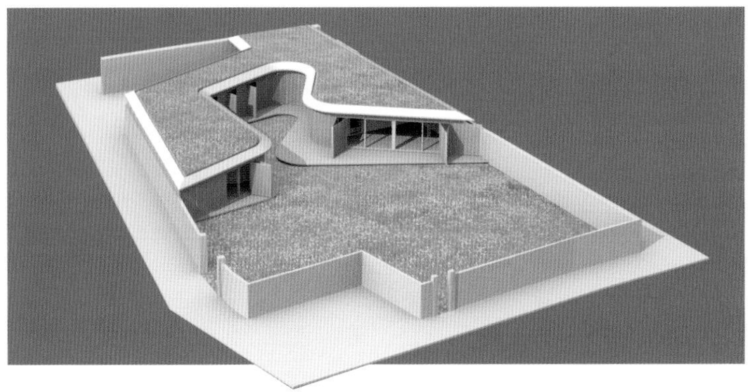

0095

When considering ventilation and cooling and heating services, aim to install them strategically in a location that will allow for short oversized duct runs with few bends. Fan and pump sizes will be substantially smaller, increasing the opportunity to achieve energy efficiency. This should be done in combination with correct solar orientation.

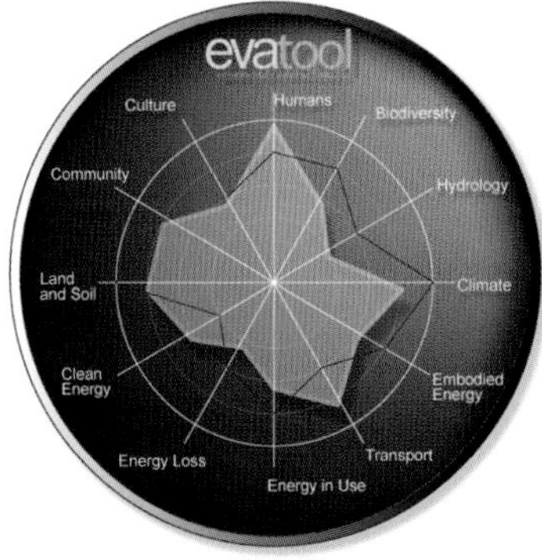

0096

Trotter House straw bale construction

The embodied energy of a building is a considerable source of carbon emissions. Try to source local, low processed materials to minimize these and to contribute to the architectural traditions and economy of the local community.

0099

Try to find ways to include living systems within the building form

Plants can contribute positively to enhancing water management and air quality factors. Life creates the conditions for life. By including ecology-enhancing strategies we create vibrant, life-affirming places.

0097

Always go back to the building and learn from it

Speak to its former occupants and to local inhabitants. Find out if their ideas worked well. By including a "feedback loop" within our design processes we have a better chance of evolving good architecture that enhances the life that interacts there and surrounds it. At KFM, to assist our process we are involved in developing EVAtool—an environmental management tool that helps with building a knowledge resource for sustainably designed projects.

0100

Learn nature's way of doing things; it is a great mentor

How does the natural world create such beautiful, elegant forms so efficiently? This can be the key to unlocking our ability to design a sustainably built environment.

0098

Turn liabilities into assets

This mixed use project for the north of Scotland made positive use of the extensive tidal flats along the loch shores to create an internal leisure feature for residents. A lightweight transparent roof provides protection during the winter months. During the summer, the external envelope becomes more dynamic as the building opens itself up to the outside views and water features.

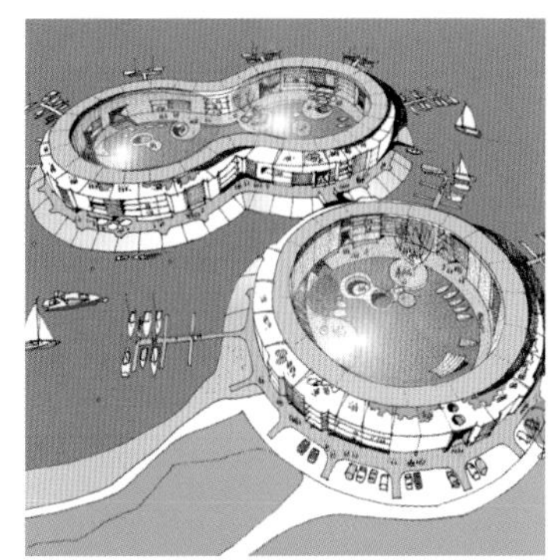

Ingenhoven Architects

Plange Mühle 1
40221 Düsseldorf, Germany
P.: (+49) 21-13-01-01-01
www.ingenhovenarchitects.com

◄0101

The striking tubular glass roof spans the entire 557-ft-long (170 m) and 165-ft-wide (50 m) structure. Its combination of very lightweight glass and steel structure enables maximum daylighting and transparency.

◄0102

The new European Investment Bank building in Luxembourg is designed and equipped to adapt to the new generation of working patterns and new communication requirements. Working conditions are multifaceted, team-oriented, communicative and motivating. Communication and spontaneous interaction are enhanced in zones where there is prevalence of great openness.

© H.G. Esch

0103

The building concept of the University College Dublin Gateway will be a new benchmark for energy efficiency and sustainability. The proposal has a very convincing key design concept based on the ecological concept of a sustainable campus without CO_2 emissions. Consequently it will receive an excellent rating in the British Eco-Standard BREEAM certification, even exceeding some certification criteria.

0104

The comb-like plan of the new Lufthansa Headquarters in Frankfurt Airport, with ten wings, uses enclosed landscaped gardens as buffer zones. Plants chosen from five continents are used to symbolize Lufthansa's global connections. All the 1,850 work stations have views over the glass-roofed gardens and can be naturally ventilated. The gardens create an ecological and healthy ambience.

© Peter Wels

© H.G. Esch

© H.G. Esch

◄0105

The Breeze Tower in Osaka is the first environmentally friendly skyscraper in Japan with a glazed double façade that allows the interiors to benefit from natural ventilation. It has a versatile layout that can adapt to suit all requirements. The nine-story podium structure, with multifunctional opera and concert hall for 960 people, restaurants, and conference facilities, creates, along with the central mall, an important new pedestrian connection.

0106►

The design of the high rise building 1 Bligh Street in Sydney is based on a fully glazed tower, equipped with a double skin façade and ventilated by an atrium stretching the whole height of the construction. The building process will utilize the most advanced technologies in order to address the challenges of the future and meet the needs of the workforce of tomorrow. The ecological concept of the tower is not only unique for Sydney but for the entire Australian continent.

© Simon Perry

0107▼

The aim of the International Criminal Court (ICC) architectural project was to construct a permanent building between the North Sea dunes and the city of The Hague. It was necessary to separate the three main areas of the ICC, although architecturally speaking the building functions as an open house. The layout of the floor plan is clear, allowing easy orientation.

© Peter Wels

0108

Ecology, economy, and technology are as essential to the new Main Station Stuttgart as comfort and security. The supporting structure is characterized by minimal height surfaces and diameters. The intelligent use of natural energy resources minimizes the building's carbon footprint.

© Holger Knauf

© H.G. Esch

0109

The Neue Messe, Hamburg's new trade fair center, is woven into the fabric of the Hanseatic city's center. It is an exhibition boulevard envisaged as a vivid, living city space along the Karolinenstraße.

The central connecting axis is the trade fair center loggia, fully glazed and linking all areas to one another. The façade divisions and the eave heights of the roof shell integrate harmoniously into the city's structure.

SLA

Carl Jacobsens Vej 29 A
2500 Valby, Copenhagen, Denmark
P.: (+45) 33-91-13-16
www.sla.dk

0110

The more we work with public spaces and landscape architecture, the more we are convinced that a stochastic pragmatism is the most sustainable answer to contemporary planning.

0111 

One of the noblest endeavors of landscape architecture is the transformation of planes into space. We find that the vocation of our work is lifting a two-dimensional plane into a three-dimensional space. These new spaces provide both the user and the visitor with experiences that are sensory, that are of change, of nature, and of materiality, offering surprises and encouraging social activity.

0112

Designing public spaces can be said to be the art of synthesizing the fundamental conditions of modern existence into a composition of space. This is a composition of surfaces and textures able to generate a universe that is both meaningful and accessible to the public. These conditions address the questions of ethics, knowledge, and beauty.

0113

In terms of knowledge, public space can serve as a platform for understanding the world around us. The logic and reason of the space should somehow reflect the empirical, rational, and social make-up of the world we live in.

0114

A complete or absolute picture is beyond the scope of perception. A comprehensive or overall view is replaced by shifts between various states.

0115

In a physical sense "the real" is that matter which surrounds us, which we perceive through our senses as trees, rocks, plastic, wind, clouds, and light. Regardless of its origins, matter's single most important purpose is the elucidation of the present and the sensory. Whether the matter or material in question stems from Denmark, Spain, China, or Mars is not the issue.

0116

The urban space consists both of a state of nature and an urban state. When one is distinct the other is blurred. Looking into a specific site, I plan with the distinct and the blurred.

0117

Beauty serves as the lens enabling us to focus our attention on the important issues in life. By contrasting these issues with the ordinary we can achieve an accentuation of communication, order, and harmony and thus become part of a collective memory and awareness.

0118

Contrary to the architect who builds buildings, the landscape architect possesses the means to create an amenity value, a factor of pleasure and delight. An amenity value is an expression that stimulates our intuitive perception of the world, where we sense before we think. The landscape challenges us, forces us to question and to look at ourselves, instead of merely perceiving the landscape as a representation.

0119

Landscape architecture as I see it, can provide the shift from one state to another by working with contour and lighting.

Landscape architecture is a matter of lightness and the senses. It is all about a light touch; a sensory encounter between life and matter.

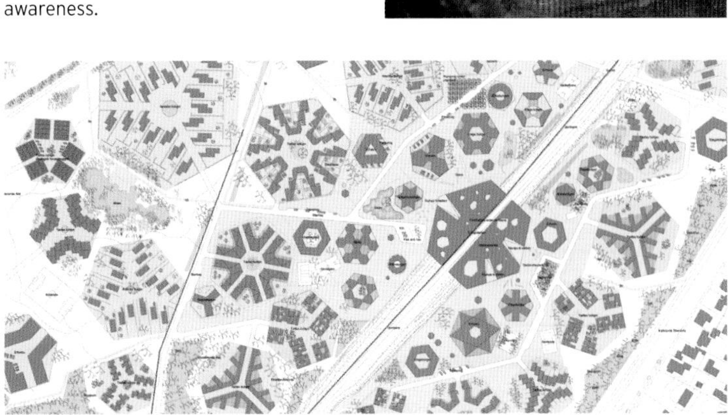

Min | Day

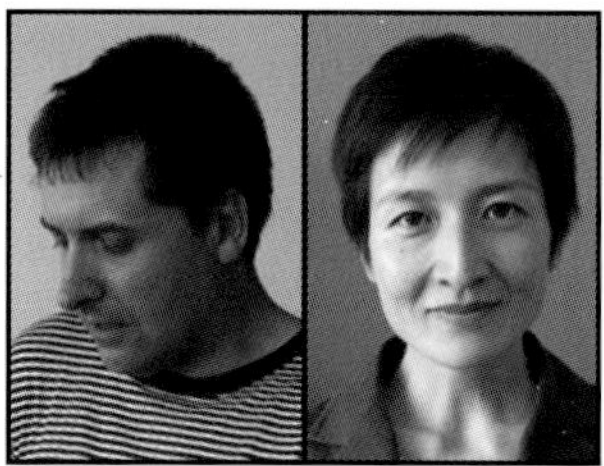

5912 Maple Street
Omaha, NE 68104, USA
P.: (+1) 402-551-0306
www.minday.com

2325 Third Street, Studio 425
San Francisco, CA 94107, USA
P.: (+1) 402-415-5551

0120▲
"This project is successful because it makes my disability less apparent to me," says our client of this universally accessible swimming pool. Rather than seeing accessible design as a problem to be solved with a compromise to a preferred agenda, we view the necessity for access as an opportunity for innovative design. As Marcel Duchamp claims, "there is no solution here because there is no problem."

0121►
Our interest in color comes, in part, from our immersion in the thought processes of landscape architecture. Unlike many architects, landscape architects are not afraid of color, nor are we. We see it as an important tool for space making, an additional layer that can reinforce or contradict the other components of spatial geometry, intensifying the experience or adding complexity.

© Paul Crosby

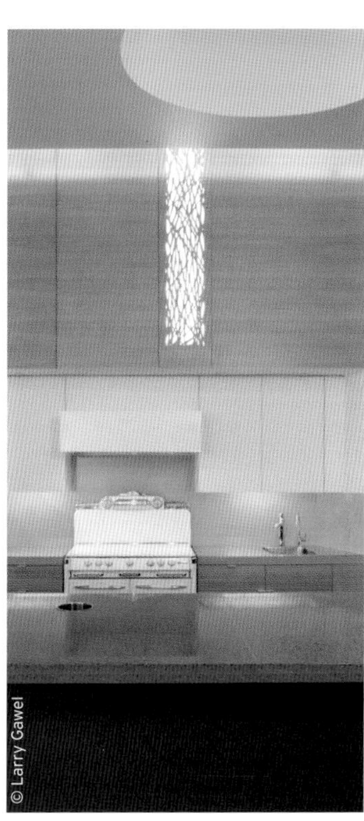

© Larry Gawel

◄0122

To color a skylight is to color light. By painting the sides of the shaft that leads to a skylight above, the light entering the room is infused with color, in this case a warm yellow-orange that complements the warm oak paneling. Treating skylights in this way develops atmosphere and mood.

0123►

The apparently floating cloud tactically hides ductwork, roof drains, and audio speakers in this renovated loft apartment. The white-painted surface also acts as a light diffuser, spreading ambient illumination throughout the space. As with the other new architectural elements in the loft, the cloud maintains a clear separation from the exposed surfaces of the historic building in which the loft is located.

© Larry Gawel

0124►

This house sits on a diminutive lot on a dense lakeshore where old cottages and new McMansions nestle tightly together. Our strategy resulted in a deceptively simple footprint while allowing for a series of complex spatial frames within the house that focus on the view while excluding the neighbors. This allowed for a sense of total privacy within the house itself.

© Paul Crosby

0125▲

In many projects we find ourselves questioning the norms of architectural convention. This often results in subtle challenges to the expectations of inhabitants in their everyday interactions with a building. Here, we installed a flush rolling door instead of a swing or pocket door. The door is now part of the wall with no visible hardware except for a small flush pull.

0126▲

The spatial frames of the house are interior tubes organized around view axes running through the site, perceptually linking the lake through the forest to the fields beyond. These view-framing tubes are literally voids in the mass of the house bounded at their ends only by glass. Light and air also enter these rooms through operable windows on the side elevations set behind the slatted wood cladding.

0127►

This domestic *portmanteau* alternately presents and hides various functions of a tight loft apartment. The inhabitable cabinet encloses a pantry, kitchen storage, dog fence, and a desk with a pullout bench that can be stowed when entertaining demands orderliness. Cabinetry as inventive and compact as a yacht cabin also acts as the fulcrum about which everyday events in the loft revolve.

><

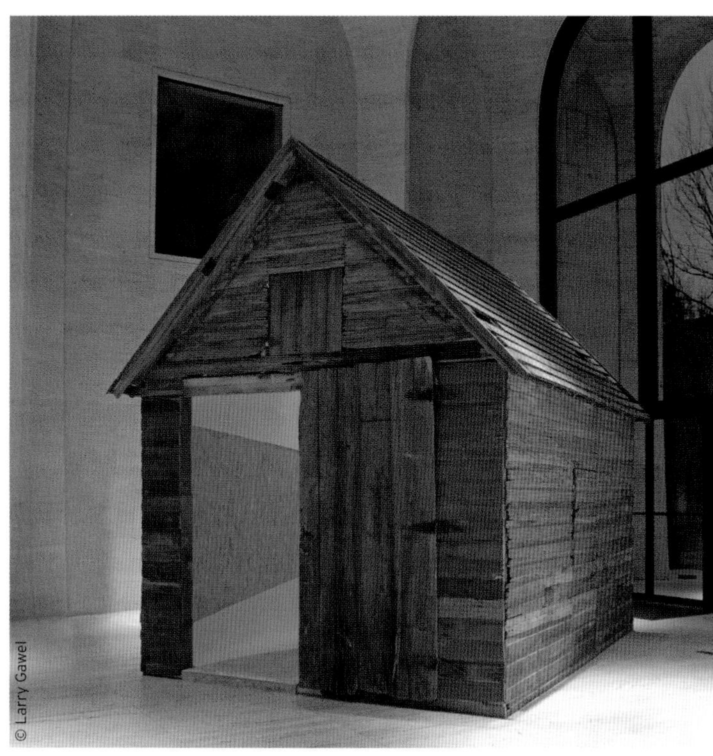

© Larry Gawel

0128

Artwork and architecture produced at Art Farm tackles the multiple histories of objects and buildings, reinterpreting them, and giving them new life and new narratives. As part of a strategy for the sustainable development of the site, the reuse of salvaged materials involves a radical juxtaposition of old and new. This suggests a pragmatic aesthetic for sustainable development as opposed to nostalgia for historical forms.

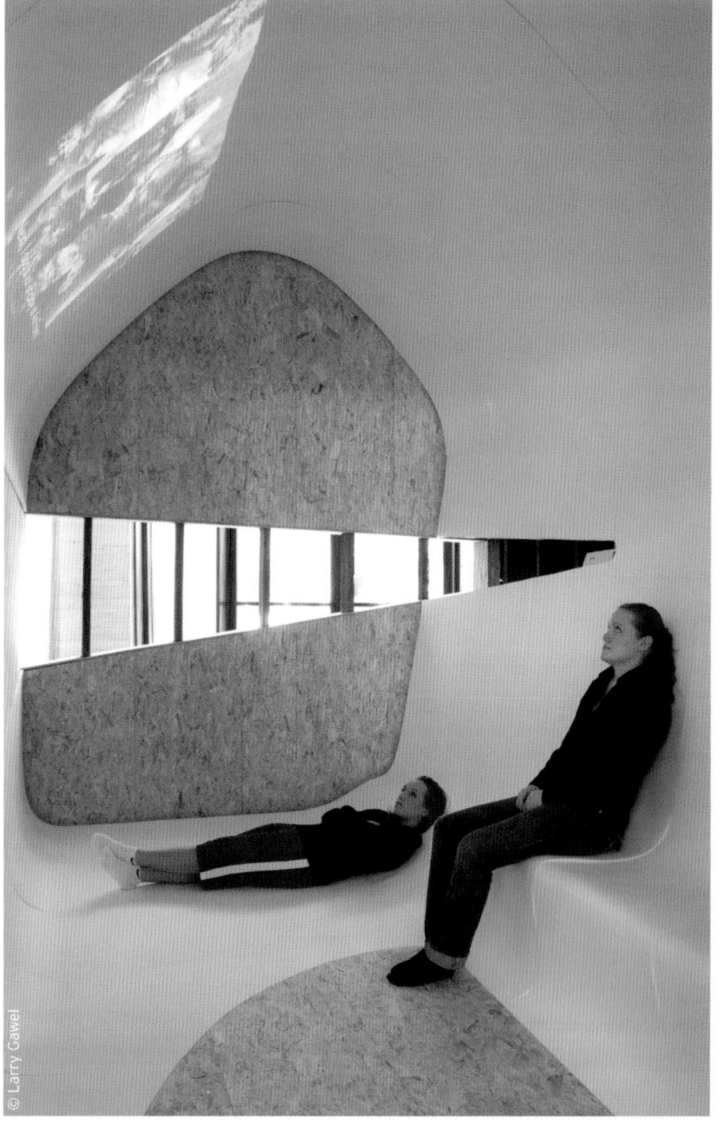

© Larry Gawel

0129

We treated the interior of this 100-year-old shed as a continuous surface for human occupation; in a sense the entire interior is one large lounge chair for watching video art. The space challenges users to find their own mode of inhabitation; one can sit in an area formed for upright sitting, or lie on the soft floor—or find any position in between.

Clorindo Testa

Av. Santa Fe 1821, 6° piso
1123 Ciudad de Buenos Aires, Argentina
P.: (+54) 11-4812-6030

0130

This building is located in the city center. We wanted the Bank of London (1966) to form a plaza in the corner. The façade of the building in form is the bank's façade.

0131

The building is located in a public park. The Argentinean National Library (1962) is a building that rests on four legs. When looking upwards, the interior of the building looks like an x-ray.

© Gustavo Sosa Pinilla

© Daniela Mac Adden

0132

In Casa en La Barranca (1992) one of the columns supporting the pool, facing the river, is the trunk of the concrete tree. It is a fake tree that seems to be real.

© Daniela Mac Adden

© Daniela Mac Adden

0133

The floor plan of the Colegio de Escribanos (1998) is a square with a large central column. Upon entering, a ramp leads down to the garage in an undulating profile with several landings, floors, and metal staircases. Above are the offices.

0134

The terrace of the Auditorium of the University of El Salvador (1998) overlooks the city on one side, and on the other it looks toward infinity.

0135

Altera Gallery (1998) is located in a Spanish seaside town called Pinamar. It is an art gallery built amid trees, in a location out of the town center. It was in need of a little color.

0136

Extension of the Legislative Palace Library (2004).

In 1956, I won the competition to design the Civic Center of the city of Santa Rosa, the capital of the province of La Pampa. Twenty years later we won the competition for its extension, and one year later the Legislative Palace was designed. Fifty years ago we designed the small library in the Legislative Palace.

0137

The Casa Verde (1999) is almost in the countryside, where the city ends.

0139

Completed in 2003, this house is located in a gated community near the city of Buenos Aires. All the homes in this community have to be white with a gray roof. For this reason the color is on the inside.

0138

The staircase of the Konex Cultural Center (2003) was the result of a competition to build a large cultural center. Only the metal staircase was built as the whole project was not completed.

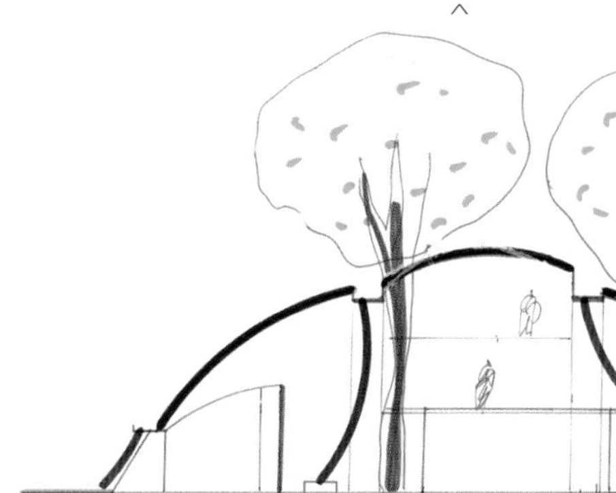

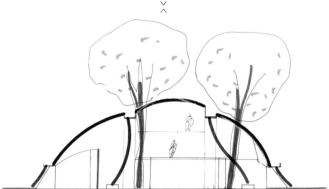

Kris Yao/Artech Architecture

6F, Dun Hua South Road Section 1
Taipei, 10689, Taiwan
P.: (+886) 2-2711-5050
www.artech-inc.com

◄0140

Nature is often the best inspiration and reference. Located at the seashore east of Taiwan, where abundant slanted cubic rocks can be found, Langyang Museum takes the form and color from this dominant landscape element.

0141►

Three strokes of Chinese ink-brush. First one is a thick, dark stroke full of ink, the second one is a dry, dragged movement of the brush, and the third one is with a wet brush, with ink seeping into the paper. The three strokes intertwine.

The architecture for the Weiwuying Performing Arts Center is composed of three parts: the solid concrete curved form houses the back stages and service functions; the reclining, but parallel, curved form houses the audience side of the functions; and the transparent volumes attached to the above two are for the lobbies and cafes. The three elements also intertwine as the brush strokes do.

0142

Again, nature is the theme for this design. The two major elements in the imaginary nature of the traditional Chinese landscape painting—cloud and stone—set the tone for this Fine Arts Museum in the ancient capital of Nanjing in China.

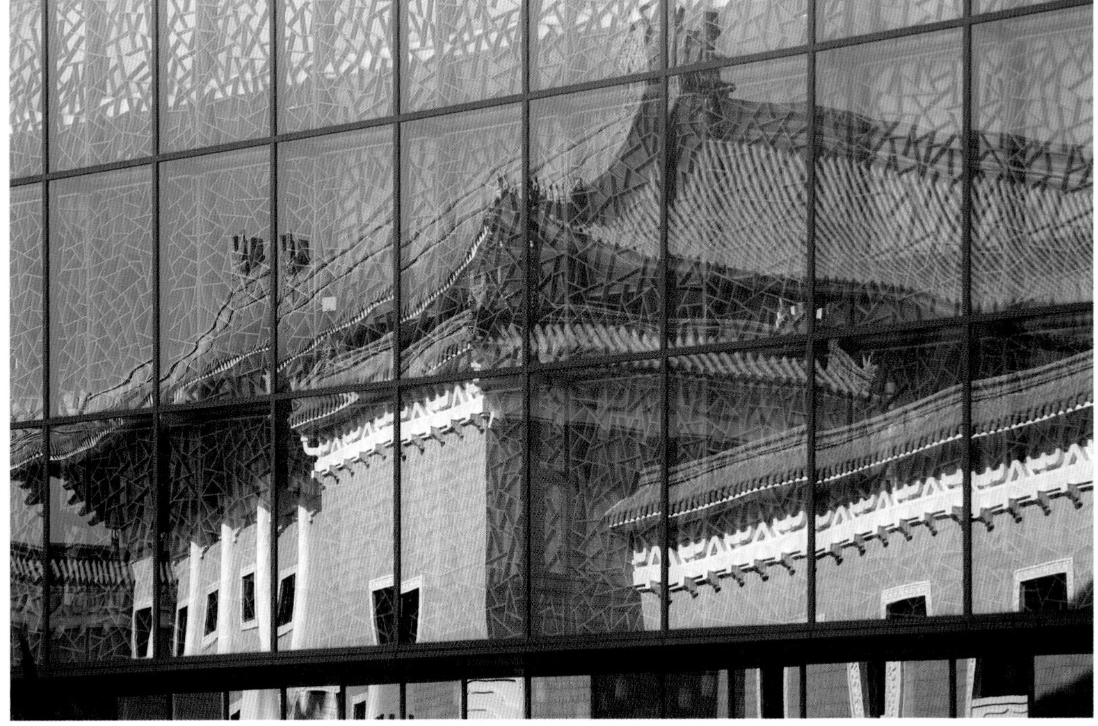

0143

The "gap" between the floating volume (the "cloud") and the pieces that protrude from under the ground (the "rock") intensifies the conflicting qualities of the two elements as the public enters the museum itself.

0144

A modern restaurant building is to be placed within the complex of the world-renowned traditional-styled Palace Museum in Taipei. The strategy is not to compete with but to compliment the surrounding old buildings.

0145

A piece of jade is being unearthed from under the sand at this half-revealed/half-hidden moment. It is full of power and imagination.

This Asian Museum with its circular form embracing a body of water, is designed with such an image. The visitors will explore the museum as if visiting a traditional Chinese garden—with constant changing views towards the same central pond.

0146

The colors for the new building—green, mustard yellow, and brown—are all carefully chosen from its surroundings. With the double-layer exterior wall, the building in the daytime reflects the graceful but colorful surrounding buildings, while at night the "ice-cracked" second layer is more prominent under the special lighting effect.

0147

A series of solid cubes in a void box, and a series of void cubes in a solid box (the interplay of Ying and Yang originated from the Chinese art of seals) is the theme for the China Fine Art Museum proposal.

0148

The exhibition and storage functions of the museum are located in solid pieces with controlled natural light, and they are clad with various color, texture, and sizes of granite on the exterior; while the void volumes in between are the public lobbies and cafes, with their glass roof and walls, ample lights are brought into the interior spaces.

0149

I like to compose complex forms in a simple manner so that the complexity is easily perceived and understood. This High Speed Train Station wraps the complex functions and structure in a relatively simple gesture: a one-pointed roof, an oval glass volume, and a pair of parallel concrete platforms.

Karres en Brands Landschapsarchitecten

Oude Amersfoortseweg 123
1212 AA Hilversum, The Netherlands
P.: (+31) 35-642-29-62
www.karresenbrands.nl

0150

Always imagine your project in bad weather.

0151 

Give beauty of the unexpected a chance.

© Jeroen Musch

0152

In order to make a strong design, sometimes it's best to repeat one good detail.

0153

Listen to the land. Use your intuition and your senses. Talk to people. Architecture is a very personal experience.

0154

The design not only determines uses, it's also determined by users.

0155

Touch and feel your projects. Spend as much time as possible on site. Use your own hands.

0156

Accept that future users will change your project. Plan with the unexpected.

0157

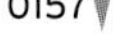

The stricter the system the more freedom is possible.

0158

Keep it simple and make it BIG!

0159

Sometimes designing is very tempting; sometimes not designing is the answer. Often silence is required instead of shouting.

Massimiliano Fuksas

Piazza del Monte di Pietà 30
00186 Roma, Italy
P.: (+39) 06-6880-7871
www.fuksas.it

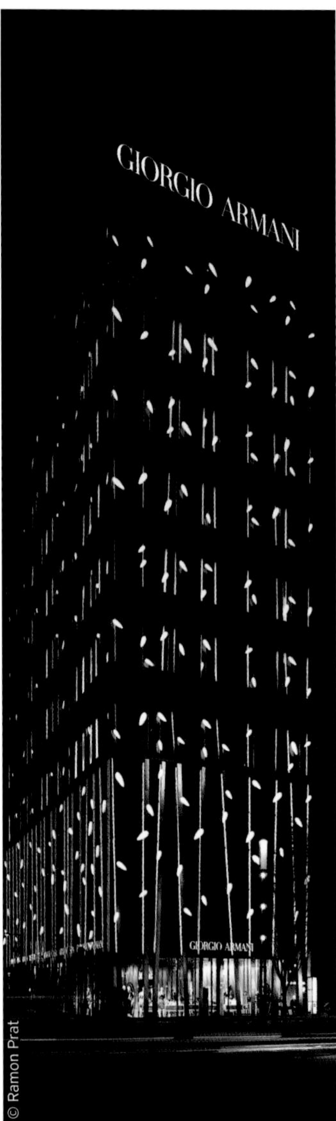

◄0160

We explored a whole host of ideas; we experimented with new textures; we modeled, sculpted, emptied, and dematerialized spaces using light, as the evanescence of an intimate sensation which comes from the exterior. The key element we wanted to incorporate in the inter-zone pathway was the element of surprise. The quest to incite emotion is as much the remittance of the architect as it is of the designer.

0161▼

The services are located within the building's double skin. The superstructure is made from steel, which is much better than concrete as it is easier to control. The glass is transparent and there are depressions and skylights. It is like a musical composition, like a wave. We wanted to create the sensation of a moving manta fish. After passing through the check-in area, travelers enter a *piazza*, where they can sit and enjoy a cup of coffee. The interior design is very important.

0162▲

It's the light that defines the space and it's the light that makes this project so magical. Its always light that directs our vision towards tectonic creations. Filling empty concrete spaces; projecting anamorphic volume into depths and penetrating even beneath ground level. It's an image that is both horizontal and vertical. It's an equation seeking solutions to conflicts between the solid and immaterial, between harmony and disharmony.

0163

The project was conceived from the desire to bring the natural environment into this highly technological complex in order to create a comfortable working ambience. Light, water, and bamboo are used in a way that transforms this building into a landscape. This project is the evolution of a new poetry genre of lightness.

© Colarossi

0164

The cloud—a totally free form housing the conference halls—is the distinguishing mark of this creation. It appears to be suspended inside the shell, halfway between the floor and the ceiling of the large illuminated hall. Built out of steel and Teflon, it is supported by a dense mesh of steel ribs, braced and resting on three elements.

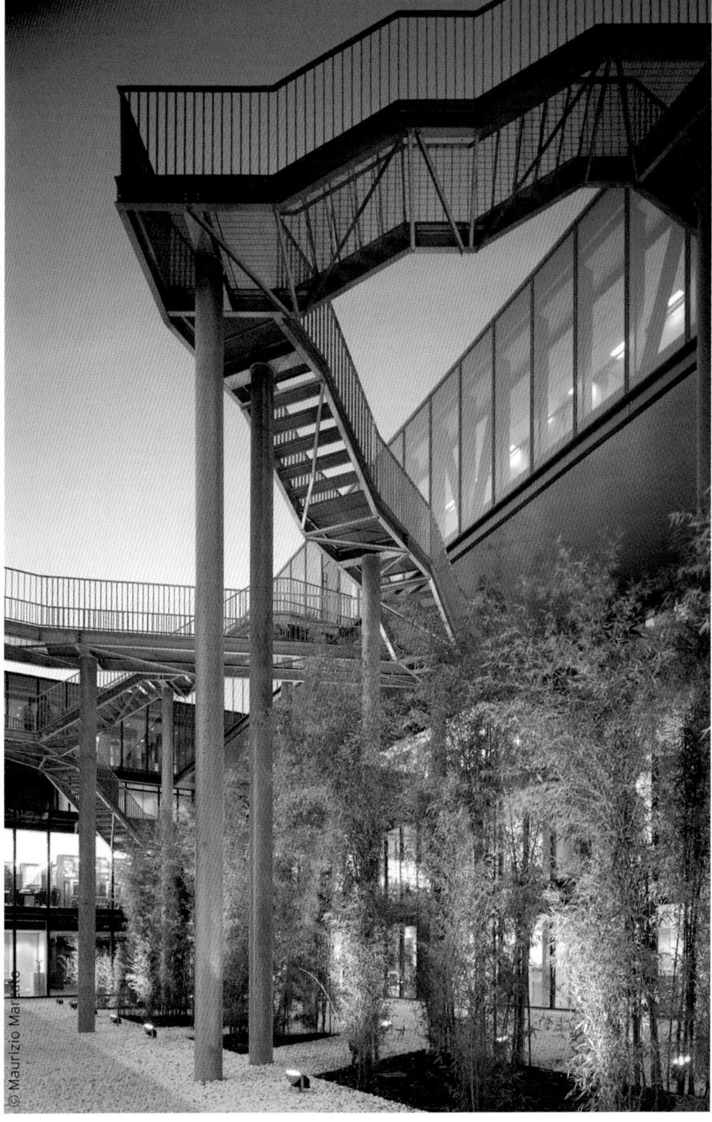

© Maurizio Marcato

© Moreno Maggi

◄0165

These façades are pulled taut across the entire complex, like garments over a human body. There is a place of communication between the individual functions of the building. This connection is strengthened by the verticality of the white steles, shaped sculptures that draw the view upward and visibly connect the levels.

0166▼

This building was designed as an autonomous and sculptural architectural element. It has a symbolic role as a space for performances. The volume is light-enhanced though the use of a membrane stretched across the elliptical rings screwed around the structure. The materials are simple and elegant: canvas, steel, and cement for the structure. The exterior finish is a red PVC membrane.

0167►

The New Milan Trade Fair is part of the recovery of wide urban spaces, and of the territory that goes beyond the city borders: areas that aspire to become geography and landscape.

The glass and steel molded roof was conceived as a roof landscape. This feature aims to set up an interplay between architecture and geography, and is a motif repeated throughout the pavilion, which is quite plain.

© Philippe Ruault

© Paolo Riolzi

0168

The building exterior is formed by alternate layers of concrete and translucent glass. During the day, the transparent glass filters the light inside, and by night it projects light outside, forming a magical image inspiring a special, spiritual message.

This project is a venue for encounters, debate, reasoning, and solutions.

© Moreno Maggi

0169

Architecture is not a mere act of creation; it is a democratic act which aims to bring together the community. This place is imbued with sensibility; it is a meeting place and a place for emotions. Because, above all, architecture is an emotion. Creating a building is a form of Humanism. Zenith is a space for sharing; a space for enlightenment. Zenith is also the way of understanding "air."

© Moreno Maggi

Dekleva Gregoric Arhitekti

Dalmatinova 11
1000 Ljubljana, Slovenia
P.: (+386) 1-430-52-70
www.dekleva-gregoric.com

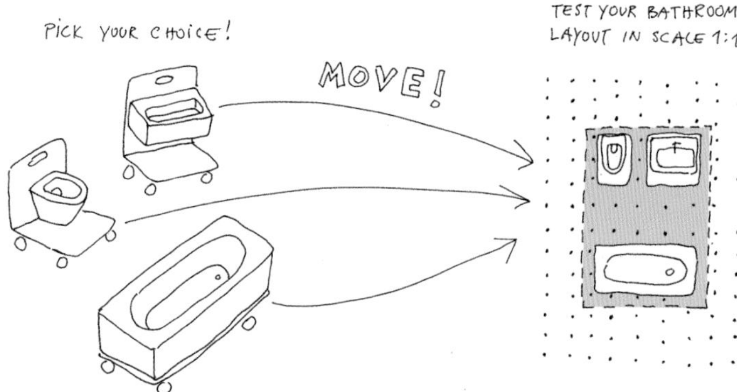

0170

Encourage user interaction through mobile bathroom elements.

0171

Think in sections.

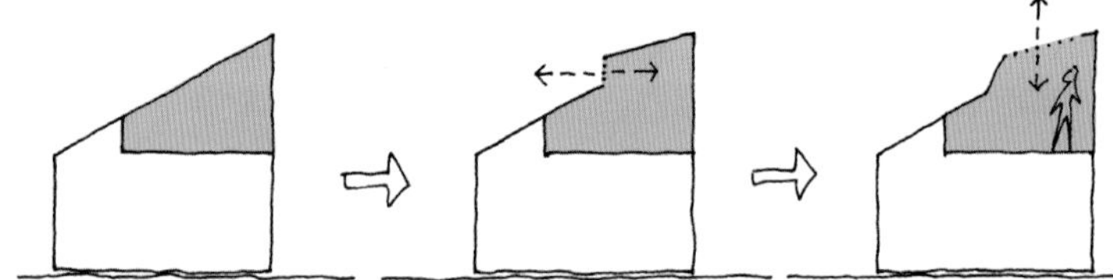

0172

Curtain partitions have several functions: space definition, background unification, light diffusion, and acoustic regulation.

0173

Challenge the obvious: twisted roof light shafts providing more light and better celestial views.

◄0174

Challenge the use of materials and expose their true nature: exposed welding details on the steel stairs.

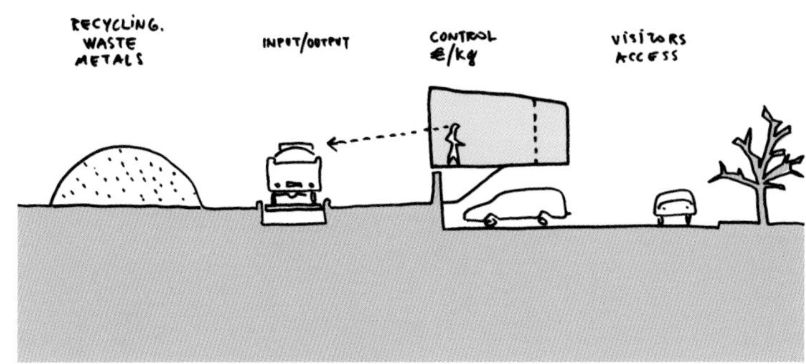

0175►

Respond to specific conditions.
A 100 percent metal building (structure + facade) can be easily recycled on site when it is no longer needed.

0176▲

At a metal reutilization plant, the recycling production process is the key input.

◄0177

Be explicit with materials.

0178►

Structure the volume to improve scale: 3 for 1, three buildings instead of one.

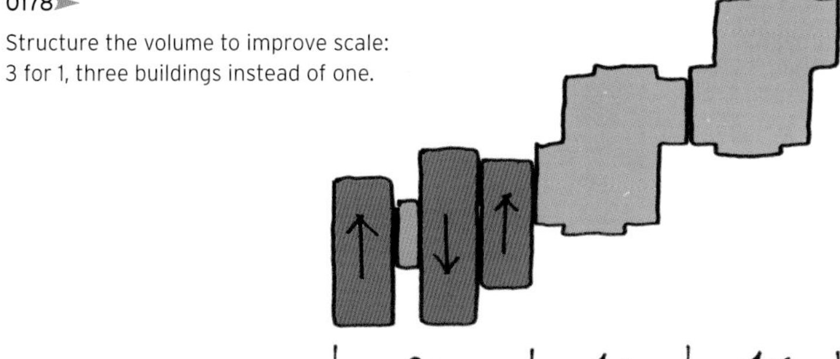

0179►

Pay attention to details, regardless of the project scale.

Felipe Assadi + Francisca Pulido

Carmencito 262, of. 202
7550056 Las Condes, Santiago, Chile
P.: (+56) 2234-5558
www.felipeassadi.com

0180

Separate the structure from the ground
Not only does this prevent contact with damp rising from the earth, it also broadens the visual horizon and increases the project's autonomy.

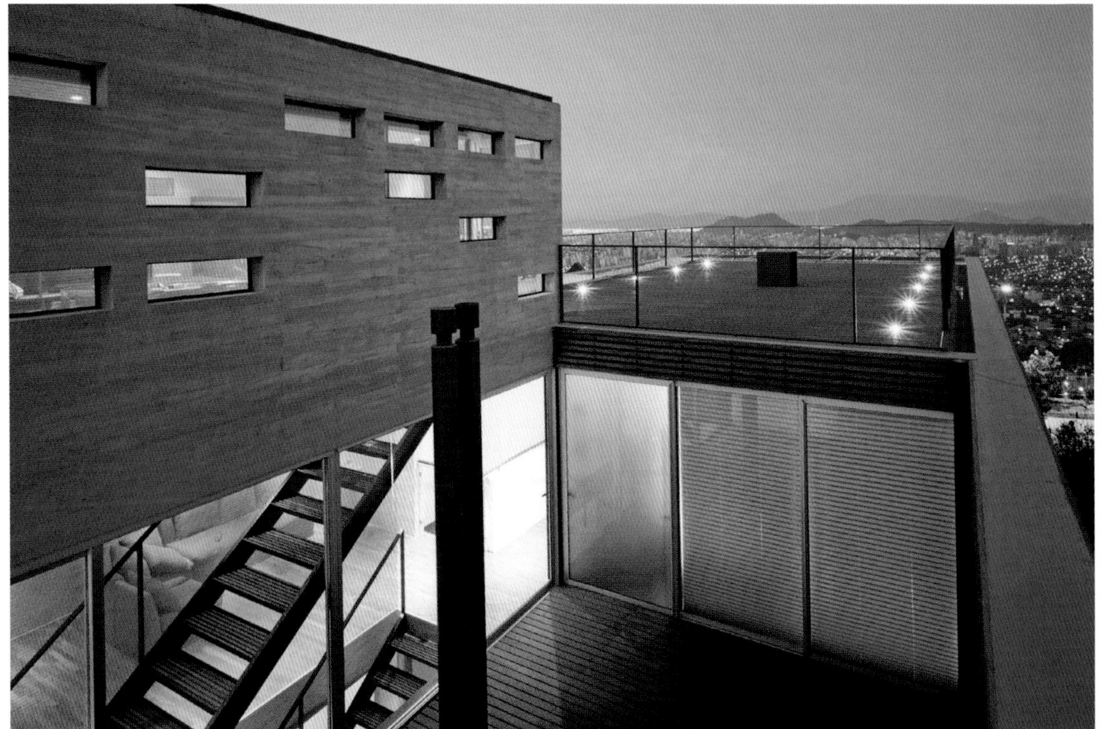

0181

Add a roof terrace whenever possible
Return approximately the same amount of earth that you have removed from the house.

◄0182

Build in furniture

Some buildings are designed to house a certain type of furniture that is best to build during the building's construction stage. This is also the more economical option.

0183►

Whenever possible, create an interior courtyard

It will provide ventilation and natural lighting in large-scale projects.

0184

Double skins

These are very useful in dwellings in close proximity to one another and when residents need isolation from their neighbors. These examples allow interesting interpretations of lighting.

0185

Add a water mirror

We mostly use this technique in minimalist courtyards, as the mirrors preserve emptiness. Otherwise, the space would be filled with objects, furniture, etc. In some cases, such as in this project, water mirrors reflect light to the surrounding spaces.

0186

Make volumes independent according to their use or the program

0187

Skylights

When these are visible, they create a new element in the landscape.

0188

Integrate a pool into the house

This saves resources if it is dug into the foundations of the house. This also conditions its use in accordance with the dwelling program.

0189

Disorder generates interest as it contradicts what is natural

We generally use disorder to organize façades, windows, flooring or, as in this case, to arrange lamps.

Josep Lluís Mateo/ MAP Architects

Teodoro Roviralta 39
08022 Barcelona, Spain
P.: (+34) 932-18-63-58
www.mateo-maparchitect.com

◄0190

The photographer describes the buildings as they were contemplated: a mass that breaks up toward the sky. At street level there is complexity and fragmentation, human details in a nutshell.

0191►

The building in relation to the sky. The folds of the surface and the material are interlocutors of the reflection, transparency, brightness, light, and shade.

0192 

The photographer describes the material, light, depth and concealed parts (water harvesting systems on the lower roof, the beam of the overhang, etc.) that are of great concern to the architect but normally invisible. Our work is not a quest for effects, it is something more essential.

0193►

The light moving from the interior to exterior spaces creates a special transparent effect. I normally prefer a more complex barrier between interior and exterior spaces instead of pure transparency.

Cold. Material freezes like the ground despite the interior light, and, when seen from outside, evokes fire.

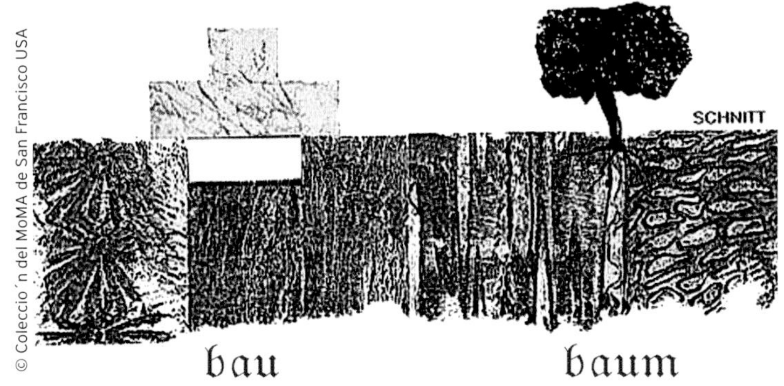

0194

Concept: the expression of an idea in words and images that is essential for communication.

0195

Space: descent. Our study is invisible from the street; it falls toward the center of the earth. Piranesi and his prisons.

0196

Location: the horizon cuts the house in two. The sea crosses it.

0197

Materials: stone. A pixel in the hands of Portuguese quarrymen available for magic.

© Beat Marugg

0198

Structure: the façade is the structure. The form is the pure exhibition of the movement of loads across the surface.

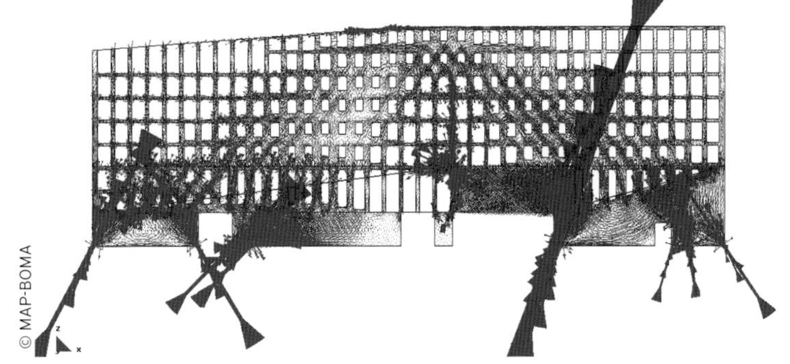

0199

Construction: moments that are ephemeral yet charged with energy. Later on, the building condenses these. They are hidden, invisible, yet real. They give soul to the buildings. That is why I am interested in being involved in construction.

Alonso Balaguer i Arquitectes Associats

Bac de Roda 40
08019 Barcelona, Spain
P.: (+34) 933-03-41-60
www.alonsobalaguer.com

> <

© Josep Mª Molinos

0200

Incorporate graphic design into architecture

Buildings with signs all over telling you what to do and what not to do can be bothersome. Graphic design brings joy and relaxation to architecture and can be accompanied by industrial designs that contain symbolic elements of the building.

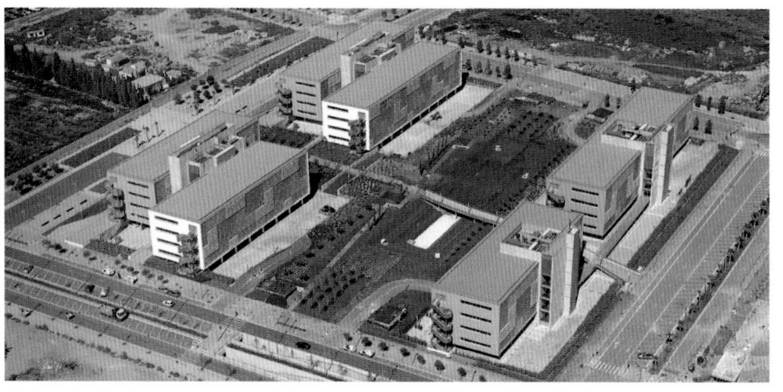

0201

Architecture should give the necessary flexibility

The changes in social patterns, habits, and technology in our lives are increasingly rapid and intense. But architecture is usually very inflexible with respect to future adaptations: the combination of a double skin façade with external communication nuclei was the solution used in the Viladecans Business Park.

0202 

Compact the city

The oil slick growth of many Spanish cities during the last decades is not sustainable from any standpoint. Compacting our cities with vertical growth in specific areas is an important formula for urban regeneration. Our proposal for the old Repsol warehouse in central Malaga, is a prime example of this technique.

◄0203

The importance of the 5th façade
The forgotten 5th façade, the roof of the building, often visually abuses and mistreats its environment. A poorly ordered storeroom to store systems and machinery. A minimum of architectural sensitivity helps to convert it into a real façade.

0204►

Functional promiscuity is a key to the future
Our historic Mediterranean cities based their success on a mixture of uses, which in recent decades has been lost with the growth of strong mono-functional ghettos. We believe it is important to design cities and buildings with promiscuous functions, and that sustainability also stems from the extensive use of buildings. Las Arenas is one example where culture, leisure, sport, commercial, and office space coexists.

0205

Externalize vertical communication elements and services

Something as simple as preserving the useful area of the building and externalizing stairwells, elevators, pipes, services etc., adds value to the architecture as it gives great flexibility.

© Josep Mª Molinos

© Josep Mª Molinos

0206

Use double skin façades as a sustainable, flexible element

On one side, this provides the sun protection that is so necessary in Spain, on the other, it gives modular flexibility to the interior skin. A wide range of materials and solutions can be used, including silkscreen glass, ceramics, wire mesh, stainless steel, and more.

0207

Use water as a landscaping element
This urban spa in Barcelona has extraordinary views of the adjacent park, with a stainless steel pool that overflows on the side facing the park, achieving an effect of a reflected landscape without limits. This forms an extension of the park inside the Sports Center.

0208

Expose systems
Serious problems in maintenance and repairs are common and these systems unfortunately tend to be installed behind false ceilings and floors.
We try not to conceal these systems, but instead to enhance them through correctly locating them, and, in some cases such as the Hesperia Tower, locate them near the center of gravity of the building, thereby saving energy.

0209

Use the defining characteristic of a city and its landscape
Every city has a characteristic that defines, differentiates, and characterizes it: a smell, a sound, or a color. That was the case in Peñafiel, whose view from the historic castle was a reddish-brown, typical of tiled roofs. We opted for a solution to ceramically coat the vaults, which are visually integrated into

Baumschlager Eberle Lochau ZT GmbH

Lindauer Straße 31
6911 Lochau, Austria
P.: (+43) 557-443-079-16
www.baumschlager-eberle.com

0210

Architecture lasts longer than mechanical services. Architectural resources can therefore be used to lend greater durability to the cooling and heating of buildings. The balconies on this laboratory building vary in depth depending on the cardinal point. The planners can thus exercise exact control over the shadowing of individual parts of the building, thereby greatly reducing the technical outlay for cooling.

0211

This large housing estate never looks the same. Foldaway sliding elements protect the private sphere of each individual home. But they also allow light and air into the private open-air spaces as and when required.

Interestingly enough, if all these story-high elements were to be closed, the estate would be transformed into an outsized copper sculpture.

0212

Residential buildings on steep slopes are mostly positioned parallel to the contour lines. The advantage of a radial arrangement is that the houses re-establish contact with each other, creating a settlement structure with an emphasis on community. The distance residents frequently wish to keep from their neighbors is preserved by the space between the buildings, and the view of the countryside is retained.

0213

Everywhere these days lifts compete with stairs. Walking up stairs saves energy, but if people are to actually use them they have to be made attractive. Crucially, they need the right proportions to ensure that walking up and down them is a pleasure rather than a pain. A useful approach would be to have the first step designed so that it hovers about a hand's breadth above the ground.

0214

Maximum transparency is a standard requirement in modern office design. In this case the façade consists of two parts. The light-refracting, layered panels of the outer skin transform the building into an emerald emitting a sparkle that changes with the daylight hours and can be seen for miles around. The inner façade safeguards the rights of the occupants, who can open the windows individually as they please.

0215

The central corridor accesses in the seven-story students' hostel called for an innovative approach to the lighting direction. Wells were cut out of the central corridors, allowing much more light into the access levels. The residents can look a long way into the floors above and below. Three-dimensionality becomes an attractive feature and the area outside the apartments acquires an element of privacy.

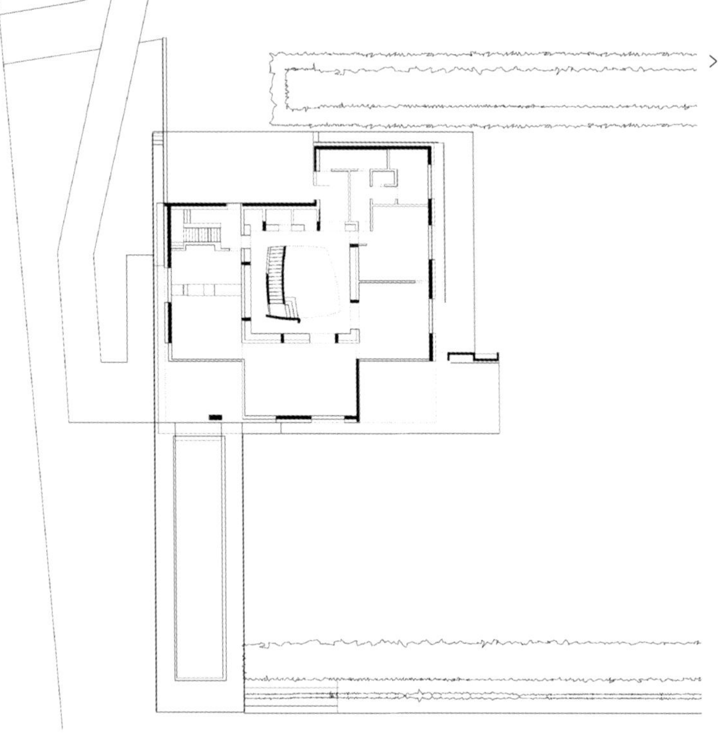

0216

Like in a classical villa, the private rooms on the upper floor are situated above a dynamically shaped hall. The spacious apartments for the client's children can function as independent units. The individual character of the residential units is reinforced by loggias inserted into the skin of the building, thus emphasizing its sculptural nature. The children will probably want to stay with their parents for a long time.

0217➤

The gravitational pull of the earth is to architecture what the wind is to sailing. The idea underlying this port building was to defy the elements by overcoming gravity. Concrete is the best material for fulfilling this dream, and it also has a distinctly practical benefit. The port area can be flooded during bad weather, but the owner of the port can still survey the scene.

© Eduard Hueber/Arch Photo Inc.

0219▼

Defining the borders between the interior and the exterior: supporting elements in the façade of the port clubhouse reflect the vegetation in the water. Contrasting with this irregular structure are the regular rectangular shapes of the glass panes that are decorated in a completely random manner. The interaction between the orthogonal and the biomorphic draws boundaries and allows them to disappear.

© Eduard Hueber/Arch Photo Inc.

◄0218

The idea behind this detached house was to enable the inhabitants to look out without others being able to look in. The completely transparent inner glazed cube offers a superb panoramic view of the attractive surroundings. But the residents did not wish to live a life of "complete exposure" and so a slatted wooden frame was installed in front of the inner climate barrier to serve as a privacy screen and offer protection against the sunlight. The slats are closed at ground level but open at different degrees of inclination on the residential floor.

© Eduard Hueber/Arch Photo Inc.

Atelier Hitoshi Abe

3.3.16 Oroshi-machi Wakabayashi-ku
Sendai-city Miyagi, 984.0015 Japan
P.: (+81) 2-2284-3411
www.a-slash.jp

0220

Design Tools

The design tools that adapt to each person connect your vague internal ideas with the external world. Design does not exist only inside you or outside, but at the boundary between these spheres. Therefore, the better the design tools are, the closer you and the world become to enabling creativity. The criteria for these tools are that they must adapt to your body, can be used quickly, can be observed, can be redone, and are easy to operate. At the moment, my favorite design tools are a whiteboard, marker, tracing paper, sharp pencil (0.5 point), post-its, digital camera, PC, projector, voice recorder, scissors, scotch tape, a calculator (large), and copy machine, etc.

0221

Change scale

In order to comprehensively grasp a problem, a project has to be analyzed from various viewpoints. Changing scale is an effective method of maintaining a wide range of viewpoints. Change scale between a bird's eye view (1:10,000) from above to an insect's point view (1:1) from the ground. However, if you observe randomly from all scales, your idea might become rather disperse. What is important here is to define both extremes of problematic scales, in other words, to find out the minimum and the maximum scale you have to deal with in a project. This will help you define a frame of a "world" in the project. Then you can set up intermediate scales between them to give focus.

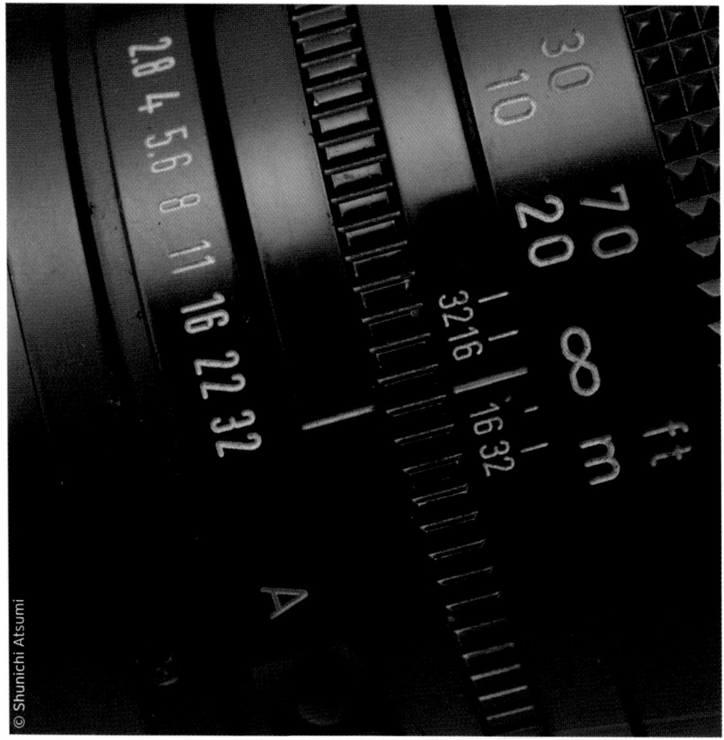

0222

Let's set up a place

Just like nomads who keep traveling, for intelligent adventurers who explore the unknown field of a project, a base camp supporting their activity is important. Six principles for an ideal workplace:

1. Big table
2. Wide wall
3. Easygoing library
4. Comfortable and light chair
5. Marginal space to escape
6. And do not tidy up

0223

Meetings should be 4 rounds of 30 minutes

Meeting is a sport. Just like soccer, basketball, or any other kind of sport, meetings should have a clear purpose and goal. And the time has to be limited. Within a limited time, you drive a meeting towards creation by using intensity and relaxation, and all kinds of artifices. From my own experience, a creative meeting should be a set of four 30 minute meetings that last no more than two hours.

0224

Take a 15-minute nap

If you feel stuck, it is a good idea to take a nap for 15 minutes. A nap has to be between 10 minutes and 15 minutes. Be careful not to sleep more than 20 minutes. The idea is not to let your brain sleep but to reactivate it.
Three tips for a 15-minute nap:

1. Be ready to wake up. Human beings have a natural self-awakening capacity. Use this ability to sleep so you can wake up.
2. Do not lie down. If you lie down comfortably, you tend to sleep for more than 20 minutes. Put your head down on a desk to take a nap.
3. Drink a cup of coffee to take a nap. Caffeine starts to work 30 minutes after you drink it. A cup of coffee or tea promises you a better awakening after a nap.

大の字で寝る。
In an X shape.

ふて寝する。
Sulking.

机に突っ伏して寝る。
Put a head down on a desk.

寝袋で寝る。
In a sleeping bag.

S,M,L,XLを枕に寝る
With Rem (S,M,L,XL).

コタツで寝る。
In a "kotatsu."

フロで寝る。
In a bathtub.

立って寝る。
Standing.

机の下にもぐって寝る。
Under a desk.

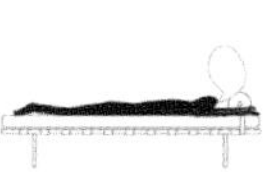

ミースで寝る。
With Mies.

椅子に座って寝る。
With Eames.

コルビジェで寝る。
With Corb.

ハンモックで寝る。
In a hammock.

電車で寝る。
In a commuter train.

正座して寝る。
In a "seiza" position.

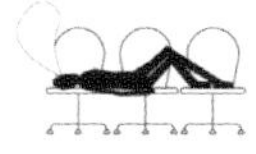

椅子を並べて寝る。
On three Eames.

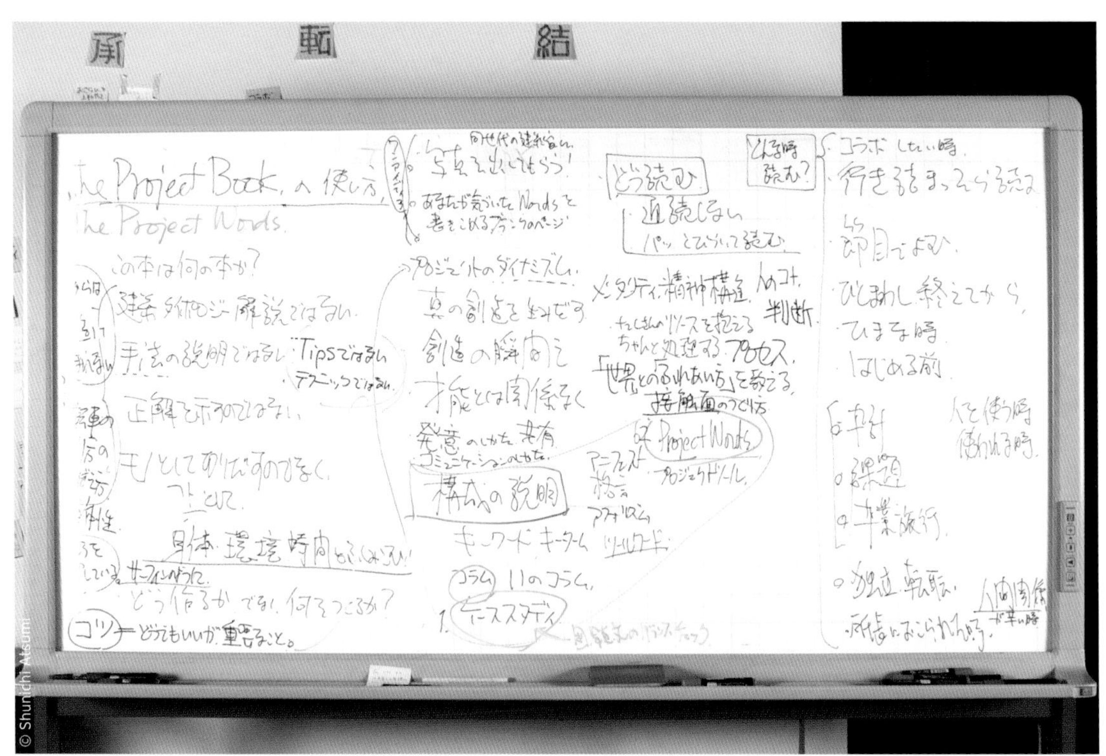

◄0225

Use a white board (combined with a printer)!

Ideas are like smoke in the air: vague, always changing form. Therefore speed and timing are important to catch them. The most effective tool so far to capture such ideas is a white board (with integrated printer). The most important characteristic of a white board is that it should stand vertically. Horizontal surfaces, such as a table, often create personal territory, on the other hand, vertical white boards enable information to be viewed globally and help to create a collaborative environment.

White boards are a tool enabling us to externalize ideas during the brainstorming process, which are fed back to us as a medium in order to encourage the next idea to emerge. Moreover, with a single click, this tool immortalizes ever-changing communications on paper.

0226►

Don't write words, draw them

Using slide shows, such as PowerPoint, in presentations can become boring. People are no longer amazed by media-rich, gorgeous presentations full of computer graphics and animations. However, texts still play a central role in transmitting information. This fact has not changed yet.

Of course, no one wants to read lengthy sentences in tiny fonts. Only large words that can be captured in an instant should be put on a screen. It is better to stimulate the great imagination of a client by letting them read between simple words.

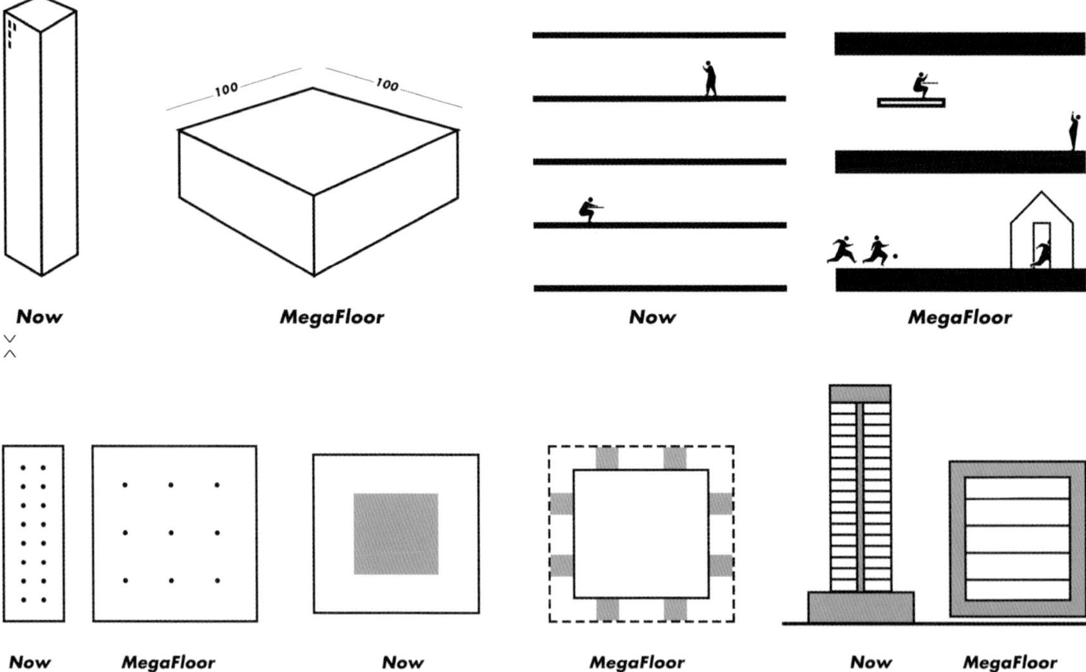

◄0227

Ten aphorisms for brainstorming

Some people say that quality is more than quantity. But in brainstorming, those two are not contradictory. Quality ideas emerge from a quantity of ideas. Below are the ten aphorisms for effective brainstorming.

1. Do not criticize
2. Do not focus on who came up with the idea
3. Overlap
4. Clarify your goal
5. Segment time
6. Place does matter
7. Positioning
8. Speak out
9. Let your eyes wonder
10. Never take notes: someone should be assigned this task

0228►

Projects change the world

During projects, clients continually change their minds. Architects, too, want to change their ideas. Nobody can stop a project from changing. A better project tends to automatically create a new scope, and it opens up a new vision of the world. A project changes the world, and also changes itself. A project is a kind of ecosystem that contains an internal feedback loop; as agents in this system, we are engulfed by the change in the world created by the evolution of a project.

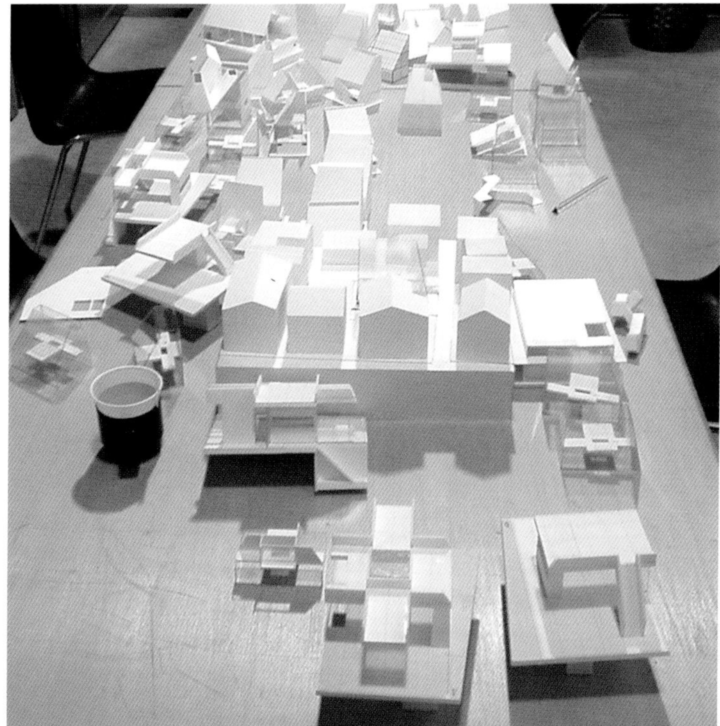

0229▼

Review to proceed

A project's work generally proceeds intermittently. To proceed effectively, reviews must be carried out. A good review does not only repeat what was done previously, it organizes past ideas and works as a genealogy in order to categorize them into groups. In doing this, members can reconfirm the direction of the project, enhance information sharing, and define the current standpoint of the team. All meetings start and end with a review.

Kuwabara Payne McKenna Blumberg Architects

322 King Street West, 3rd Floor
Toronto, Ontario, M5V 1J2 Canada
P.: (+1) 416-977-5104
www.kpmbarchitects.com

◄0230

Conceive tall buildings as vertical communities. In a world where interaction between people is increasingly digital, it is increasingly important to create opportunities for mixing and interaction in real time and space. We created a vertical urban campus for Concordia University in downtown Montreal by organizing the plan around a system of stacked atria with interconnecting stairs and lounges located near elevator lobbies.

0231▲

Every building needs a heart where people can assemble or simply find a sanctuary in the company of others. For the Centennial HP Science and Technology Center, we created an academic village organized around a *Town Square*—an informal gathering space with large Spanish steps beneath a wood-clad lecture pod for students to meet, hang out, and assemble.

©Tom Arban

0232

"There is a crack in the jar . . . that's how the light gets in"—Leonard Cohen. Rooms that receive no natural light, or light from one direction, are static. Even the smallest sources of natural light can animate spaces with diurnal and seasonal rhythms, such as the small window and skylight at the west end of the long living loft of the Reisman-Jenkinson House.

0233

Use the space between form and mass to create communal areas: the public realm. In the Japanese Canadian Cultural Center we used the space between the program to create the Gallery Hall—a space wide enough to host exhibits and events.

© Steven Evans

© Tom Arban

0234

Every building implies a city. Imagine every building as one figure within a group portrait of the urban fabric. Richard Sennet, writing about family portraits by German photographer Thomas Struth, compared the table around which the family members sit and stand to a shared public space. In this project, Canada's National Ballet School, new and old, tall and short, mass and light, create an urban ensemble, a portrait of the city within the city.

© Eduard Hueber/Arch Photo Inc.

◄0235

Subtract rather than add in order to create space in existing buildings. Openings cut through floors and ceilings provide visual connections and draw natural light into the center. For the James Stewart Center, we cut a void through a Collegiate Gothic building to open up the floor plate, providing visual connectivity between scholars and students, and drawing natural light deep into the center.

© Gerry Kopelow

0236►

Integrate performance, aesthetics, and urbanism to make architecture a collaborative endeavor between the client, architects, consultants, and builders. Be responsive and responsible for the health and well-being of users, cities, and environments. Manitoba Hydro Place, a new office tower for an energy corporation in downtown Winnipeg, was designed using the Integrated Design Process to achieve a seamless fusion of a supportive workplace, urban revitalization, and 60 percent energy efficiency in an extreme climate that ranges from -31°F to +95°F (-35°C to +35°C). It will be a model for climate responsive design.

0237

Use a limited material palette to achieve coherence and calm. For the Gardiner Museum, we added a new floor to a two-story museum, and thoroughly renovated its interior. The Indiana limestone resonates with an adjacent Beaux-Arts building. White oak and glass weave the interior together to create an intimate, quiet backdrop against which to foreground a collection of ceramic treasures.

© Shai Gil

0238

Make halls not corridors when creating spaces of movement and circulation. In the James Stewart Center we created generously scaled hallways furnished with blackboards, benches, and tables to promote spontaneous teamwork.

© Eduard Hueber/Arch Photo Inc.

0239

Maximize flexibility to adapt easily to change. Change is the only thing that is certain. The concrete loft with high ceilings, maximum exposure to natural light, and a robust structure is the most flexible and sustainable of building types and can be adapted for living, working, and recreation (Vaughan Civic Centre, under construction).

© Tom Arban

Endo Shuhei Architect Institute Inc.

2-14-5. Tenma. Kita-ku
530-0043 Osaka, Japan
P.: (+81) 6-6354-7456
www.paramodern.com

© Yoshiharu Matsumura

0240

It was originally developed to be used as a base for emergency activities in times of disaster, but in order to effectively utilize the vast area during normal times as well, it currently functions as an indoor tennis complex. Its systemized trusses form continuous asymmetrical curves, and three large skylights and a center court 16 feet below ground level create continuity in the vertical space.

© Yoshiharu Matsumura

0241

This asymmetrical shape of the dome of this tennis complex stems from the surrounding natural environmental conditions. Its irregular form has no protrusions and allows wild grass from the natural ecosystem to propagate on its green roof.

© Yoshiharu Matsumura

© Yoshiharu Matsumura

0242

The wooden, single-layer truss structure, effectively utilizing a surplus of thinned wood, forms the roof and walls of the facility, creating a continuous three-dimensional space. The three spaces are seamlessly joined together in varying form, centered around the lightwell.

0243

Three spherical bodies are smoothly connected to one another, and a courtyard positioned roughly in the center of the facility functions as a lightwell that allows light and wind into the interior and increases the stability of the structure. The exterior, covered in weather-resistant steel sheets, changes color over time, deepening the structure's harmony with its surrounding environment.

© Yoshiharu Matsumura

0244

The characteristic 425-ft-long stone wall of this funeral hall exhibits the many aspects of stones through changes in time, light, and shadows, creating both an interior and exterior environment. The two consecutive roofs create a dynamic, static space.

© Yoshiharu Matsumura

0245

The roof of this kindergarten has a wooden structure, forming a space that embodies the concept of one of nature's rational shapes: the bubble. The facility is comprised of four nursery rooms, a playroom, a staffroom, and a meeting room. The space within the structure is multifunctional, while also successfully maintaining a sense of unity with the materials and the environment.

© Yoshiharu Matsumura

0246

A steel sheet structure is created by directly utilizing the prevailing natural element of gravity. The curved roof was not designed as an objective, but rather as a result of the architecture.

© Yoshiharu Matsumura

0247

The retaining wall on a slope is utilized as an architectural element to the greatest extent possible. The interaction of the integrated roof, walls, and retaining wall creates both an open and enclosed space.

0248

The form of this guest house is established by a repetition of straight lines of corrugated steel sheets and arcs of compound materials. The various segmented spaces are linked while sharing peripheral sections such as 'front/back' and 'interior/exterior', evenly exhibiting a communion of discontinuous, spread out components, from exterior to interior and vice versa.

© Yoshiharu Matsumura

© Yoshiharu Matsumura

0249

This lavatory is formed by an inverted, continuous spiral band of 0.125 inch corrugated steel sheeting. The interior walls form the exterior ceiling and floor, which then continues on to form the exterior walls and roofs and then back to forming the interior. By means of a trajectory that advances the three precisely cylindrical, continuous sides, the structure is reduced to its geometric form.

Arkitekt Kristine Jensens Tegnestue

Mejlagde 50 bb st
8000 Aarhus C, Denmark
P.: (+45) 86-18-96-34
www.kristinejensen.dk

© Simon Høgsberg

◄0250

In this boulevard project the activity areas are placed as counterparts to the continuing green sections. The boulevard and the activity areas constitute the park as a whole and can be seen as coordinated elements. Precisely as the Egyptian hieroglyphs, the elements are placed side by side without a superior hierarchical system and without defined leaps in scale.

0251▼

When solving terrain problems on the site we actually turned these into the main landscape feature. The 328-ft-long (100 m) wall and staircase dividing the parking lot and the lower area is now the main meeting place for Egå High School students, where they can sit in the sun until late afternoon.

© Christina Capatillo

0252➤

The non-homogeneous character of space with industrial, home, traffic and city life offers the chance to test materials that are more modern than the prevalent safe choices. The materials chosen are generally unconventional. The surfaces of the footpaths have strong graphic patterns, the squares and activity areas appear as red areas in the green; there are edges in stainless steel, green neon lights, fences with soft curves, curbstones of granite, black rubber boards, etc.

© Christina Capatillo

© Thomas Mølvig

◄0253

Whereas the green sections are the connecting elements, the activity areas are seen as ruptures and crossing fields. It was necessary to enclose or screen several of the activity areas. The fence, which has no front or rear, efficiently shields the area while allowing onlookers to glimpse through. It appears as creased pieces and creates the architectural signature of several activity areas that contrast with the straight lines of the boulevard.

© Bjarne Frost

© Thomas Mølvig

0254

The parking lot at the school is normally only used during the day. As it is a large sloping area visible from both the classrooms and the nearby road, we had to make the very most of this feature. Through using traditional white stripes we turned it upside down and made it fun by defining the parking spaces using letters spelling Egå Gymnasium.

0255

In order to restore the schoolyard as a public space and structural codex on both a city level and in between the row of existing houses, we filled the gap with a circular music stage and on the opposite side we built a new wall which is almost 250 ft (76 m) long and 18 to 23 ft (5.5 to 7 m) high. This framework seems to give order and deals with orientation and stability. Tangible magnolias and colorful dots overflow in the space between the long wall and steel structures.

© Simon Høgsberg

0256

In this sense the place is organized, reorganized, and disorganized at the same time. We aimed to make a kind of place that counteracts classical terms of beginnings and endings. It was an invitation for us to work with a polyfocal space that reflects the fact that it is approached from many different angles, since it can be entered in many different ways.

0257

Materials are essential. We have tried to reconnect past and present through an architectural program in which we contradict and counteract soft with hard, magnolias with steel structures, and masculinity with femininity. The steel comes as both raw steel, Corten steel, and painted steel. The asphalt was a ready-made element from the schoolyard days and is reused as terrain with a new top layer. And the bright white graphic creates links between the houses.

0258

Coverings can be so much more. This floor covering was developed as a metaphor on an illuminated surface of water, evoking the river running alongside. The covering is made in black basalt; white tints resemble reflections in the water and blue hues accentuate the blue tone of this type of basalt.

0259

An outdoor furniture collection was designed for this project. The overall arrangement of the furniture emerged from the idea of lines of notes organizing, specifying, and keeping the different elements in place. Benches, plant boxes, or bicycle stands are joined to become one element: the strip. The continuous course is underlined by the repetition of a single material: steel. This is bent and turned like a paper chain, creating a variety of situations and spaces.

Andrew Maynard Architects

Suite 12, 397 Smith St
3065 Fitzroy, VIC, Australia
P.: (+61) 399-396-323
www.maynardarchitects.com

© Peter Bennetts

0260

You do not have to view statutory body regulations as limitations. Here, the strict dictations regarding the extension's height and setbacks were obeyed in a playful manner, generating this interesting roof form that subverts these restrictions and ultimately results in a unique interpretation of these rules.

© Peter Bennetts

0261

The eastern and western façades of this building were concealed in louvers to give the clients complete control of the amount of sun entering into their extension. This level of control and ability to monitor heat gain from solar exposure and heat loss from what would have been large exposed windows greatly reduces reliance on heating and cooling systems.

© Peter Bennetts

0262

The desire to delineate the usually distinct division between outdoor and indoor spaces, resulted in the creation of this "postless corner." Here, there is no permanent, confronting physical barrier between inside and outside, allowing these often separate environments to coexist and their boundaries to blur.

0263 

Rather than solving a single problem with a single solution, look to solve many problems with one solution: design elements that can multitask and have multiple functions. Here, this staircase also acts as part of the kitchen woodwork and storage space.

© Peter Bennetts

0264

The simple box shape is the strongest and most economic architectural form available. The "tattoo" on the external facade was a playful solution to strict regulations on second story screening, while allowing as much light to filter into the building as possible, in line with the client's program. The graphics, inspired by neighborhood trees, create an interesting dappled interior lighting effect.

© Peter Bennetts

© Peter Bennetts

0265

Breaking up a large mass into smaller fragments enables the creation of interesting forms and interiors. This arrangement of boxes of different height and depths, and the varying thickness of the walls of this extension, provides solidity to this fragmented box. The right angle layout of the larger fragment ensures increased interaction between this face and the outside environment.

0266

Good orientation for your building is vital. If not, measures such as screening and shading devices must be employed to enable the low sun to penetrate deep into your building while blocking out the higher, harsher sun.

0267

Buildings do not respond to the condition of time. Our lives are becoming increasingly more mobile—with cars, mobiles and planes—and change is imminent. So why are our buildings so static and frozen? This concept is an architectural form that can be transformed and arranged to respond to time, sex, age, mood, weather, light, and technology. As wants and need change, architecture should be able to be manipulated to suit them.

© Peter Bennetts

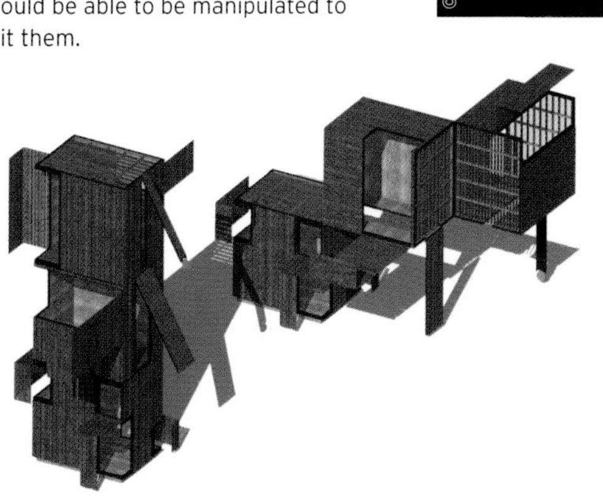

0268

Recycling and reusing building materials and found objects may not always be the most economic solution, but it means that your materials have a much lower carbon footprint, in addition to adding character and context to your design.

0269

Break down the mental thresholds and tunnel vision restricting you. Do not always use a linear and formal response to address needs, change, and the future. Respond to global environments and be forward thinking. CV08 is a response to society's reliance on cars and oil, and to what may happen when oil has run out and transportation no longer functions. Think globally and think outside of your square.

Vāstu Shilpā Consultants

Balkrishna V Doshi
'Sangath', Drive In Road
Ahmedabad 380054, India
P.: (+91) 79-27-45-4537/39
www.sangath.org

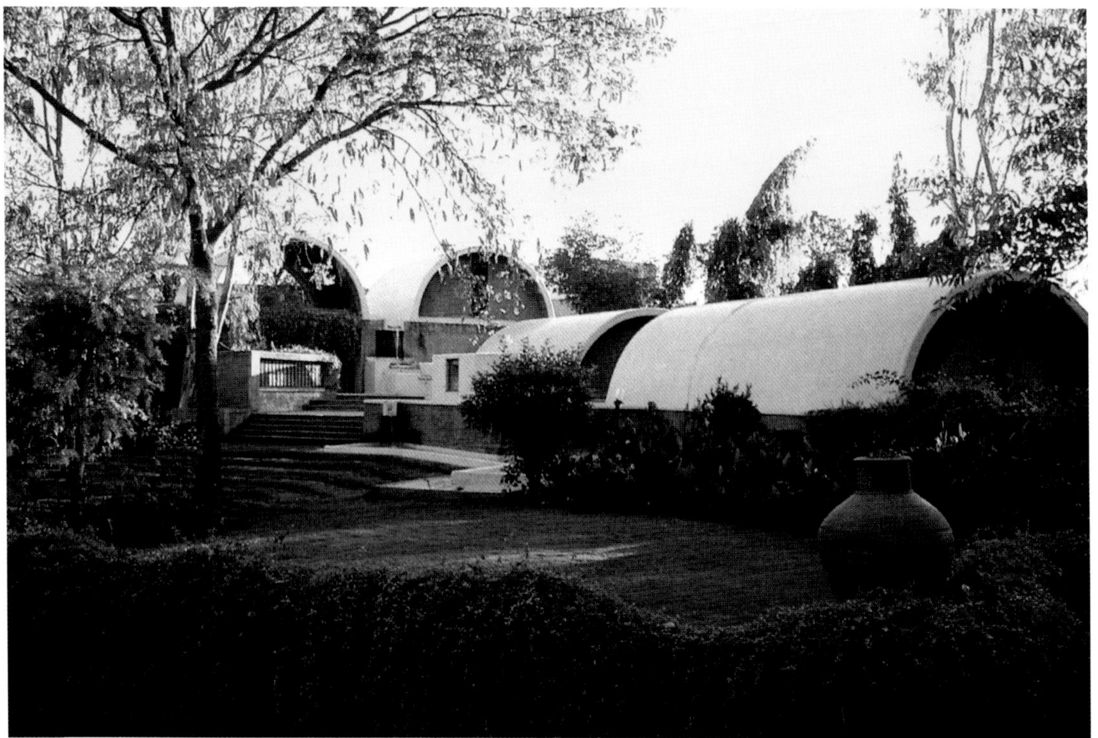

◄0270

Themes that work well in a hot, arid climate include organizing forms relatively, layering spaces, controlling interiors and exterior transitions, interrupting the skyline through varying outlines that break the sun into shadow, and opening the roof into the night sky. At Sangath–the architect's design studio–these themes come into their own.

0271►

In order to combat the vagaries of nature in a hot, dry climate where temperatures reach 113°F (45 °C), the vaulted roof is made of local clay sandwiched in the concrete slab. This provides a nonconductive layer in which the clay impedes heat transmission, and is finished with white, glossy china mosaic glazed tiles to further enhance insulation by deflecting the sun's rays.

0272

A vaulted roof creates an efficient surface:volume ratio in order to optimize the quantity of materials utilized. The higher space creates pockets of hot air since connective currents maintain lower areas relatively cooler. The upper ventilating window releases the accumulated hot air via pressure differences.

0273

The building is largely buried under the ground to use earth as natural insulation. Its outer walls are nearly one meter thick, but have been hollowed to form storage alcoves and provide insulation. There is a difference of about 46°F (8°C) between the inner and outer layers of the roof's skin.

0274

Sunlight brings heat and haze. The light is received indirectly via diffusion in order to maximize daylighting and the intensity of illumination and to diffuse heat and glare. Natural daylight ensures minimum electrical consumption for artificial light, and insulation measures have meant a 30 to 50 percent cost reduction in cooling systems.

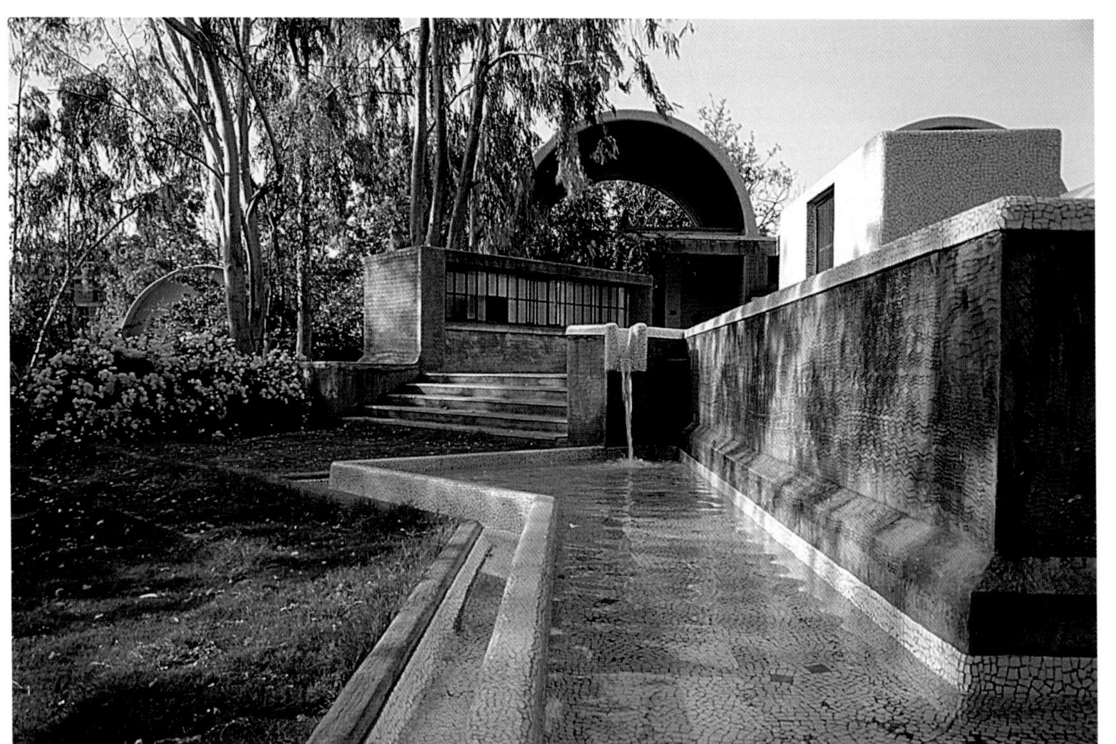

◄0275

Rainwater and the overflow of water pumped from the roof tank are harnessed through flows that run through a series of cascading tanks and water channels, culminating in a pond where the water is either recycled or utilized for irrigating vegetation. Water cascades also provide interesting visual experiences.

0276▼

A simple wire mesh and mortar-lined floor with a sagging cloth shape, evolved through scaled model studies, eliminates the need of any kind of foundation, since the basic form is continuous and efficient in optimizing the stresses and their distribution. Construction is carried out with simple manual tools and by semiskilled and unskilled workers on site.

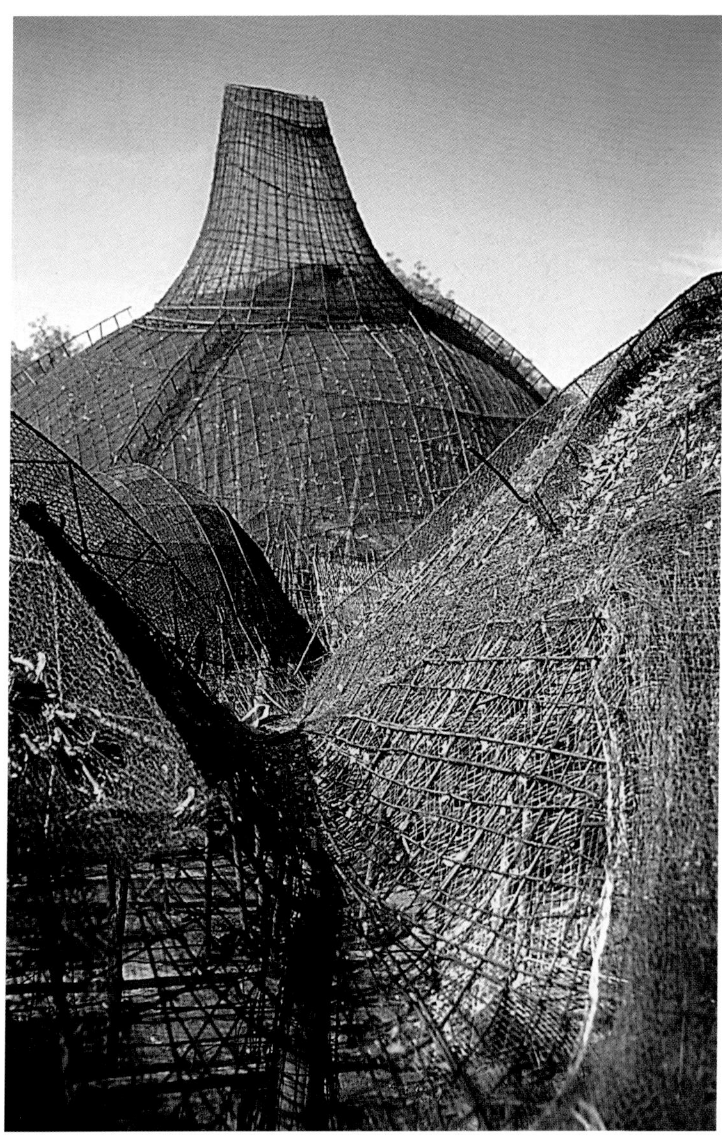

0277

Use of secondary waste material. Stone chip waste is used as a paving material whereas the roof surface utilizes waste from glazed tiles. These materials can be sourced for no cost from factories and have been creatively handcrafted and fully integrated into the design. Using materials that require skillful application also promotes our traditional heritage and craftsmanship.

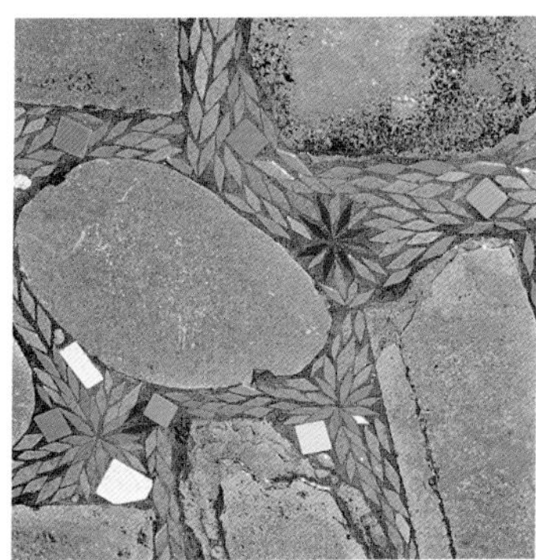

0278

The shells, domes, and skylight protrusions of various sizes and shapes float on a partially buried space and earth mounds to become an integral element in the natural landscape. Bent edges and eave gutters cantilever over the ground in order to further accentuate this feeling and anchor the object to the ground. The architecture is rendered energy conscious in an otherwise harsh, hot and dry climate through the use of buried spaces, earth mounds, raised volumes, and china mosaic finishes. Material resources are further optimized through its thin shell-like forms and ferrocement construction techniques.

0279

The shells were made in wire frame on site and manually raised to the exact location without using formwork and shuttering. Reinforcement, in the form of skeletal steel and wire mesh, was then sandwiched between the layer of hand-compacted mortar from both sides, combining rudimentary building skills with sophisticated technology to achieve optimum forms.

Studio Arthur Casas

Studio Arthur Casas SP
818 Itápolis Street, Pacaembu
São Paulo, SP 01245-000, Brazil
P.: (+55) 11-2182-7500
www.arthurcasas.com

Studio Arthur Casas NY
31 West 27th Street, 11th Floor
New York, NY 10001, USA
P.: (+1) 646-839-5063

©Tuca Reinés

©Tuca Reinés

©Leonardo Finotti

0280

The automatic door detail connects the living space to the garden and creates natural ventilation.

©Tuca Reinés

0281

Swiveling metal louvers are utilized here to create natural ventilation.

©Tuca Reinés

0282

Here, the living space is integrated with the dining room.

0283

Sliding doors are used to integrate the living/kitchen space with the garden, producing cross ventilation.

0284

Internal walls are finished with cement board.

©Leonardo Finotti

0285

This ladder accesses the solarium.

0286

Here, a bridge between the master bedroom and other bedrooms allows privacy.

0287

Glazing has been used to integrate the bedroom with the landscape.

0288

Glass doors recessed in walls open up interior spaces to the pool area.

0289

Vertical Cumaru wood pieces (sustainable origin) are used here to act as louvers, diminishing the impact of the sun's rays.

Griffin Enright Architects

Tips: Margaret Griffin

12468 Washington Blvd.
Los Angeles, CA 90066, USA
P.: (+1) 310-391-4484
www.griffinenrightarchitects.com

0290

Super graphics can be integrated with architecture and furniture systems to create layered spatial conditions for seating areas.

0291

Blurring the boundaries between architecture, lighting, and furniture creates dynamic conditions for impromptu uses.

© Tom Bonner

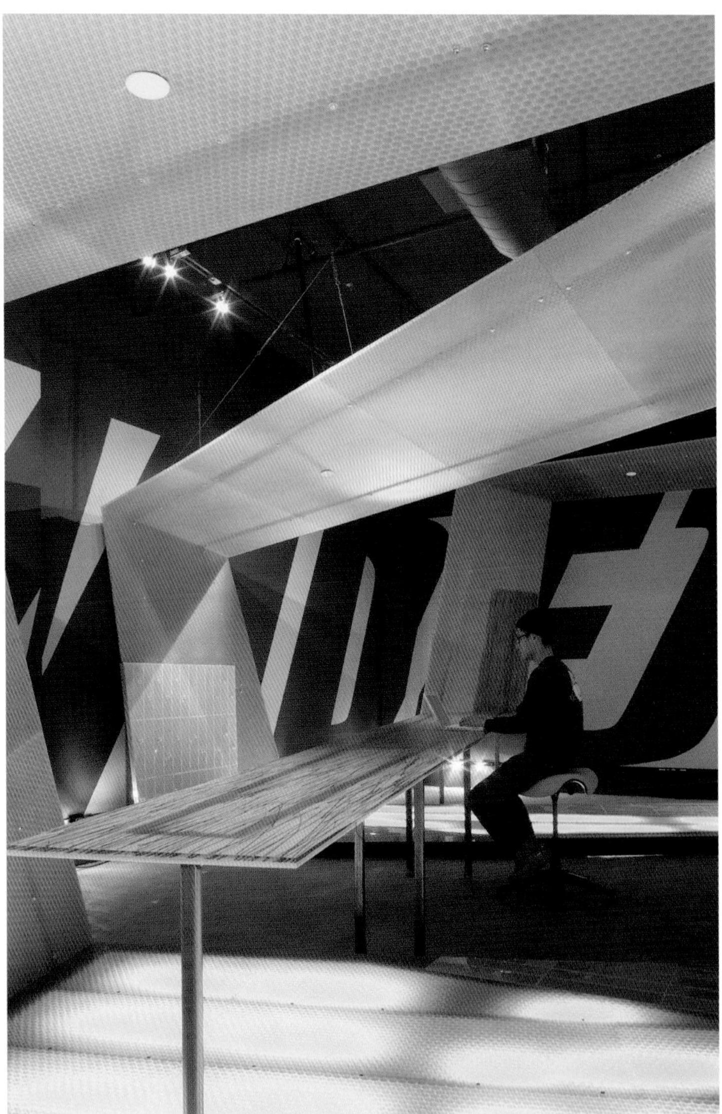

0292

A floating shelf creates an open partition between the living room and family room, while also serving to organize collectables.

0293

Intersecting custom light boxes with skylights creates area definition in an open floor plan. Cost effective track lights in randomized slots cut from plywood panels create a unique ceiling that opens up the view.

© Benny Chan

© Benny Chan

0294

The combination of book jackets, a floating fireplace, and a seamless view to nature creates a meditative library space.

© Art Gray

0295

Peel out windows provide ocean views from the rear of a residence while creating a dynamic massing condition.

0296

Bookshelf-like wood fins emerge from the library space, becoming a shading device that is then extruded to become part of the railing for a second floor terrace above.

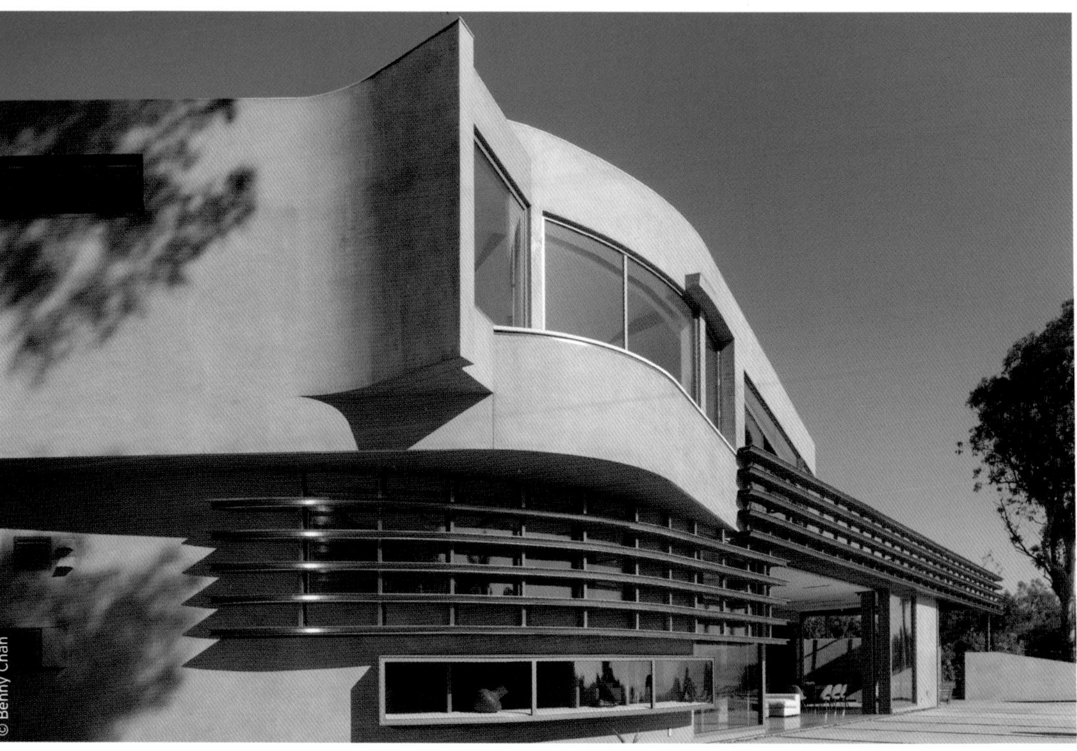

0297

A curved entry hall with curved clerestory lighting enhances the varying natural lighting conditions, while creating a dynamic threshold between public and private spaces.

0298

Tucking the steam shower and the water closet behind a floating wall allows for an open and spacious master bath.

0299

A split-level terrace creates a seating area for the outdoor fire pit.

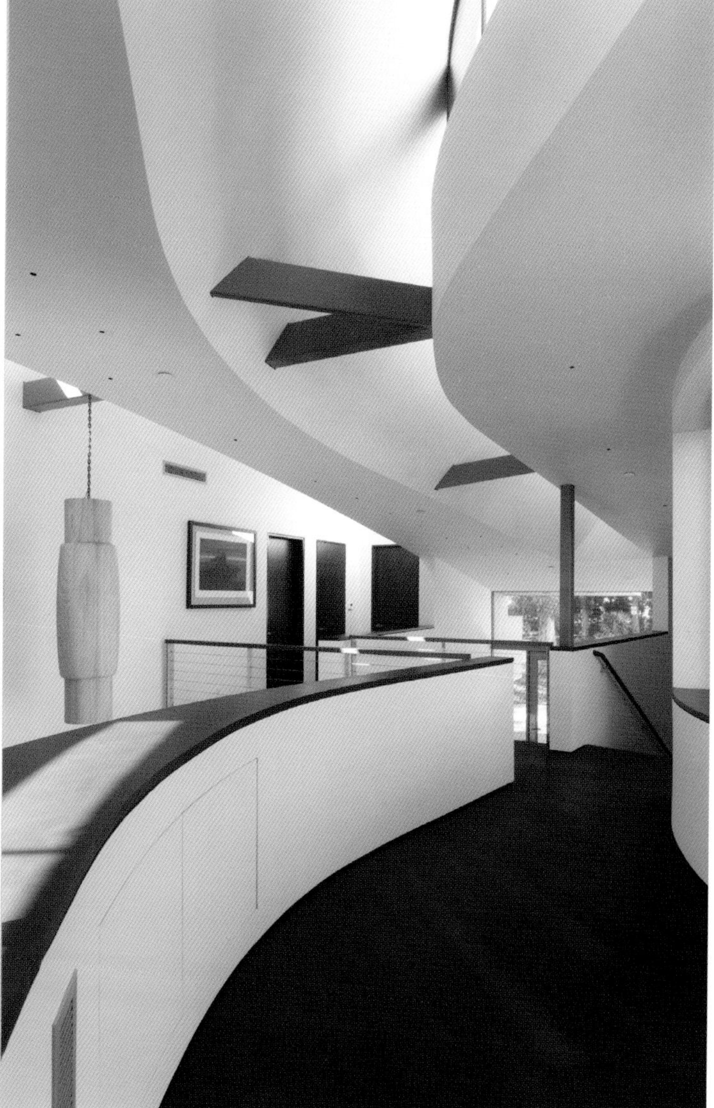

Jarmund/Vigsnæs AS Arkitekter

Hausmanns gate 6
0186 Oslo, Norway
P.: (+47) 2299-4343
www.jva.no

0300

Buildings are physical elements that affect the wind. If you need to direct the wind to control snow drifting, the building should work as an aerodynamic object.

0301

Do not place the building on the part of the lot that will be useful garden space.

0302

To create a space that appears to have been carved out of mass, use the same material for all visible surfaces.

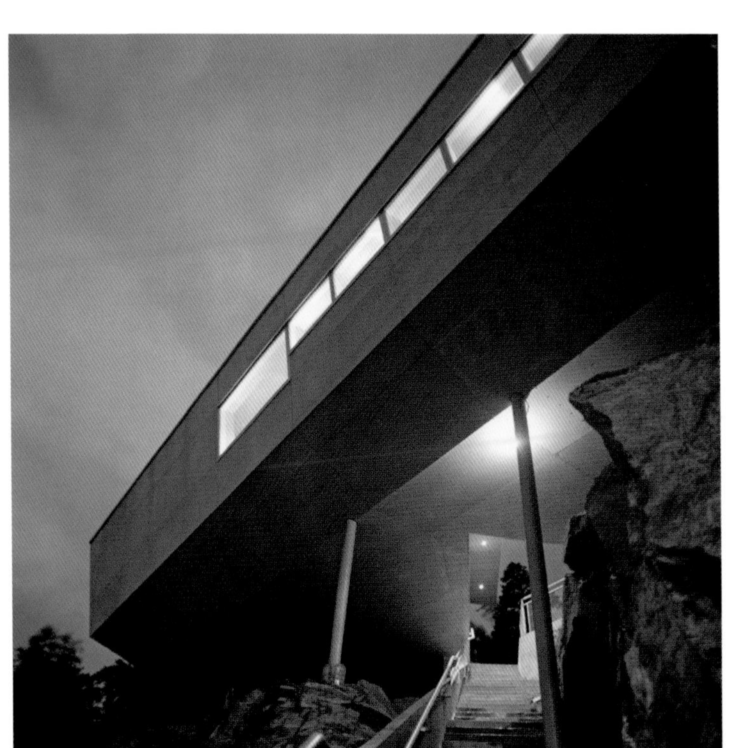

0303

How you enter the building is a major design issue.

0304

Materials can totally change identity through different details and lighting effects.

0305 

The building may respond to the landscape and climate.

0306

Organizing functions creates an opportunity to sculpturally shape buildings.

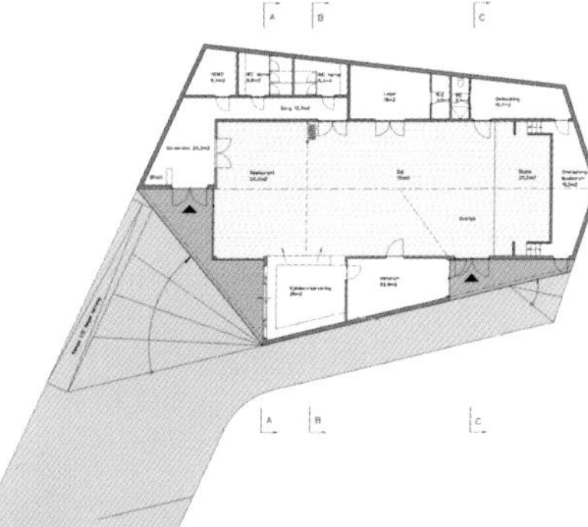

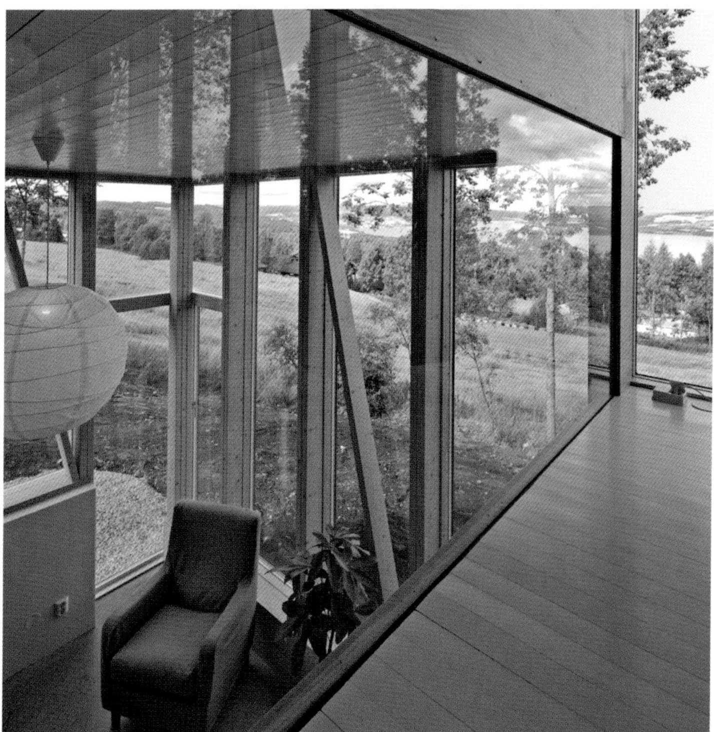

0307

Architectural focus can be achieved by limiting natural light.

0308

A small room can be enlarged by incorporating external space.

0309

Recycling materials creates opportunities for storytelling.

Pugh + Scarpa Architects

Tips: Lawrence Scarpa

2525 Michigan Ave., building F1
Santa Monica, CA 90404, USA
P.: (+1) 310-828-0226
www.pugh-scarpa.com

© Marvin Rand

0310

Double duty
Make the most of your design choices. The solar panels on our Solar Umbrella House perform a *double duty* by protecting the building envelope from harsh sunlight and providing energy to the house and to the power grid.

0311

Let the site pass through the building
To take advantage of an extremely constricted site, we transformed the existing footprint of a 1970s ranch house into a pavilion-like structure that allows the site to, in a sense, *pass through the house*, offering extraordinary panoramic views. Large 22-ft-high (6.7 m) custom sliding glass doors allow the interior and exterior to become one. Private areas are treated as loft-like spaces, capturing volume and views while maintaining privacy.

© Marvin Rand

© Marvin Rand

◀0312

Generic + specific = Sublime

The Vail-Grant House is a product of zoning setback rules and a reaction to its dramatic hillside setting. This project is directly related to the topography and engages with the landscape, diving into the hill at points and breaking away from it at others.

0313▼

Elements in dialogue

At Orange Grove Lofts we made use of two square profile balcony surrounds in the front façade in order to initiate a dialogue between them. One is small, the other large, one is open at the front, the other is veiled with stainless steel slats. The smaller one relates to the driveway gate below, and the other to the roll-up door and first-floor balcony.

0314▼

Strong definition

At Bronson Lofts, each piece of the building has a strong and clearly defined shape, such as the corrugated metal surround that encloses the second-story balcony in the east and north facades.

0315

Coherence and dynamism
The question was how to maintain continuity and coherence with the character of the existing industrial warehouse buildings at Bergamot Station without compromising formal and material experimentation and innovation. Corrugated metal, steel and glass blend in with the surrounding context, while cold-rolled steel and translucent Lexan panels create moments of distinction in the details of the building.

0316

Make the ordinary extraordinary
There is poetry in prosaic daily elements. We feel it is the architect's duty and challenge to seek out these commonplace, even throw-away materials, and put them to extraordinary uses.

0317

Let simplicity reign
Here, the interior of Bergamot Lofts is deliberately treated as a simple volume or shell in which the distinct elements of the space can more clearly emerge. An exposed steel truss and metal deck roof system continues the effect of creating a quiet background field in which feature elements can construct spatial and textural complexity.

0318

Link indoor and outdoor spaces
By creating strong visual and physical links between outside and inside, this outdoor room interlocks with interior spaces, blurring the boundary and creating a more dynamic relationship between the two.

0319 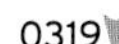

Break up the box
Wherever possible, insert small courtyards and public spaces into private multifamily residences to create social opportunities. This is particularly important in cities that are as privacy-oriented and lacking in public space as Los Angeles.

GH+A, Guillermo Hevia Arquitectos

Augusto Leguía 44, dpto. 202
Las Condes, Santiago, Chile
P.: (+56) 2724-0968
www.guillermohevia.cl

0320

Materials always give us an opportunity to contemplate on how to make our architecture. Glass is transformed into screens, like a double skin, to both project an image and provide protection. The morphology of the side façad–with perpendicular colored fins–acts like a sail, enhancing the structure's identity and allowing cross ventilation.

0321

Light, color, and transparency are architectural resources. By night the building awakens, with precise, strategic glints of light. The forms and volumes are enhanced, evoking the features of the surrounding geography. The reflections in the water form a new dimension of the illuminated tectonic body.

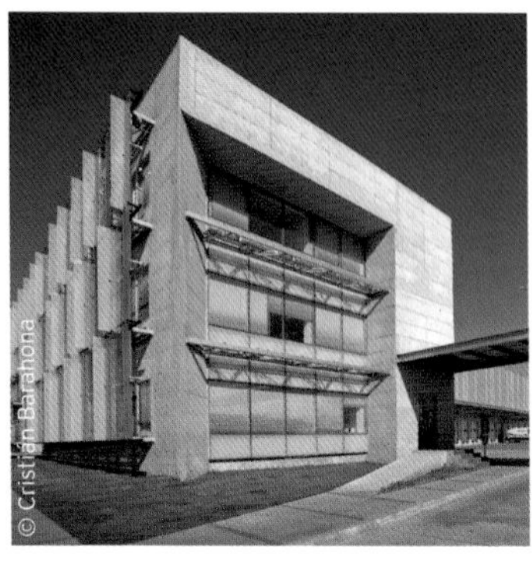

© Guy Wenborne

0322

In the Cristalchile factory architecture and geography are complementary. Architecture should belong to the setting and the intervention should belong to the landscape. Achieving this creates harmony, and pleasantly enhances forms and colors. The work may also be a reinterpretation of nature.

0323

A commercial building with transparent façades must have meaning. The building's light and the way in which it is viewed from exterior spaces create a hierarchical spatial dimension and bring the landscape inside, improving the quality of the working environment.

© Juan Purcell

◄0324

Including clean technologies in order to make sustainable architectural structures should not impede the creation of quality and aesthetically pleasing works, where the quest for beauty and equilibrium is always present.

© Cristóbal Palma

0325►

Sensitive architecture should coexist with its setting. The building and natural landscape, the forms and material, the color and light, are all enhanced and complemented, generating a contrasting harmony.

0326▲

Architecture is an opportunity to make a lot using only a few elements. The materials are elaborated in a simple manner, with straight and angular forms, recovering the natural hues of the wood, the ground and the scarce flora. They become components that emphasize the humility and the natural character of the project.

0327►

The architecture appears to rise naturally out of the setting. The lines of the olive grove are projected onto the building, creating a patterned effect on its façades. The boundary between the start of the structure and the end of its natural receptacle is subtle, almost imperceptible. Harmony is to be found in the dialog between the forms, light, color, and landscape.

© Cristóbal Palma

◄0328

A concept as abstract as "the sensuality of wine" can be manifested subtly and poetically with great power. Here, this is embodied in rolling forms and the different shades of the colors of this architectural volume.

0329▲

It is the color and the materiality of this project that have constructed a harmonious whole. The architecture is enhanced by the balance of colors and shapes, proving that abstract ideas can be embodied with delicate subtlety.

McGregor Coxall

21 c Whistler Street
Manly NSW 2095, Sydney, Australia
P.: (+61) 299-773-853
www.mcgregorcoxall.com

0330

The sweeping north deck is an exercise in balance and scale, creating a powerful yet precarious relationship between itself and its setting. It is a grand gesture that floats above the cliff face like a steel halo, mirroring the site of the former main storage tank below, now home to frog and bird habitats. It provides a dramatic vantage point that affords memorable views of the city across the harbor and allows users to engage with, and experience the ever-changing natural light and wind conditions that prevail there.

© Brett Boardman

© Brett Boardman

0331

Former BP site south deck shares many of the traits of its northern sibling in its restraint, materiality, and its ability to allow users to engage with their surrounds. Seated comfortably above a raw & dramatic sandstone bed, a clear synergy is formed between the two elements. The south stairs, connected to the south deck, lead to the pedestrian links and water's edge below. This is a clean insertion that slides between two natural walls cut in the rock and continues the clear dialogue between the design and the site's geological natural beauty and rawness.

0332

This park design as a whole integrates a series of layers including heritage, connectivity, platforms, water systems, and cultural references. It utilizes simple details and applies an honest, non-decorative palette of robust materials that echo the site's context and its industrial past.

Off form concrete, recycled sandstone filled gabions, galvanized steel and chain wire have been inserted, folded and applied intelligently. These elements are framed by native vegetation grown from seed that has been collected locally from the site, to establish a genetic bank for the diminishing harborfront sandstone woodlands that once occurred here naturally.

© Petronella Ryan

0333

Conceived initially as a series of mobile gardens, Amoeba was a flexible cellular being, capable of organic transformation and of creating temporal environments that both surprise and delight.

The 132 cells that made up Amoeba colonized a number of sites across Sydney's central business district. Part landscape and part art installation, Amoeba formed an important part of the Royal Botanic Gardens showcase exhibition: *Gardens of the Tomorrow*. Amoeba explored ideas on adaptability and transformation, on the unseen and the unexplored possibilities and potential of spaces. Constructed from recycled materials, amoeba was also a commentary on issues relating to waste, consumerism, and the environment we impact upon each day.

© HASSELL / Haycraft Duloy

0334▲

Sheas Stream is the unifying design feature of the Green Square Town Center. Framed by public and private uses arranged along its banks, the creek functions as a green spine and ecological engine that purifies stormwater. Water from Sheas Stream and its associated wetlands is used as a water source across the site, meeting needs such as irrigation, street washing, and building systems. Sheas Creek evolved from a desire to establish a sustainable and versatile green oasis within an urban environment. Indigenous native plants selected from local endangered vegetation communities have been used to reinstate original flora and fauna and encourage biodiversity.

0336▼

Our passion for place making, environmental sustainability, contemporary design, and the future of our cities and public spaces is evident throughout this design. Sheas Park is a sun-filled environment, with boardwalks, a play room, generous open lawns, and productive gardens. It is also home to a wildlife pond, supplied via a reticulation system of reed bed filtered water, reminiscent of the wetlands that once occurred here. Sheas Park provides the setting for a range of passive and active recreational needs and exploration as well as for hosting concerts and festivals. It is a place that celebrates community, the environment, culture, health, and well-being.

0335▼

The Nova Project consists of 119 apartments in four separate buildings arranged around two communal courtyards positioned above a basement car park. The project is located between two prominent public parks that meet the larger active space requirements of residents. The courtyards are caracterized by simple graphic legibility and contemporary forms and elements, which are easily read at either ground level or from the balconies overlooking them. These communal courtyards, sitting beneath a green canopy of native Eucalyptus, are arranged as a graphic sequence of "island rooms," which define the central open space.

© Haycraft Duloy

© Brett Boardman

© Brett Boardman

0337

The communal courtyards were developed with the aim of satisfying the more intimately scaled passive recreational needs of residents. These courtyards are an escape from the speed and pressure of the world beyond, and allow users to access and experience a gentler, more intimate place and to enjoy a mood and environment that enables them to simply reflect and to be. These living rooms grow and evolve with time, providing constant renewal and opportunities for sensory experience and discovery.

0338

The Green Square Town Center is a sustainable metro village project that forms the largest single urban renewal development in Australia. It proposes public and private uses, including three urban squares, a new park, a library, cinemas, bars, and housing in addition to community, commercial and retail facilities. The Civic Plaza lies at the heart of the development.

It is a dynamic and flexible environment, facilitating community gatherings, civic events and day-to-day shopping. Working on such a large scale requires an approach combining ambition, innovation and foresight in order to deliver a world-class leadership urban design that meets the challenges of urban growth in our modern world and is based on environmental innovation.

© Haycraft Duloy

0339

The Trojan sculptural installation was a collaborative award-winning entry in the *Back to the Future* art exhibition. It makes a simple but poignant social commentary that challenges our normal daily thinking and explores the topic of food, our most basic commodity, and the ethics and values behind its production. Each day freight carriers, like modern day Trojan horses, transport hidden cargo to our shores and into our cities.

Some carriers contain genetically modified seed. This silent infiltration threatens to spawn an invasion to which most of us, we the consumers, remain oblivious.

© Murray McKean

Durbach Block Architects

Level 5, 71 York Street
Sydney NSW 2000, Australia
P.: (+61) 282-973-500
www.durbachblock.com

0340

Context is our canvas.

0341

Curiosity is a muscle.

0342

Raw vs. cooked.

0343

Gardens are US

.

0344

The client, however crazy, takes you to unexpected places.

© Kraig Carlstrom

0345

Suspend judgment while testing assumptions.

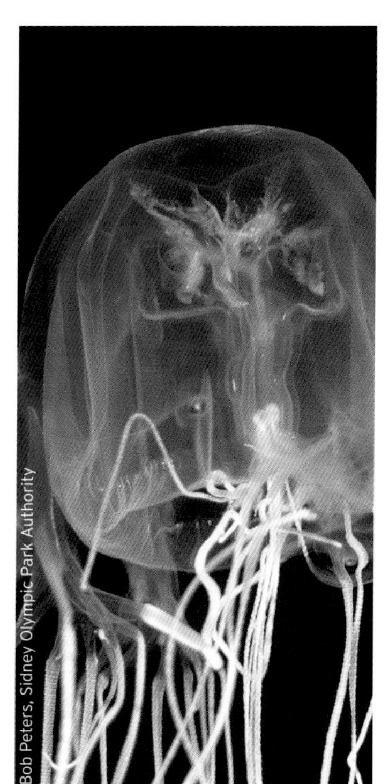
© Bob Peters, Sidney Olympic Park Authority

0346

Work analogously.

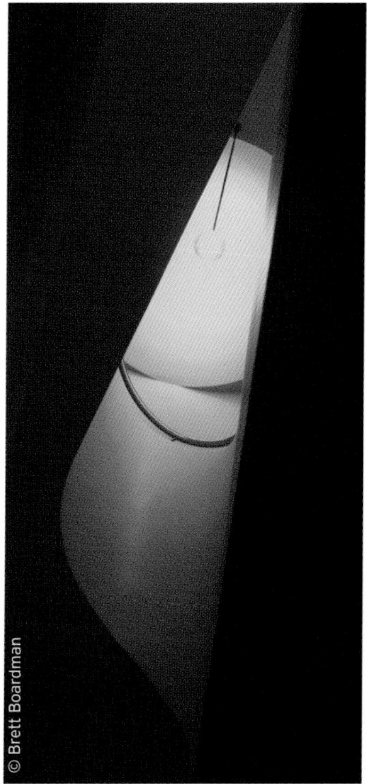
© Brett Boardman

0347

Read everything, travel everywhere.

0348

Add magic.

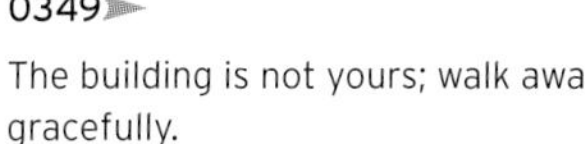

0349

The building is not yours; walk away gracefully.

Weiss/Manfredi

130 West 29th Street, 12 Floor
New York, NY 10001, USA
P.: (+1) 212-760-9002
www.weissmanfredi.com

Rather than giving advice, we make suggestions by posing a series of thoughts or issues that are important to our work. These issues, which crystallize around a series of words, continuously crop up in lectures, discussions, and conversations that we have about our work and about design, with colleagues, students, and informally in our studio.

We offer these thoughts in the spirit of a conversation. It is our hope that these thoughts and images might act as provocations for future work, for ideas as yet untested, for projects as yet unimagined.

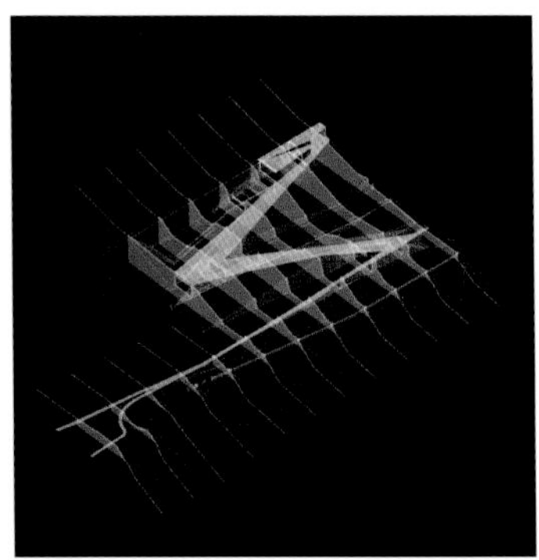

◄0350

Acupuncture

A complete project can often be designed with the lightest touch and we look for highly specific points or moments that, just like acupuncture, can galvanize an entire condition with minimum effort.

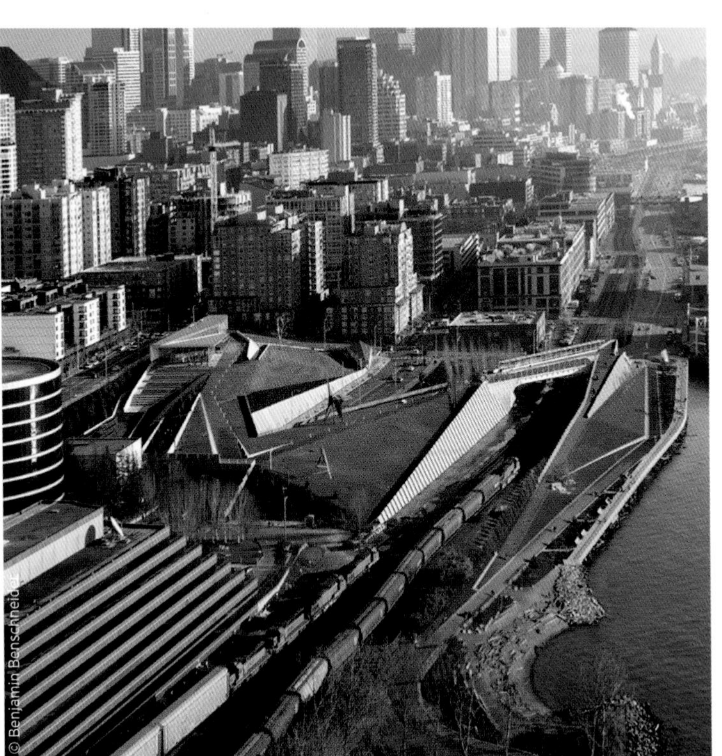

© Benjamin Benschneider

0351►

Resilience

A design strategy must be durable and robust to survive. We try to define a diagram or a resilient form that is simple enough to withstand the inevitable changes in the program, the obligations of multiple agendas, and competing interests.

© Paul Warchol

0352▲

Listen

Be good listeners; listen carefully because there is usually some other fabulous thing that you are not aware of, and can be used to make the design richer and stronger. Listening can be energizing.

0353

Context

Context is not a given, neutral, and immutable condition. You can never simply read a site or simply respond to the context, because as soon as you intervene, the context has changed once more.

0354

Wait

Postpone conclusions. Often the question not asked can become the driving force behind a design strategy. Experts often talk of immediate requirements and specific needs. Wait to discover what is not discussed or asked; this can become the most important part of a project or space.

0355

Peripheral vision

Design creativity has the capacity to resolve competing interests and agendas that often cannot be resolved in a linear fashion. Be synthetic and lateral in your thinking; design settings that encourage offhand encounters and peripheral vision.

© Benjamin Benschneider

Bruce Moore

0356

The visceral

Expand your sensory repertoire beyond the visual. A project has to operate at a visceral as well as intellectual level.

How you experience it, how you feel it, how your body moves through it, all matter. Foreground haptic elements. Architecture can transform an idea into an immersive and sensual reality.

0357

Weight

In an effort to offset our interest in the ephemeral and the lightness of things, we find weight and gravity a necessary and real counterpoint. Weight is the friend of lightness.

0358

Topography

We imagine architecture as a topographic condition that liberates us from the limited conventions of building or sites, inside or outside, allowing us to see these as continuous experiences. A topographic interpretation gives privilege to the continuity of plan and section where surface and subsurface can become a continuous condition.

© Benjamin Benschneider

© Benjamin Benschneider

0359

The temporal
Often design is confused with control and we are seduced into trying to design every condition. Instead, we hope to incorporate the ephemeral, the temporal, and the unexpected affects, such as the play of car lights on a metal surface to enrich and animate a design.

0360

Choreography
Movement through space defines architecture; we think of design as a form of choreography. The pattern of movements of a group, or the solitary slalom of a wandering individual all play off a set of surfaces. How bodies move through space in both expected and unexpected ways is one of architecture's great gifts.

© Jeff Goldberg

0361

Debris
Each project generates its own debris: model studies, material explorations, texts, drawings and even ideas. This debris is a precious intellectual and creative resource that has the potential to inform other work. The castoffs and forgotten elements of one project can become the generator of another.

A final thought: architecture and design is primarily a visual art. However, given its social dimension, it is a social art. It is impure and its capacity to deal with ideas and words is compromised. It is messy, contaminated. But because of this it becomes a much richer and more vital reality.

Schmidt Hammer Lassen Architects

Tips: Kristian Ahlmark

Aaboulevarden 37
8000 Aarhus C, Denmark
P.: (+45) 86-20-19-00
ww.shl.dk

0362

Explore form
The organic envelope of this design proposal for the National Symphonic Concert Hall and conference center cloaks a sequence of complex and curvilinear interior volumes, partly inspired by the shape of the symphonic instruments to be found in this venue.

0363

A luminous sculpture
The glazed façade is constructed with a mesh of stainless steel, which reflects the continuously changing daylight. During the dark days of the Icelandic winter, integral lighting dramatically enhances the opulent and dynamic interior, which can be seen as a glowing, organic unit by visitors approaching the building.

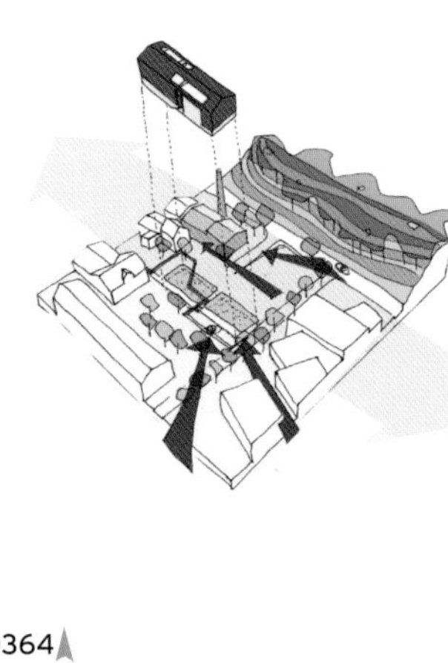

0364

Building on contrast
The aim of this project was to provide an optimal physical environment in order to encourage fellowship and cooperation in a folk high school, where educational and social aspirations form an integral part of the curriculum. The building has been designed to connect the folk high school with the town by offering a vibrant setting for the local community, including cafés, a music theatre, cinemas, and a media centre.

0365

Building in motion
After night falls, the interior lights shine through the circular apertures incised into the façade, transforming the building into an animated beacon shining its light over the surroundings. The building therefore appears to be in perpetual motion, becoming a "performer."

© Schmidt Hammer Lassen Architects

0366

An open-open office
A flexible office building has a central atrium that doubles as an internal public square; open 24 hours a day. This public space connects to the Karlinska Nam Park and the leafy river promenade beyond. Typical Prague paving stones are laid throughout the square in order to reinforce its connection with the city.

© Schmidt Hammer Lassen Architects

0367

Expressing materials
This building is a celebration of its components; its internal, ducting, and ventilation systems are honestly expressed. Externally, the new building is clad with boldly perforated rust-red steel panels.

© Schmidt Hammer Lassen Architects

0368

Inner court: public square
The building's heart is a vast atrium, a high-tech and innovative public space which also operates as a covered public square complete with hanging terraces, water features, trees, and flowers: an inviting place that both creates and reflects the civic life of the community.

The Danish artist Anne Marie Ploug has collaborated with Schmidt Hammer Lassen to design the atrium's internal screen decoration, which takes the form of suspended foliage, inspired by the feel of the Amazonian jungle.

© Schmidt Hammer Lassen Architects

0369

Dynamic synergy
The school's dynamic design, with its four distinct axes, is intended to create opportunities for academic exploration, knowledge sharing, and social interaction right across the student community, as a visual metaphor honoring the ethos of the man after whom the school is named.

0370

Stacking program
The layered design for the new Thor Heyerdahl Upper Secondary School is simple but effective, clustering its various elements in a compact, flexible, and vertically oriented building. The main structure comprises an open square plate into which openings have been incised, allowing natural light to penetrate deep into the building. A corresponding plate above is turned 180 degrees on the building's axis, creating a series of single and double height spaces.

© Schmidt Hammer Lassen Architects

0371

Atrium vortex
The rotational effect and plate displacement creates outdoor terraces, while providing internal visual connections between the floors. The lift and twist effect created by this rotation also forms a central space that widens toward the top, increasing the natural light flooding into the building.

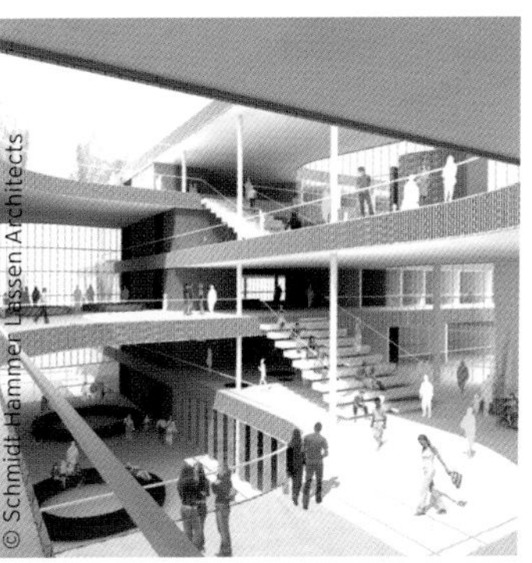

© Schmidt Hammer Lassen Architects

Pete O'Shea ASLA FAAR/ Siteworks Studio

826C Hinton Avenue
Charlottesville, VA 22901, USA
P.: (+1) 434-923-8100
www.siteworks-studio.com

0372

Create tactile juxtapositions
Find opportunities to create contrasting textures and material qualities to establish a tactile dialogue in intimate spaces. In Steel & Stone Garden, Charlottesville, we juxtaposed a steel clad wall and terraces with dry-stacked stone walls. Both define site topography and contain plants. While each weathers according to its own individual material properties, both are defined by this juxtaposition and by the constantly changing plantings.

0373

Create interactive surfaces
This monument to the First Amendment to the United States Constitution protecting the right to freedom of expression provides an interactive and dynamic venue for the public. A public chalk wall is constructed of local black slate with a stainless steel chalk tray. The wall is cleaned two to four times a week and is filled with writings and art work within hours. Located in front of the city hall, this piece has become the default venue for all manner of public discourse, debate, and protest while tapping into the inherent human desire to leave evidence of our presence and opinions.

0374►

Textured surfaces & integrated seating

When we were told that the budget of a project to pave a major plaza in a new sports and entertainment arena would only stretch to standard cast concrete we sought to optimize the application of a common material. We combined conventional flat unfinished concrete and exposed aggregate concrete in a carefully modulated pattern to create a sense of movement and scale in a space that can hold from fifteen to fifteen thousand people. This approach was echoed in the creation of an overall site structure of a woven pattern of paving and seat height site walls that help to orient circulation flows, providing ample integrated seating and collecting stormwater run-off.

0375▲

Salvage and transform memory

For this public playground we engaged the history of the site through research and the transformation of locally salvaged materials. We marked the location of a mansion that once stood on the site with a series of seat-height walls constructed from salvaged granite slabs that once served as local street curbs. These materials, which we found in the city yard under a tangle of vines, were transformed into seating, balance beams, an interactive play fountain, and a visible tracing of the site's physical memory.

◄0376

Render site flows visible

A broken and undersized pipe presented an opportunity for rendering visible the flow of rainwater across the site's surface. A planted rock-lined channel replaces the pipe and leads to a galvanized steel scupper and concrete weir wall that feeds a trough of horsetail. This system is animated each time it rains, creating a temporal fountain from a utilitarian requirement and a stimulating visual and auditory experience for the adjacent student center, the Averett University.

0377 ►

Sculpt utility

All bioretention facilities require a device that establishes a ponding height for stormwater collection. In this project we created a series of sculptural stone troughs set inside a native bioretention meadow and birch grove. These elements stand as a constant structural reminder of the utilitarian function of this garden located in a prime public plaza adjacent to a newly constructed basketball and performance arena.

0378 ▲

Articulate site hydrology

An underground utility with no place to go but out of the side of this wall begged to be articulated as a meaningfully formed element. A bronze and stainless steel scupper was designed to house this pipe opening and to transfer the flow of stormwater run-off into an adjacent bioretention garden. Located in a sunken bamboo grove, this rainwater fountain provides a sculptural focal point for the glass-enclosed boardroom.

◄ 0379

Integrate illumination

We used translucent polycarbonate panels attached to a steel frame to create a fence for our studio entrance walk, which would provide privacy without blocking sunlight. This fence functions as an illuminated scrim registering the shaded tracery of the neighbor's garden and the ever-fluctuating quality of light throughout the course of a day.

0380▼

Capture reflections

By using a laminar flow of water across a highly polished black granite surface we were able to capture the reflected images of all that surrounds this fountain. This highly finished surface was combined with a heavily rusticated, inverted and stepped cone that creates an agitated flow and pleasing sound below the still, mirror-like disc of the fountain top.

0381▲

Fuse inside and out spatially

While it seems so simple, it is surprisingly rare that the indoors and outdoors are truly spatially fused. For this café space we wanted to create a seamless connection between the plaza and outdoor dining area. By using accordion folding glass doors and carefully determining exterior grades, we were able to create the sense of unity and continuity between these two spaces. Connected by the free flow of air, space, light, sounds, and the movement of people, the café and the plaza are virtually undifferentiated.

Marmol Radziner + Associates

12210 Nebraska Avenue
Los Angeles, CA 90025, USA
P.: (+1) 310-826-6222
www.marmol-radziner.com

© David Glomb

0382

Create ample transitions between interior and exterior spaces.

0383

Place natural elements close to interior spaces to connect them with the landscape.

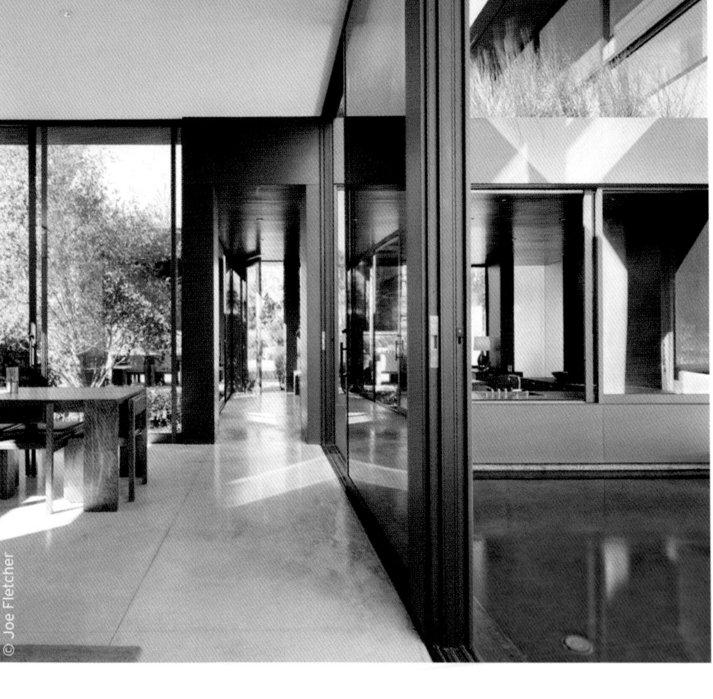

© Joe Fletcher

0384

Eliminate upper cabinets in kitchens to create openness.

© Joe Fletcher

0385

Locate banquettes in close proximity to the exterior environment to make residents feel as if they are dining outdoors.

© Joe Fletcher

© Joe Fletcher

0386

Create a spa feeling in bathrooms by using natural lighting and textured materials like stone and wood.

0387 

A minimal palette of materials adds openness to small spaces.

© Benny Chan

0388

Use books as a design element to add color and texture to a space.

© Benny Chan

0389

The sound of water adds a sense of tranquility to projects and connects spaces to the landscape.

© Benny Chan

© Joe Fletcher

0390

Covered exterior spaces with fireplaces extend living space year round.

0391

Use windows to frame views of the surrounding landscape.

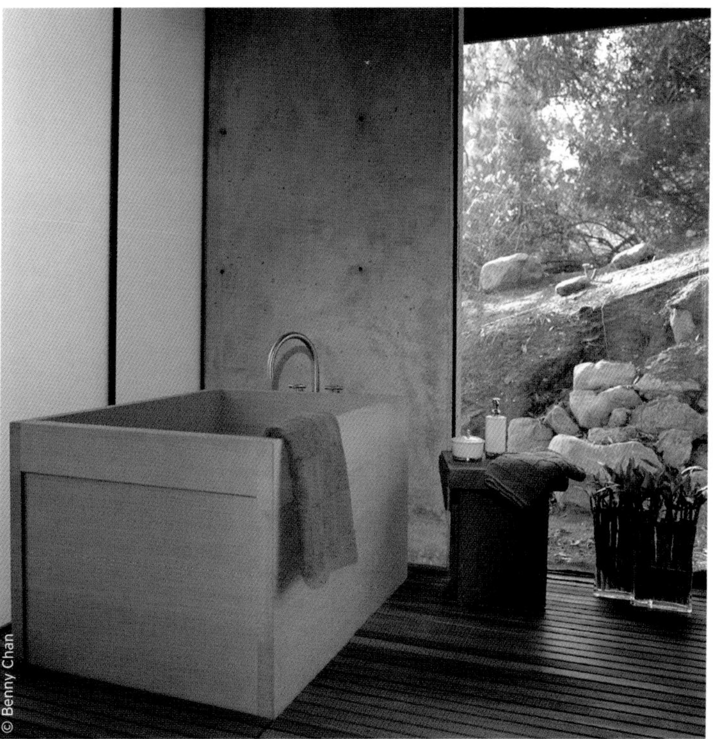

© Benny Chan

Carl-Viggo Hølmebakk

Sofiesgate 70
0168 Oslo, Norway
P.: (+47) 22-46-76-00
www.holmebakk.no

0392

The Norwegian painter Harald Sohlberg created his famous *Winter Night in the Mountains* nearly 100 years ago. In 1914, after working with the motif for fourteen years he said, "pray to who controls your fate that this work must succeed! This single painting would be enough for me to be satisfied with my life's work." Today the statement sounds somewhat high-flown—it is good to look at paintings.

0393

One important thing was to find out how to conserve the trees. The project started out as a flexible steel structure resting on top of the ground, moving along with the ground frost. But the structure became more and more intricate and complicated. The engineers struggled, and we needed to ask if the choice of a steel structure was the right thing, or even possible?

0394

Eventually we changed the material to concrete. At first I felt this was a great defeat. In retrospect I think it is important to make decisions like this one. A new foundation system was developed, using thin steel poles piercing the ground all the way down to the bedrock, some places more than 40 feet below the ground surface.

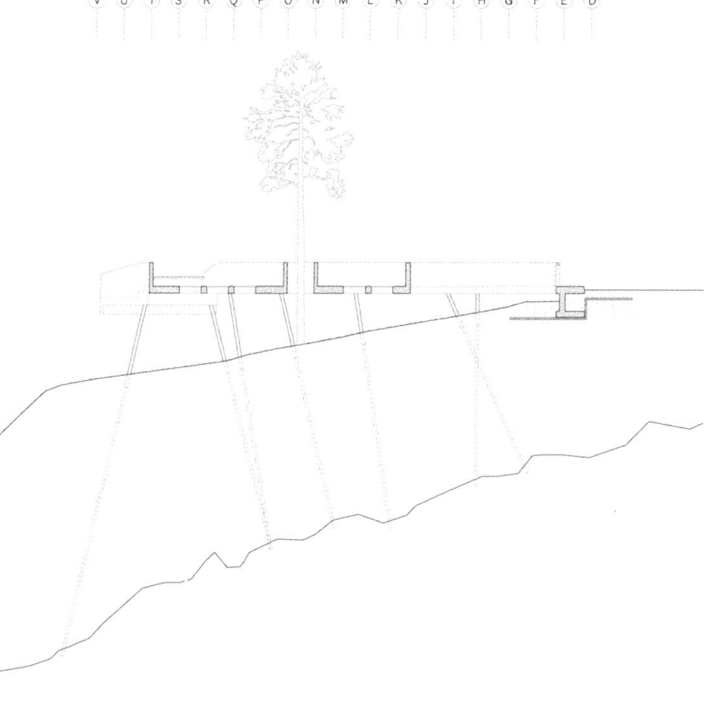

0395

The relationship between the position of the pine trees and the geometry of the platform is close, although not consequentially mathematical. We went to a cottage nearby to borrow a ladder and climbed almost every tree at the site in order to understand the views and experience the space between the branches.

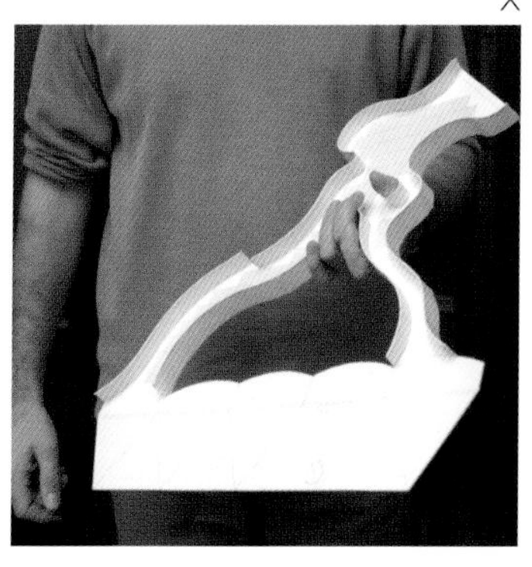

0396

The Sohlbergplassen Viewpoint was to be erected at the spot where Sohlberg studied the motif. The intriguing challenge was to interpret something already so strongly captured. What could be added? Was it at all possible to speak of an architectural precision towards this natural spot? What was the right question to ask?

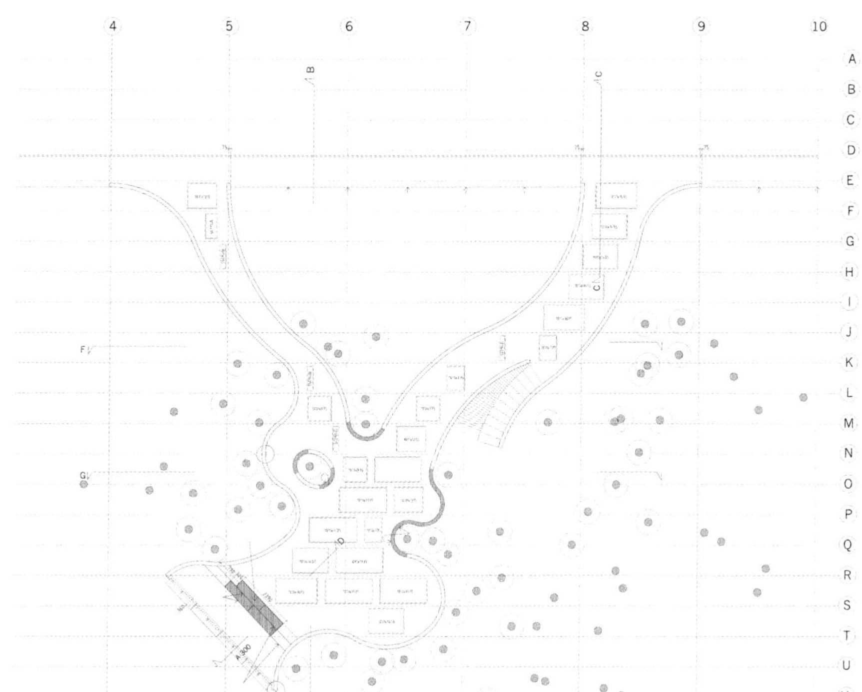

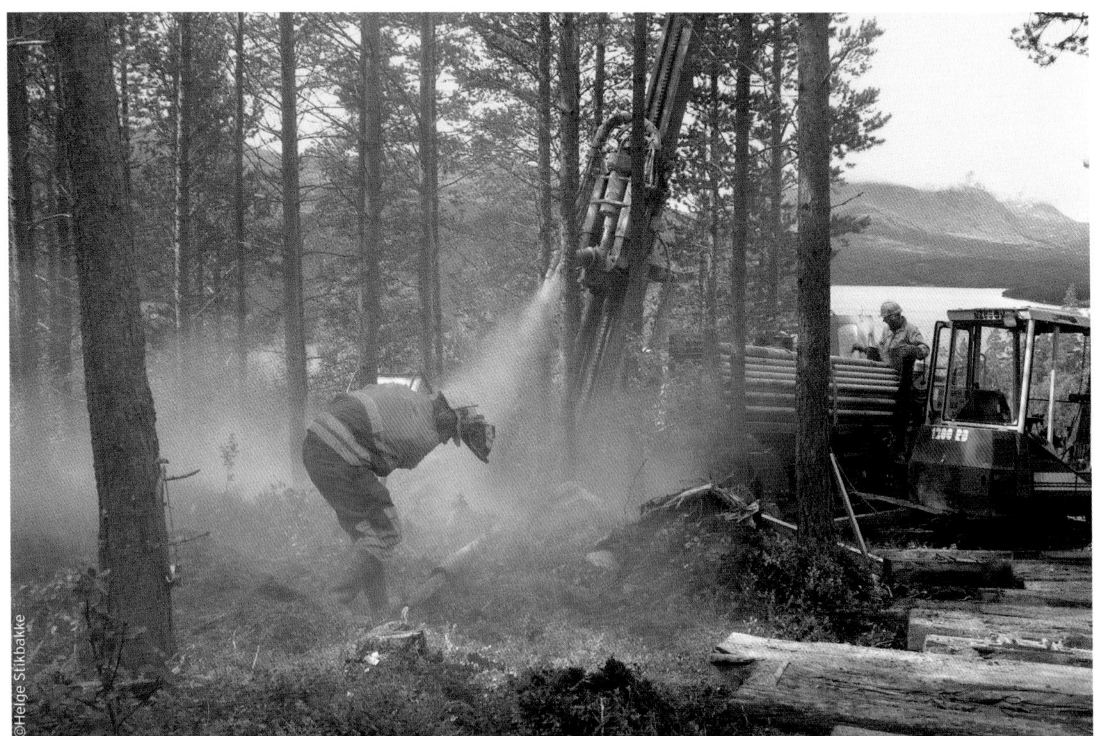

0397

I got a phone call from the man maneuvering the drilling machine. He missed by just 4 inches (10 cm) when entering the rig into the central area of the site and wanted to discuss which tree to cut. He had a suggestion, could I please look up drawing number. . . I felt bad thinking of my numerous complaints at building sites. Operators should be given the information they need, and be trusted.

0398

The steel poles were drilled into position with the use of a GPS, giving an accuracy of a few tenths of an inch (millimeters).

0399

It is important to remember that a concrete structure is always the result of another structure and another material. The distance from the tree trunks to the concrete railing was determined by the space needed for the formwork shutterers.

◄0400

During the design process most projects have places or parts no one really cares about. I believe such places often could be developed to add significant qualities. The openings in the floor let daylight and rain down to the ground below. Already after two seasons the natural growth of moss and mountain cranberry is spreading back under the platform.

0401►

To me it was decisive that the circumferential railing was also the primary beam of the structure. I have noticed that people who hear this, even architects, are not especially interested. I also explain how the floor has a slight 1-ft (0.3 meter) tilt from the road to the outermost point in order to slowly "pull" the visitors toward the distant view.

Office of Mobile Design
a Jennifer Siegal Company

1725 Abbot Kinney Boulevard
Venice, CA 90291, USA
P.: (+1) 310-439-1129
www.designmobile.com

© Benny Chan/ FotoWorks

0403
Green economy.

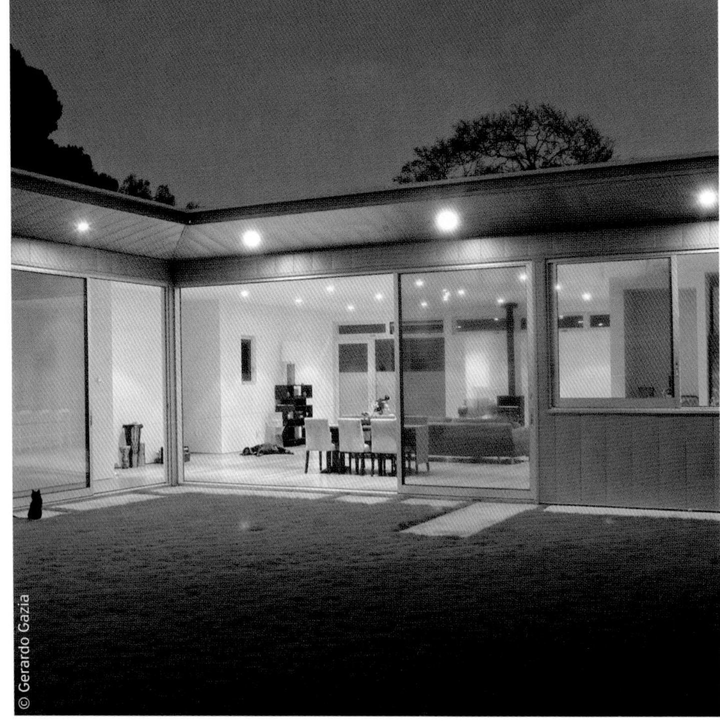
© Gerardo Gazia

0402
High + low technology.

0404
Do-it-yourself movement.

© Benny Chan/ FotoWorks

0405
Do you know the weight of your house?

0406➤
Hard + soft space.

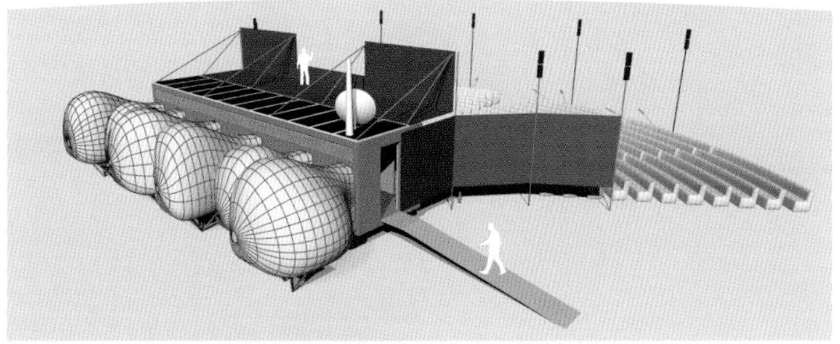

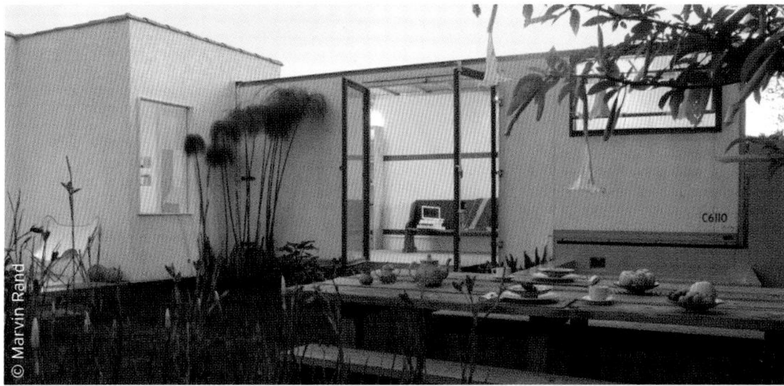

© Marvin Rand

0407➤
New nomadism.

0408
Death of distance.

© Undine Prohl

0409

EcoLogic.

0410➤
Futurism.

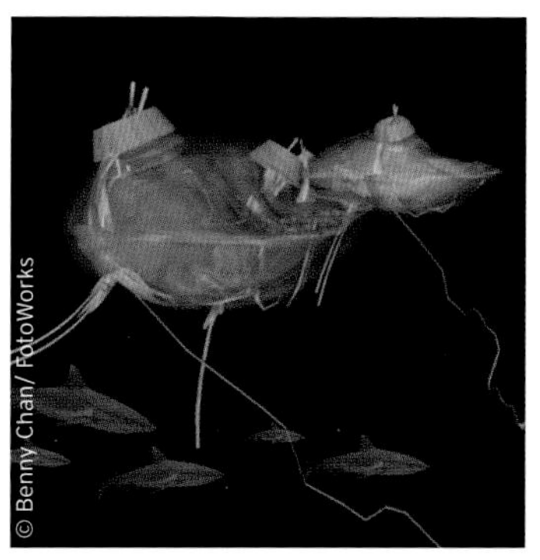
© Benny Chan/ FotoWorks

0411
Generation mobile.

Studio Pei-Zhu

B-413 Tian Hai Business Center 107
N. Dongsi Street
Beijing, 100007, China
P.: (+86) 10-6401-6657-805
www.studiopeizhu.com

© Liu Wentian

◄0412

The design concept should be clear in the construction

This building functions as an information database for the communications industry. Computers and machines make three quarters of the program and hence three of the four masses. This program does not require light so the cladding is predominantly stone with a glass pattern that resembles circuitry. The fourth mass contains office functions, mirroring the formal relationship. What was stone for the machine function is glass for the office function, what was glass is now a graphic LED installation.

© Fang Zhenning

0413▲

Use low-tech to create a high-tech building

Building systems are becoming increasingly intricate, international, and complicated. Yet construction methods and techniques remain regional, using unskilled local labor. Use simple materials and detailing for ease of construction while employing modern systems and planning for contemporary experiences and comfort.

0414

Reinforce the old and introduce the new, compromising neither

The old building sits still, freezing the memories of the past. It is important to honestly restore the courtyard house to its original condition. The new addition is detached, a floating pure form utilizing a reflective titanium-aluminum alloy surface to soften the visual impact. Maintain a strong presence of the past while introducing a soft and "invisible" reference to the future.

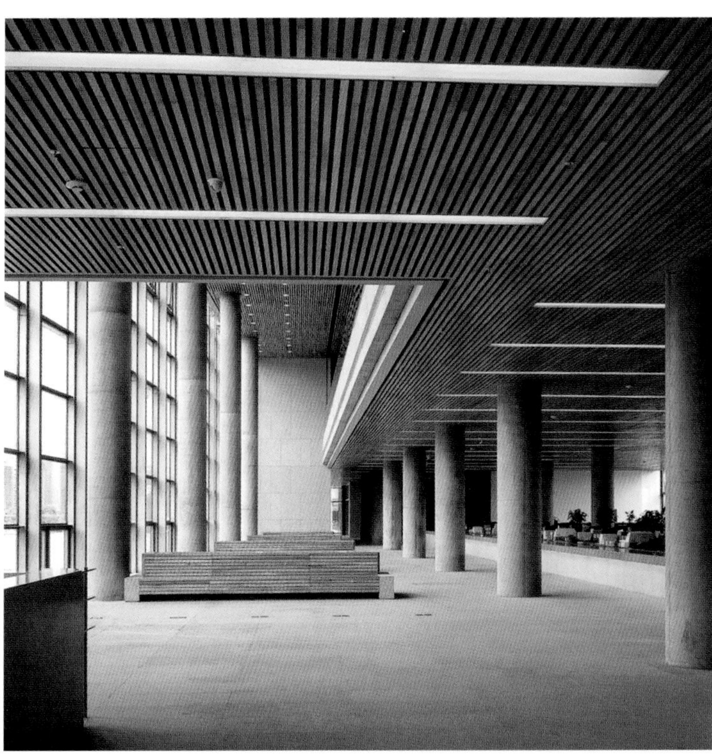

0415

Particular and special requests of clients inspire distinctive and unique forms of architecture

Time and memories are contained in the existing building. Enhance these memories while introducing modern functions into the space.

0416

Materials matter!

Thoughtful, natural, yet simple materials determine the quality of the designed space. Light enhances the texture of materials and increases people's enjoyment of the space.

© Fang Zhenning

© Fang Zhenning

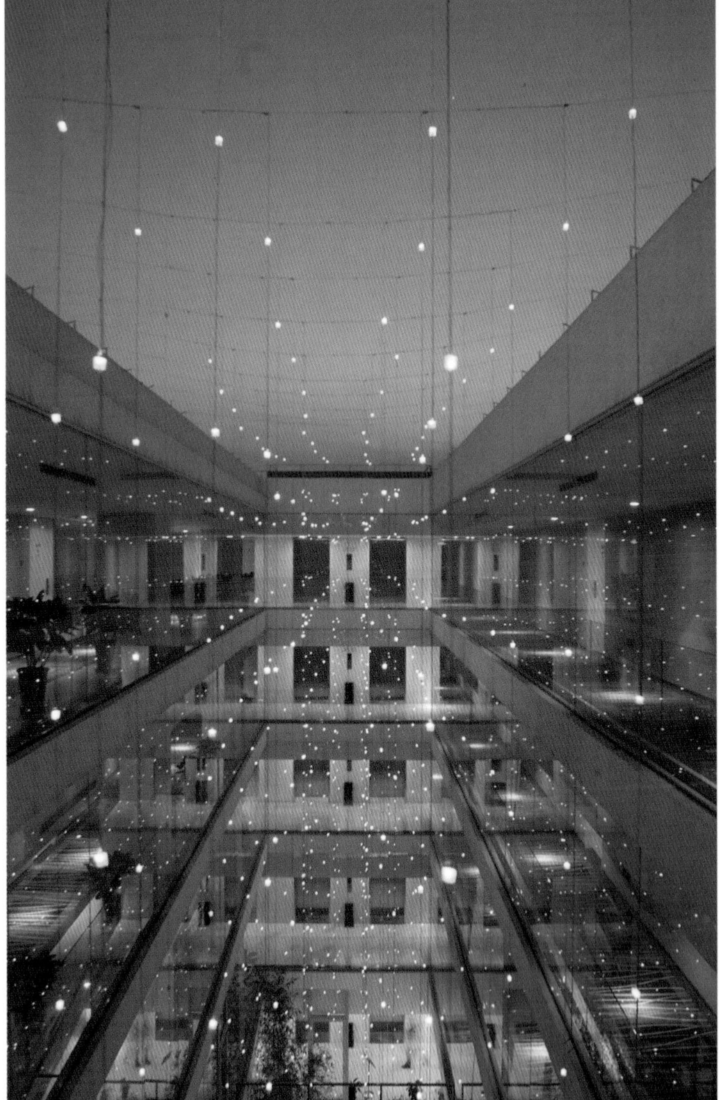

0417 

Green building strategy

Similar buildings are usually demolished or uninhabited. This is a massive waste of materials, built resources, and space. Use the existing structure as a framework to create new works and to reuse materials and resources.

0418

Invisible architecture

Adjacent to the Forbidden City in a 200-year-old Hutong neighborhood, the hotel is a minimal insertion in this traditional Beijing setting. The progression of modernization has led to mass materialization that disconnects the spirit and self. In Chinese philosophy, the process of experiencing art through architecture can refine and inspire the human spirit, alleviating physical invasion and restoring balance to the self. Art is the immaterial content of space that stirs the heart and sparks humanity's dreams. Instead of being too eager to occupy space, we need to return buildings to nature when they are not in use. The buildings melt into the context and reappear when they are needed.

© Li Yongquan

0419

Urban revitalization
Stimulate a decayed context through energetically injecting provocative contemporary space and converting an old, private, internally focused building to a new, public, externally open building.

0420

Create spaces for chance meetings between people
Publishing is a creative field; chance occurrences increase communication and invention. Provoke external reaction of spatial relationships by creating multiple terraces for public use. Provoke internal questioning of the working links within the space by using various creative centers to house multiple user groups and diverse functions.

© Li Yongquan

© Li Yongquan

Architecture & Hygiene

Kalkin Co/Quik Build
59 Mine Brook Rd.
Bernardsville, NJ 07924, USA
P.: (+1) 908-696-1999
www.architectureandhygiene.com

© Peter Aaron/Esto

0421
12 Container House
Large holes are slimming.

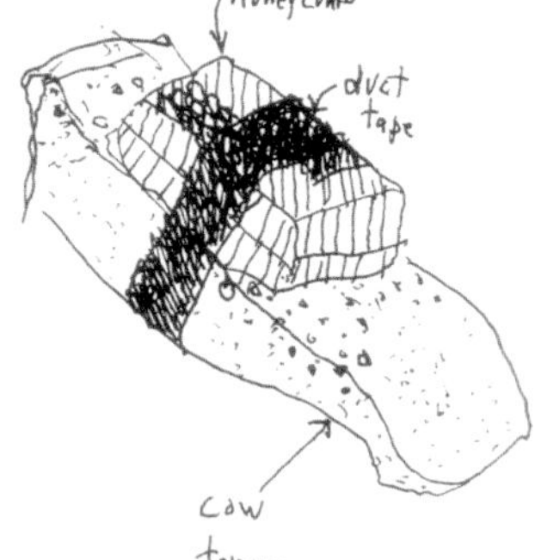

0422
Cow Tongue
Duct tape yokes the moistest parts.

0423
Bunny Lane 1
Things inside of things inside of things. . .

© Peter Aaron/Esto

© Peter Aaron/Esto

0424
Bunny Lane 2
Bright colors work well in dark rooms.

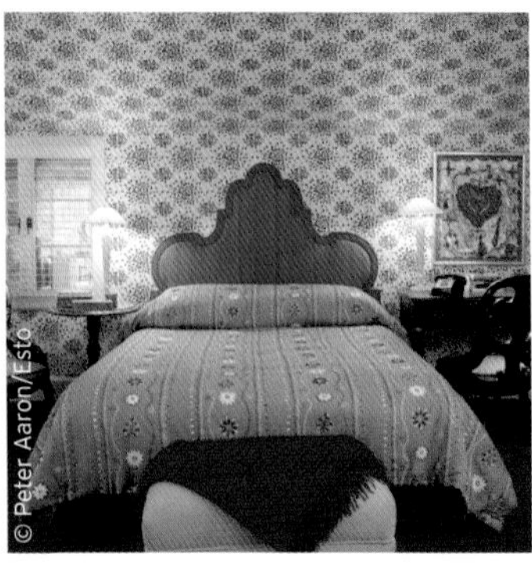
© Peter Aaron/Esto

© Peter Aaron/Esto

0425
Califon
Don't apologize.

0426
Push Button House 1
Use a low horizon in small spaces.

0427

Target
Every house is an oasis.

© Peter Aaron/Esto

0428

Suburban House Kit
Make the television as large as possible.

© Peter Aaron/Esto

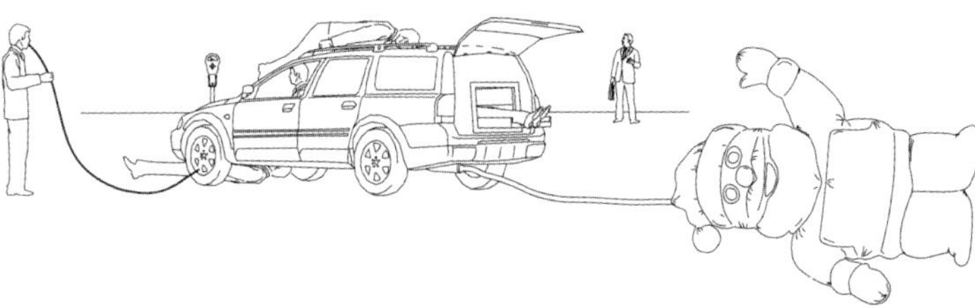

0429

Car Museum
Cars are efficient museums.

© Peter Aaron/Esto

0430

Push Button House 2
Pack houses tightly for moving.

© Peter Aaron/Esto

0431

Museum without walls
For $20, the museumgoer is entitled to more risk.

© Peter Aaron/Esto

fieldoffice

Martha Skinner, Douglas Hecker Principals
272 Riggs Drive
Clemson, SC 29631, USA
P.: (+1) 864-653-5025
www.field-office.com

0432

Concrete details

The concrete base of the project has numerous CNC cut formwork inserts to form the fixtures and the programs related to water and fire in the house. We have begun testing ahead of construction the concrete mixtures and CNC formwork inserts. This test (the H_2O sink) is based on two drops of water touching.

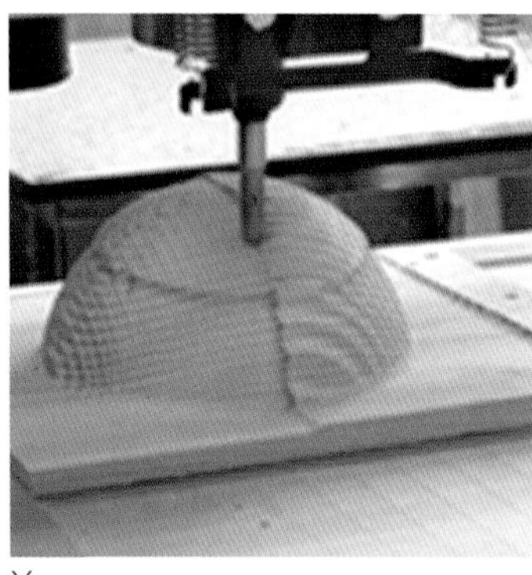

0433

View from marsh

The project proposes the house as a harvester of views, sun, rain, and wind. This off-the-grid house lies at the edge of a salt marsh on Florida's west coast with a southern orientation that "harvests" the site's exposure to the elements and views. The roof has an "elastic" form in order to mitigate the competing demands to capture these disparate resources by transitioning smoothly from collecting sunlight, to collecting water, to collecting views. The project continues our research into fabrication and customization technologies in the timber industry and is constructed using a CNC cut timber frame.

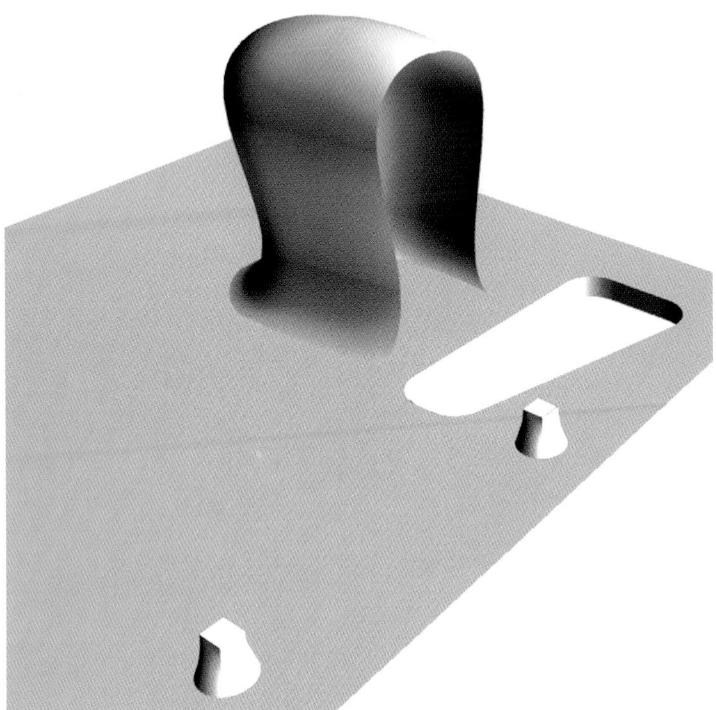

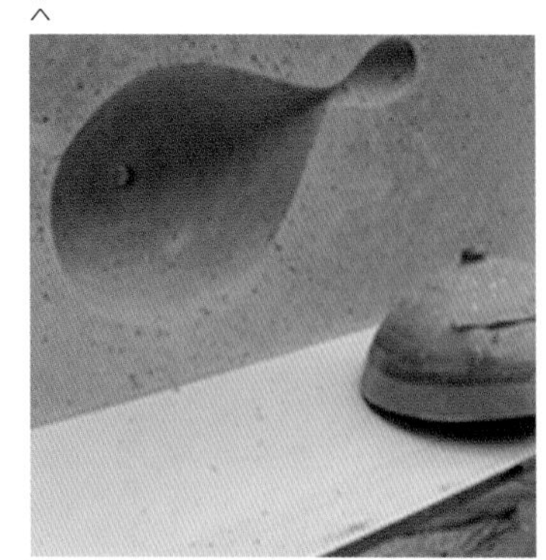

0434

Siting

The house is placed at the transition from salt marsh to pine forest to take advantage of two distinct spaces (forest and marsh) and the numerous site resources to be "harvested" while minimizing the impact on the existing ecosystem that it straddles.

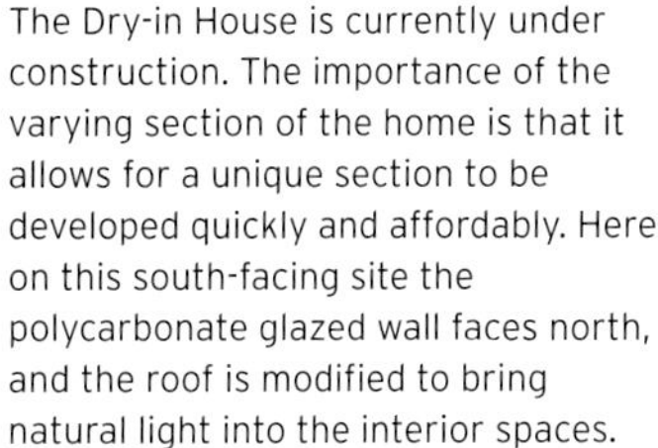

0435

The Dry-in House is currently under construction. The importance of the varying section of the home is that it allows for a unique section to be developed quickly and affordably. Here on this south-facing site the polycarbonate glazed wall faces north, and the roof is modified to bring natural light into the interior spaces.

© Jackson Blalock

0436

Diagram of sun, wind, and rain

The house is oriented to capture the prevailing winds, while the roof form is designed to maximize the harvesting of sun through the photovoltaics on its south face, while acting as a catchment for a grey water system.

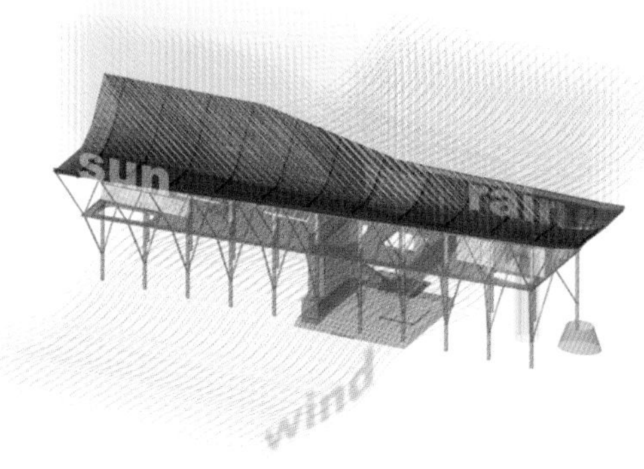

0437

The dwelling has a fixed plan but flexible section, allowing the homeowner to customize the section to their needs, sites, and desires affordably. Homeowners are sent a one-page design worksheet in the mail to sketch out potential roof and ceiling configurations for their new home. These images show the Dry-in House and the initial sketch made by its homeowner.

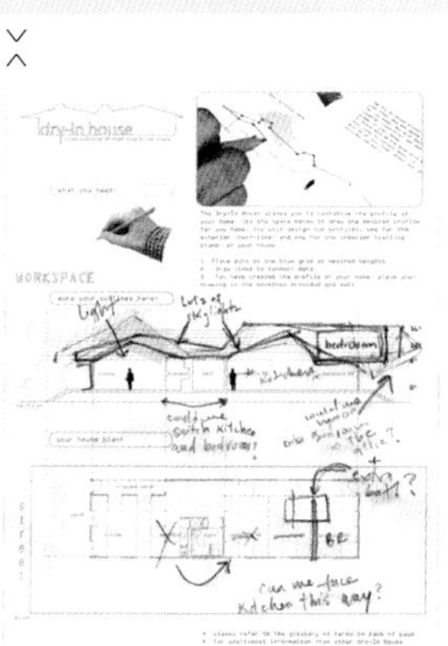

0438

This diagram shows an overview of the idea and how information technology can be utilized in conjunction with automated fabrication platforms (in this case, the wood plate trusses) to mass produce customized homes that reflect both their owners and unique building sites.

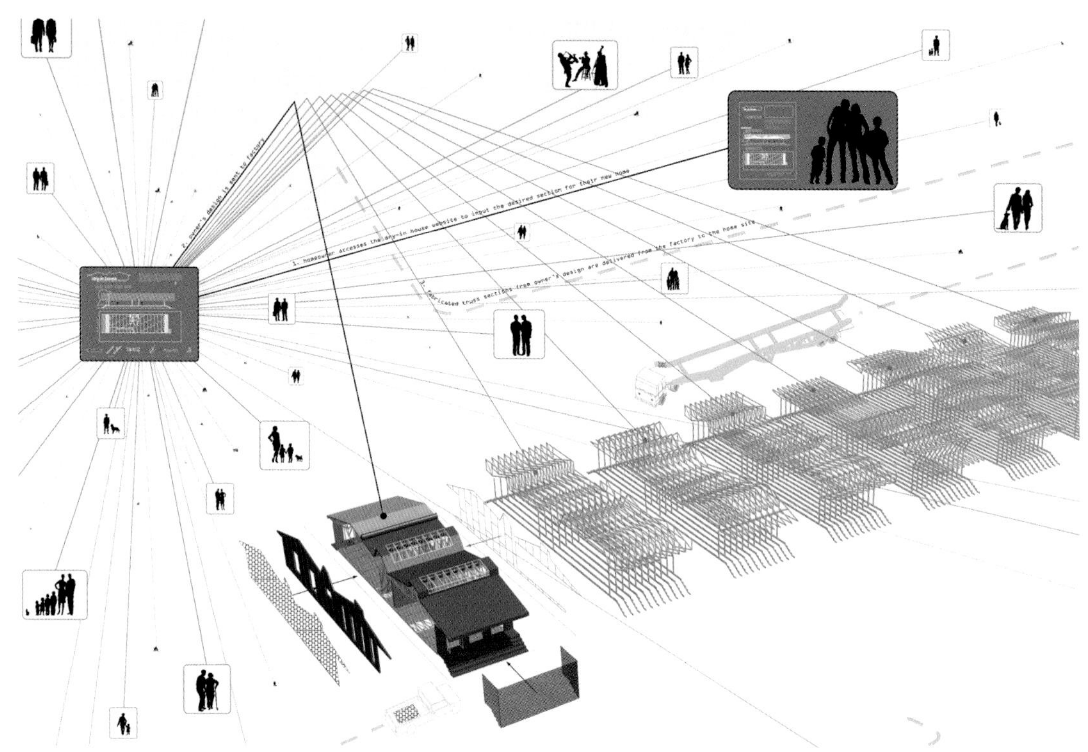

0439

A bird's eye view of a typical block in New Orleans, showing the variety of possible mass-customized designs along with Dry-in House. The "chassis" of the design is the lower portion of the project and remains largely the same, ensuring a lively street life, with natural light and ventilation for the interiors.

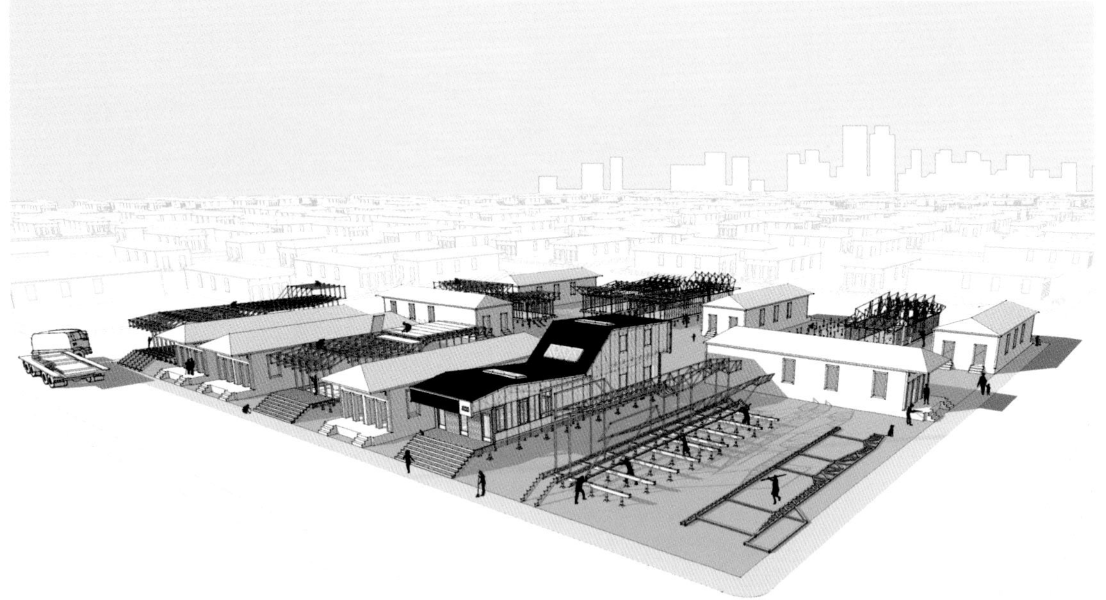

0440

The house's "truss sections" being raised by volunteers. The framing of the house is constructed in a series of parallel sections that are based on the homeowner's original sketch, and then input into parametric engineering software that calculates the structural sections quickly and affordably.

0441

The homeowner accesses the Dry-in House website where they are able to input the profiles (roof and ceiling) of their new home. Using a simple Flash interface and working with a design volunteer, the owner can pull the "elastic" roof and ceiling profiles to produce the desired configuration. Scripts in the interface prevent users from putting in design information that cannot be engineered or constructed. The design proposes a system that, once in place and constraints determined, provides a level of design input on the part of the owner that is currently unavailable in affordable housing in the United States.

0442

Interior view from the entry porch. The ethos of the project is to provide a dried-in shell that is designed in such a way that it can be left as a finished home. Homeowners also have the option to layer on additional finishes within their means and own timeline.

© Melissa Vandiver

0443

The finishes in the house (rubber roofing and siding, polycarbonate siding, exposed wooden trusses, and exposed OSB) are designed in such a way that they can be left as is or layered on with more finishes.

Bektaş Architectural Office

Üryanizade Street 15
34674 Kuzguncuk-Üsküdar
Istanbul, Turkey
P.: (+90) 216-310-0774/495-6857
www.cengizbektas.com

0444

The International Industry and Trade Bank (Bakırköy branch) is situated on the corner of two narrow streets, projecting its interiors onto the street outside. Employees experience a blend of interior and exterior sensations.

The project used exposed concrete; its outer walls were designed to collect heat in winter and to insulate against the heat in the summer.

0445

The National Turkish Language Institute structure is 100% reinforced concrete. Its interior divisions, cabinets and furniture are made of wood. It was voted by architects as one of the top twenty buildings with typical republican architecture.

0446

This ten-story mall building in Denizli was located on a site where even a two-story shopping mall had previously been unsuccessful. The whole structure is sloped. The Babadaglilar shopping mall has been a successful facility for the last 35 years, becoming a symbol of the city.

0447

The lot of Halil Bektas primary school is situated in a built-up area. Wherever possible the building has been designed to open up in the direction it is faces: south-south-east. This gives the classrooms suitable lighting. The design aims to show reality to the children: pipes are left exposed, and casing has not been used to hide elements.

0448

Mersin, once a small city with 100,000 inhabitants, has experienced a population boom. It is now over ten times that size. This building was built on a former brown site and has easy access from the ring road. It has been designed to represent the growth of the city center. Located on one side of the skyscraper, the shops are all arranged on a circular slope, enabling car access to the top floors. In the centre of the shopping area there is a pool, and in the middle of the pool a stage: a space for a theater. Below the pool there is a multifunctional space containing a theater, concert hall, registry office, etc. All the spaces flow into each other. Underground there are three floors of car parking.

0449

The Olbia Social Centre is the socio-cultural complex of the Akdeniz University in Antalya. Uninterrupted pergolas follow the lines of the slopes. The spaces flow into each other. This construction is shaded by greenery and offers multifunctional uses. The materials utilized were wood and the travertine stone that was unearthed when the foundations were dug. The walls have been left unplastered.

0450

This lot, measuring somewhere in the region of 21,500 sq ft (2,000 square metres), is located in Göltürkbükü, on the Bodrum peninsula. The Gulsema-Lutz were a couple living in England. The brief was to design a building to be used as a summer house for several years and then as a permanent residence. Like any typical Bodrum house, this house was designed around a living space of a kitchen with a fireplace opening out to a terrace through sliding glass doors. This space can be enclosed in winter by simply closing the doors. The morning sunlight floods into the house, however the house turns its back on the unbearably hot midday summer sun and any noise from the road. The bedroom is one floor up, surrounded by a roof garden. The whole roof is garden space.

0451

The Afrodisias museum extension has been designed as a steel construction built on piles. The piles do not touch any remains of the ancient walls, and no trees were cut down. Visitors can walk underneath the structure and see everything. The walls and roof have two ventilation layers.

Mario Botta Architetto

Via Ciani 16
6904 Lugano, Switzerland
P.: (+41) 91 972 86 25
www.botta.ch

0452

With two spaces, different in function but unified in their design and need for spirituality, the Cymbalista Synagogue and Jewish Heritage Centre in Tel Aviv is a place for prayer and a place for discussion, functioning as both a synagogue and a lecture hall. The two square-shaped volumes rise into a conoid, which takes a circular shape at roof level. Both towers are constructed with the same materials and both interiors have exactly the same down-lighting systems.

0453

In designing the new Banca del Gottardo offices my aim was to give the town a new image. This was not because of the grandness of the site or its intended use. In fact, I think a bank, like a post office, a church, or a theater, is a part of a city as it serves the community.

0454

The chapel of Santa Maria degli Angeli in Mount Tamaro "detaches" itself, as it were, from the mountain to form a new horizon, the starting point of a perfect viaduct. The overall structure is more than just a new building; it is a manipulation of the existing landscape. The plastic forms, the transverse composition, and the innovative configurations make up a kind of "negative" image gathered beneath the horizon of the walkway.

© Enrico Cano

© Pino Musi

0455

The SFMOMA, San Francisco Museum of Modern Art, is an energetic response to the density of the downtown area and sits within a highly varied cityscape. In its design, the architect has acknowledged this reality, and throws down a challenge to the contemporary city by using masses that are loaded with material and color.
Partner architect: Hellmuth, Obata & Kassabaum Inc., SF

0456

In the hope of making a house for man, I designed the Cathedral of the Resurrection in Evry as the "house of God." To build a cathedral today is an extraordinary opportunity to create and enrich the environment in which we live. It offers a moment of silence, of reflection and prayer, and speaks of man in relation to the rapid changes and contradictions of life.

© Pino Musi

0457➤

At MART, the Museum of Modern and Contemporary Art in Rovereto, the plaza, covered by a glass dome, becomes the heart of the structure and also the image of the museum complex that is organized around it. It is the empty space, the covered plaza, that becomes the true matrix of the architectural composition. Partner architect: Giulio Andreolli

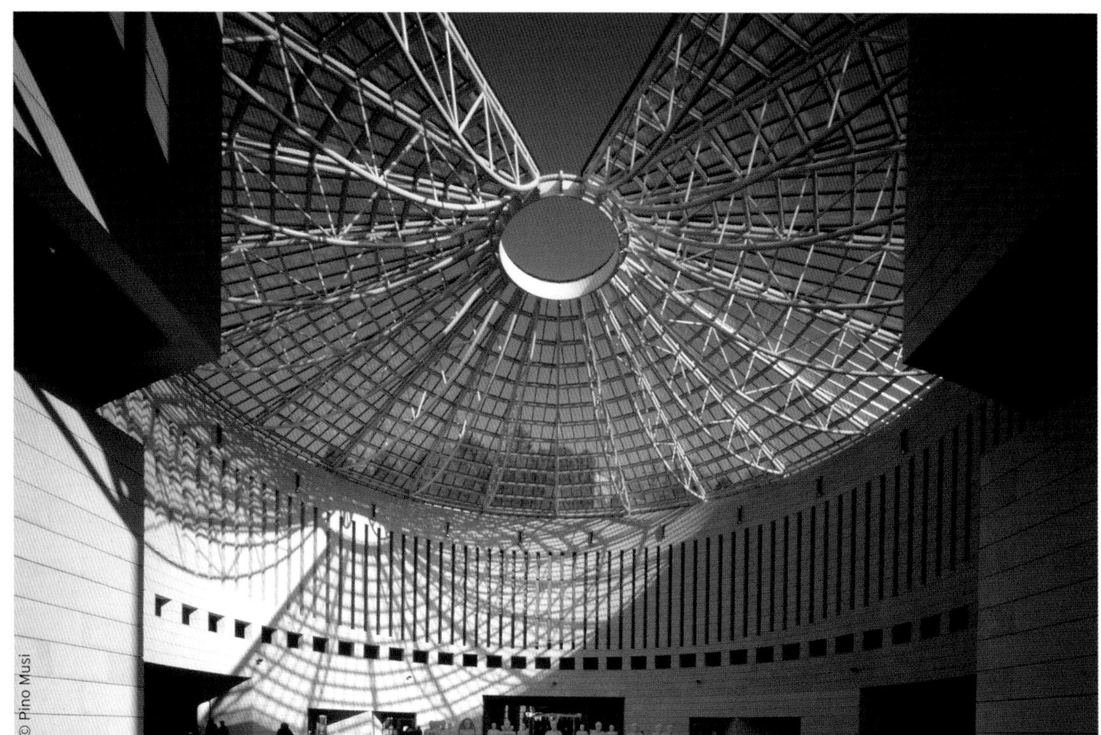
© Pino Musi

© Enrico Cano

◄0458

At the Tschuggen Bergoase Wellness Centre in Arosa we imagined building without building in order to affirm the presence of the new building through emerging bodies—trees of light—and to leave the great volume interred within the functional program. Partner architect: Fanzun AG, Chur

0459▼

The church of Santo Volto in Turin edifies a church devoted to the face of Christ displayed at the back of the altar. It has a heptagonal plan surrounded by seven towers that are connected to the lower volumes of the chapels. The chimney of the former steelworks, transformed into the church belfry, becomes a symbol of the old and new utilization.

© Enrico Cano

© Studio DIM Associati_Florence

© Young Chea Park

0460

The Bechtler Museum of Modern Art in Charlotte project has a central glass heart housing the hall. The interplay between voids and swells created by the glass core gives the construction a strong plastic force. The building is developed on four levels, the last of which is zenith-lit by skylights and juts outwardly. This configuration embodies distinctive characteristics by drawing a plaza inside the museum's primary volume.
Partner architect: Wagner Murray Architects

0461

For Kyobo Tower in Seoul, the idea was to create a gigantic construction, compact and with seemingly blind fronts in order to form a contrast with the glass and steel structured buildings in the surrounding area. Straight as a medieval tower, this new architectural presence helps people to orient themselves in the modern city.
Partner architect: Chang-Jo Architects, Inc., Seoul

NSMH-Nevzat Sayın Mimarlık Hizmetleri

Icadiye cd. 81
34674 Kuzguncuk-Üsküdar
Istanbul, Turkey
P.: (+90) 216-310-08-70
www.nsmh.com

0462►

Yahşi School is an example of a self-sustaining building constructed through employing local workers, maters, and technologies.

◄0463

Umur represents a distinctive, colorful space in a printing house where all staff and visitors enter by the same entrance.

0464▲

Fethiye shows how to build a building today with simple construction materials and following traditional methods.

0465►

Gön Leather Factory is a helter-skelter back neighborhood; a quiet, plain experiment that we think will serve as an example for what comes later.

0466

Evidea is an attempt to bring 470 dwellings together in such a fashion that they will create their own worlds.

©Cemal Emden

0467

Irmak is an educational building that allows one to clearly read how it was constructed.

0468

Banvit: an entrance building for an industrial plant with heavy in-and-out traffic.

©Cemal Emden

©Ali Bekman

©Cemal Emden

©Cemal Emden

0469

Santral Istanbul CAC is a contemporary art center which by day looks completely closed and at night turns into a discreet icon thanks to its own light.

0470

The Santral Istanbul Communications Faculty is a unique educational building designed adhering to supremely simple and familiar schemata.

©Cemal Emden

0471

Göksu Office is an example of how traditional knowledge of wood can be used today.

Imre Makovecz

MAKONA Architectural Studio
Kecske utca 25
Budapest, 1034 Hungary
P.: (+36) 1-388-1702
www.makovecz.hu

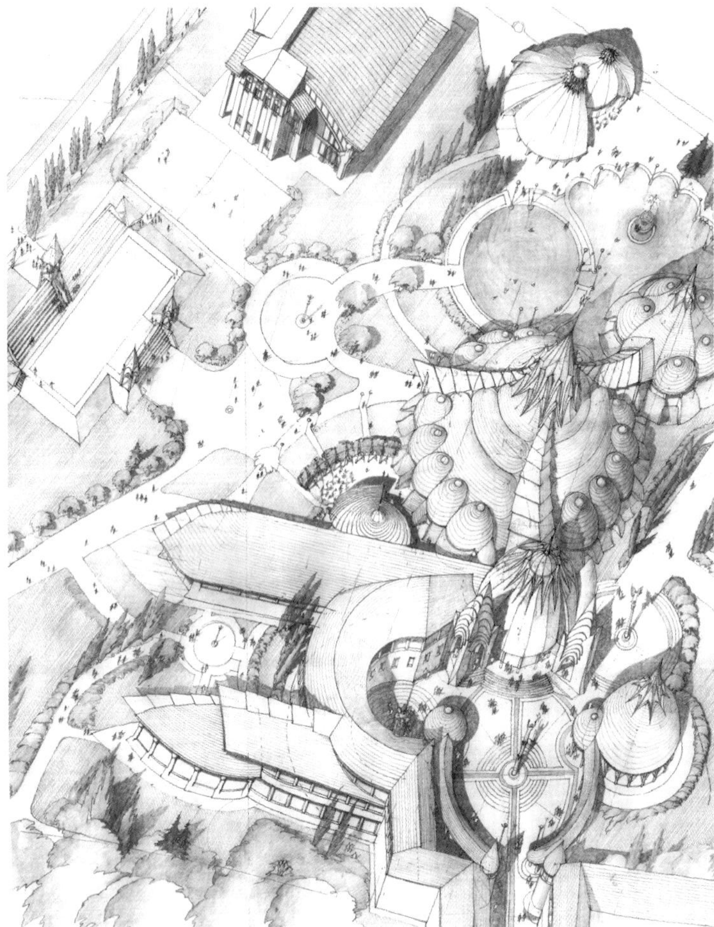

◄0472

Makó, a city renowned for its onions, is planning a new pool and a fitness-wellness center, which will fit into the texture of the town, as witnessed shown in this photograph.

0473▼

The Onion House in Makó is the town's theater, as well as the venue for its celebrations.

0474

The tower on the left is the German Tower. Inside and behind it are local government spaces and a bank, because the Germans are better at this. While the tower on the right is the Székely Tower with the big hall dedicated to celebrations, dance, and words, because the Székelys are better at this. The pub where the Germans ask for a spritzer, and the Székelys for a *fröcss*, is situated in the middle. What good is a central headquarters if it divides people?

0475

The centralized world of communism and the world of finance are two sides of the same coin. It was in the face of this that we built the so-called "village houses" in the 1970s, when communist policy targeted the destruction of villages. The population of Kakasd is comprised of Germans (Swabians) and Székely Hungarians from Bukovina. After World War II, the former were killed or deported to Germany, while the latter were expelled from Romania to find a home here.

0476

In Csíkszereda (Miercurea-Cius, Romania), ancient six- and seven-hundred-year old cross-shaped tombstones lean against the extant medieval church. One was used for the two towers of the new church. Four bronze angels guard the central skylight of the main building.

Budapest
Roman catholic church
Architect: Makovecz Imre

◄0477

The Church of Upper Christinatown of Budapest rests on earlier layers. Building began during World War II but was discontinued under communism. They built one story on top, which was used as a disco. Blasphemy!

0478▼

In Kolozsvár (Cluj, Romania), this was the realization of an old plan that for eight years Mayor Funar had vetoed. But in the end the Székely Towers, the ribbed interior, and the gates were finished as well. The Székelys are Romania's Irish or Scotch.

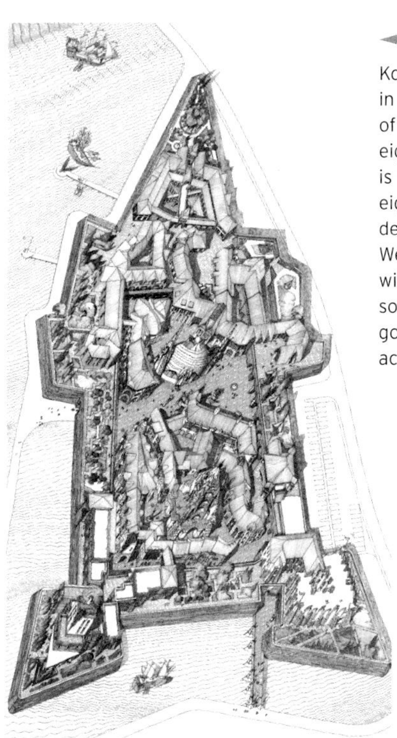

0479

Komárom (Komarno, Slovakia) was built in the 12th century at the confluence of the Duna and the Vág rivers. On a eighteenth century etching, the town is within the castle walls. In the eighteenth century the town was demolished to make room for a fort. We have rebuilt the city on blueprints without cars, noise, or air pollution, so that even a child should be able to go to kindergarten without being accompanied by an adult.

0480

Catholic University, Piliscsaba. In 1990, after the occupying army left Hungary, the state gave the former Soviet barracks to the Catholic Church. We started construction after clearing away the mental, spiritual, and physical filth. The Stephaneum received its name in honor of St. Stephen. The first of its kind in Hungary, the building is about the space-time continuum, where what counts is not Euclidean geometry, but the drama inherent in the interplay of space and time.

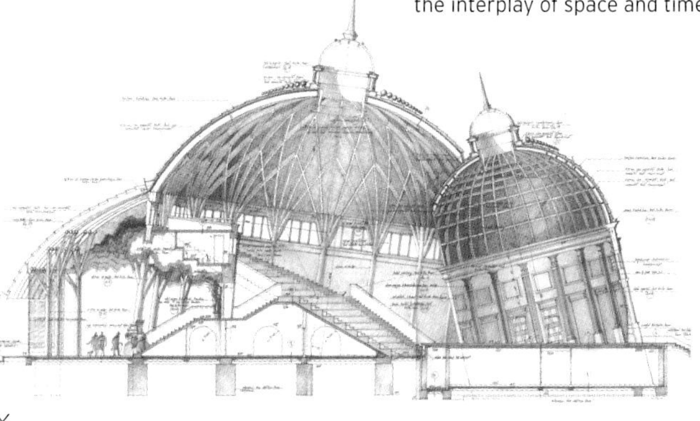

Acconci Studio

20 Jay Street, #215 Brooklyn
New York, NY 11201, USA
P.: (+1) 718-852-6591
www.acconci.com

0481

Cannon Center for the Performing Arts
Push & pull. Roof like a liquid flung over the plaza.

0482

Mobius Bench
Continuous surface, endless space.

0483

United Bamboo Store
Bubble. Bulge. Ooze.

0484

Subway Station, Coney Island
Wave. An architecture of flow.

◄0485

Fold. Enfold. Embed.
Screens for a walkway between buildings, buses, and cars at Shibuya Station curve up like shells to shield the walkway from the surrounding buildings and traffic, and the bare walls of the ramps. The screens are like Venetian blinds; the surroundings flicker, as if in a movie, a kaleidoscope, a flipbook. At the bottom of the screen you sit on light; light bounces up, mirrored from slat to slat and is reflected back onto the walkway.

◄0486

Light Street, Canseco Garage
Emergence. Growth. Architecture from inside out. Architecture from bottom up.

0487▲

Mur Island
Twist. Warp. Morph.

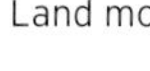

0488▲

Park in the water, Laakhaven Hollands Spoor
Land moves. A mix of land and sea.

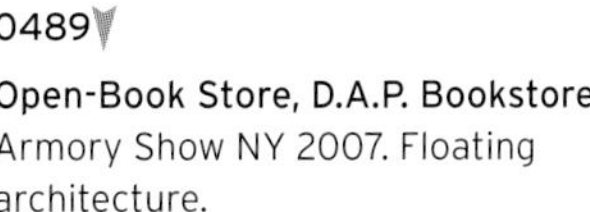

0489▼

Open-Book Store, D.A.P. Bookstore
Armory Show NY 2007. Floating architecture.

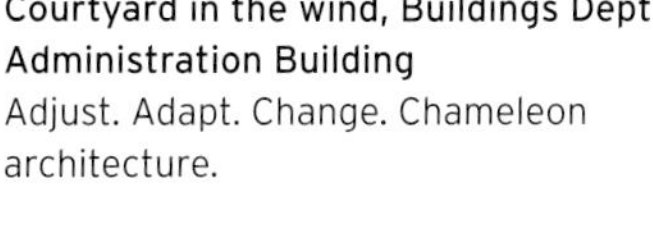

0490►

Courtyard in the wind, Buildings Dept Administration Building
Adjust. Adapt. Change. Chameleon architecture.

5+1AA Alfonso Femia Gianluca Peluffo

© Maritati

Via Interiano 3/11
16124 Genoa, Italy
P.: (+39) 010-540-095
www.5piu1aa.com

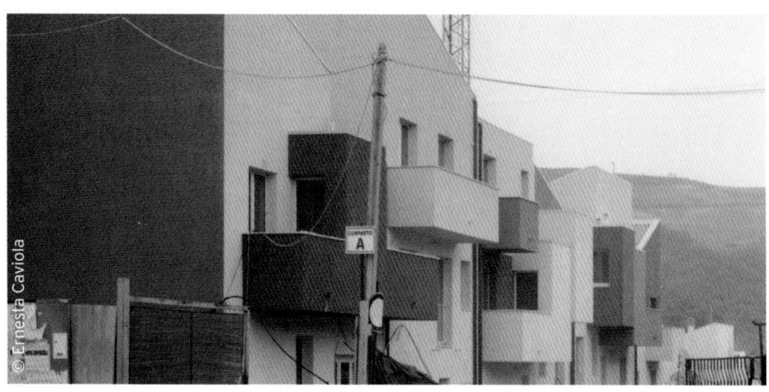
© Ernesta Caviola

0491

Reconstruction of San Giuliano di Puglia
Places. Non-places do not exist. Non-memory exists. The fear of what we do not understand exists. The terror of our memories and possible futures exists. The confusion between news and the present exists. So we spend years worrying about surrogates of truth: It is simple and convenient. But deadly.
Partner Designer: A.Spalla

0493

Italian Space Agency (ASI) building, Rome (under construction)
Navel (dreams). Our mouth for nine months. We often find ourselves gazing down at it, perplexed. Sometimes it is just an excuse not to look up and face reality. Yet, all in all, it is by no means reassuring. After all, you cannot see its end. It is the part of our body where dreams started and still hide. We must look up and free those dreams.
Partner Designer: A. Spalla

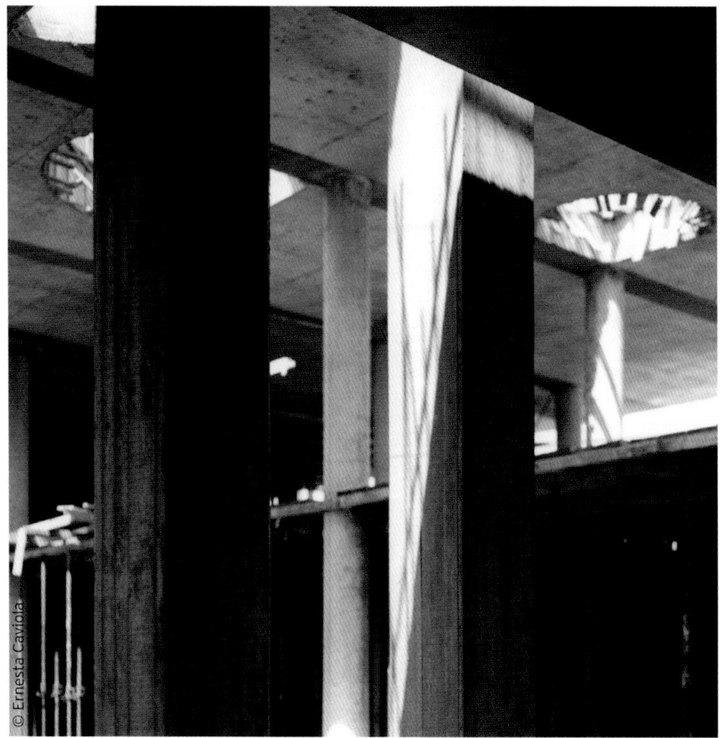
© Ernesta Caviola

0492

MOdAM, Museum and School of Fashion, City of Fashion, Milan (International competition, 2006)
Palm of the hand (South). Mediterranean culture, as the culture of all Southerners, communicates through touch, with the sensitivity of the palm of a hand. The back of the hand is tension, technique, a spring, a structure. The touch of a hand is the ability to grasp and let go, to clutch. Greco-Roman wrestling does not kill. Boxing does. We can assimilate millions of pieces of information through the palm of a hand. We can even read the future.
Partner Designer: R. Ricciotti

0494

Milanese ice factory, Milan (2008)
Stomach (Fridge). You open the Fridge and peer inside. All too often it's a desolate sight and your stomach growls in protest. Terrible, deep noises, as if from Purgatory. You must cook something, with what there is, with the leftovers your forgetfulness and that rude guest have left you. But the image of a good dish is stronger than the reflection of the cold light of the Fridge, and those distant noises from Purgatory are already a presage of Paradise.

© Ernesta Caviola

0495

Retail Park – Area D4 Assago, Assago
Sex (what you do with whom). That's a tricky question. How do you identify the thin line that separates sensuality from pornography, pleasure from violence. Being from possessing. Professionalism from being servile.

0496

Parfiri Low Emission Building, Vado Ligure (Competition, winning design, 2005)
Back. Beauty and Ethics. Beauty is Truth when it doesn't become an idol, an image, but when it is born like a chiasmus from the air that you breathe between two different things, inside a dualism. The space between two opposites is the place of beauty. Being ethical, being upright means tirelessly working there in the middle. Even if you make mistakes. Whatever it takes.

© Ernesta Caviola

© Ernesta Caviola

0497

Territorial tower, Rozzano (under development)

Feet (speed). When did we start running? How many times did we think we could understand better by slowing down, stopping? It was just an illusion. The duty of the contemporary is one of Hercules' tasks thrown at mad speed. Forget it: we must stop believing that slowness is possible. We look at the world with a terrible horizontal speed. But we try to understand deep down. As often as possible, as deep as possible.

0498

New directional buildings for Sviluppo Sistema Fiera, Rho (under construction)

Ear (echo). We can never listen directly. The promise of happiness from our childhood returns in the form of an echo. The promise of happiness from our childhood returns in the form of an echo. We listen and build on the basis of these echoes that we transform, through the duty of the contemporary, into feelings of shared space. Modern. The echo brings us forgotten futures. Partner Designer: J.B. Pietri – Italiana Costruzioni spa

0499

New Cinema Palace of Venice, Venice (under construction)

Heart. It's a choice. We have decided not to use our minds any more. It was pointless anyway. So, at each moment, we try to react with our heart and stomach. It means you still nourish a romantic, sentimental hope that you will be able to understand reality and transform it. You will be able to find forms you can share, a catharsis. Understanding.

Partner Designer: R. Ricciotti

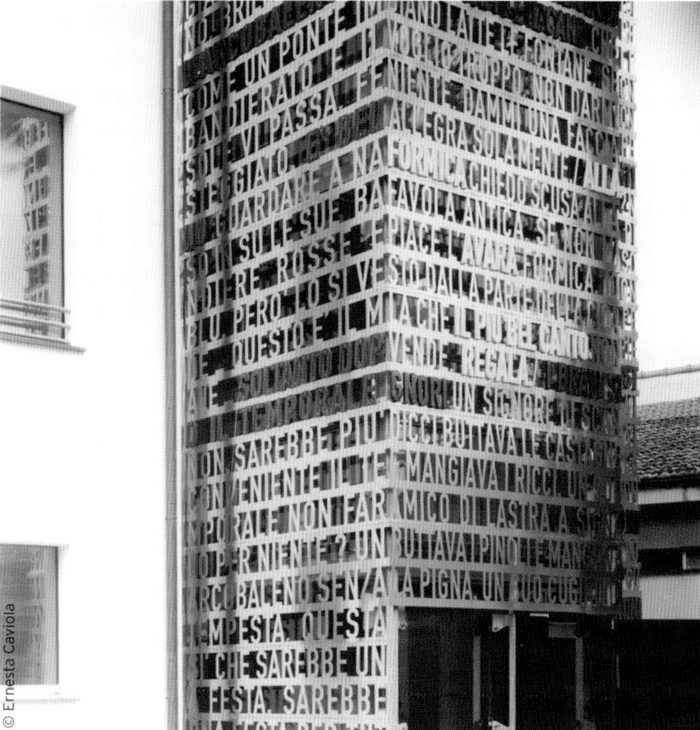

0500

Library, games room, and auditorium in former Villa Sottanis, Casarza Ligure (2008)

Soul (feelings, love). What affects our soul makes us exist, forms the world, and so forms us too. Architecture must be a slow, tireless sentimental education. Not without mistakes. By no means, not without mistakes. The relationship of our soul, of ourselves, with life allows us to conserve, cultivate and develop something moving, the illusion of a miracle, amazement. Women often guide us with their emotions through this amazement.

JML Consultants

Eusebi Guëll 12-13
08034 Barcelona, Spain
P.: (+34) 932-80-53-74
www.jmlwaterfeaturedesign.com

© Communauté Urbaine de Bordeaux

0501

Trust in the public's creativity
A thin layer of water covering a *piazza* can be used in many ways: wading, cycling, skim-boarding...

0502

The art of creating attractive water features through observation
This project reproduces the famous natural flooding of Piazza San Marco in Venice.

© JML Consultants, Michel Corajoud Paysagiste, Pierre Gangnet Architecte

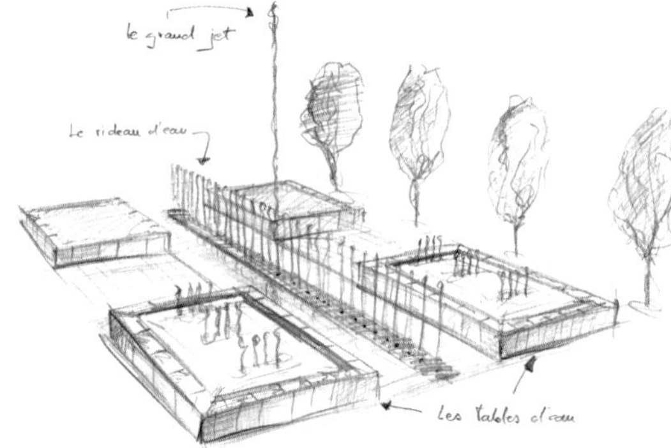

0503

A fountain where kids can play with water, interacting with liquid: an urban oasis
A water feature is a gathering place, a community experience. A simple design is sometimes the best way to achieve great results.

0504

This project reuses a former warehouse located on the banks of the River Garonne. It has been transformed to house all the mechanical systems that artificially flood the 29,062-sq ft (2,700-sq-m) *piazza*.

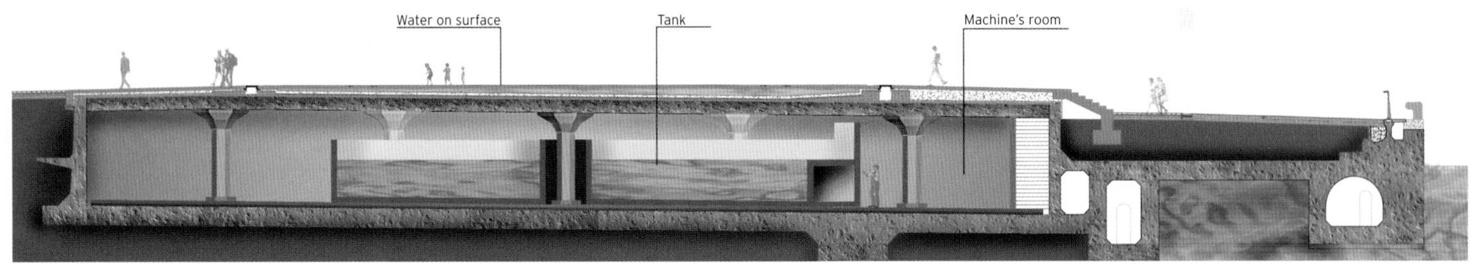

0505

The surrounding architectural context is part of the project
The high jet lays down a challenge to the high tower. And the two vertical signals can be seen from miles away.

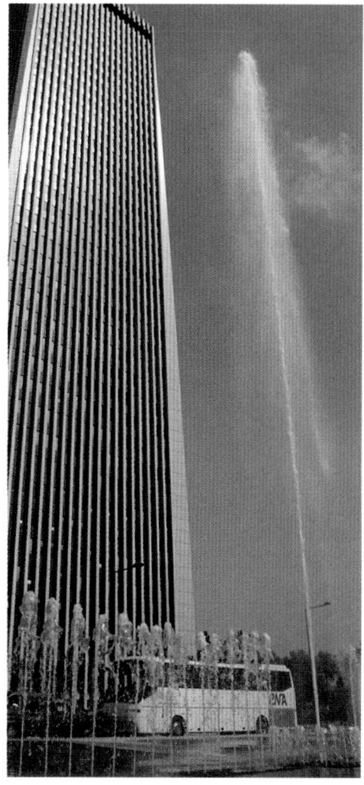

0506

Play with emotions

0507

A water shape can be used as an architectural element
It has a strong hypnotic power and can become an integral powerful element in the urban landscape.

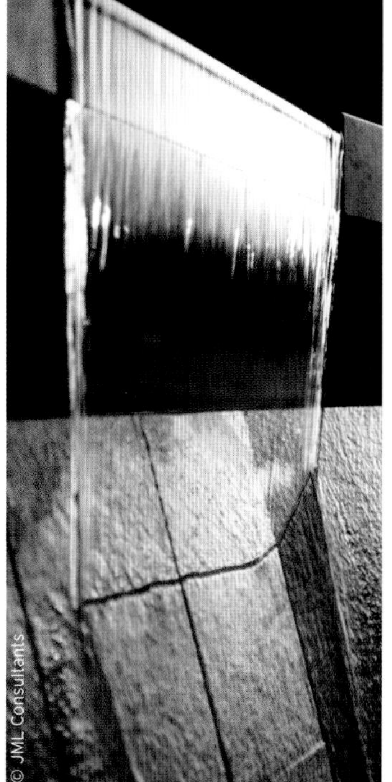

0508

Water has a formidable capacity for metamorphosis
In our projects we try to utilize all the different aspects of water. Modern techniques allow us to modify its state, artificially recreating pressure or temperature differences in order to solidify or vaporize it.

0510

Attention to detail
Water has the power to reveal constructive quality and details or, on the contrary, faults. Designing with water is challenging. Take care of the details. If you want to achieve the best effects, your creation has to be perfect.

0509

Transform a simple stairway into a great chill-out area through doing something as simple as running water through stairs.

Estudio Luis de Garrido

Blasco Ibáñez 114, puertas 7 y 9
46022 Valencia, Spain
P.: (+34) 963-56-70-70
www.luisdegarrido.com

Bertran 6-8, entlo. 1ª, esc. A
08028 Barcelona, Spain

0511

The iSleep Hotel, in Zaragoza, is the first demountable, expandable and portable budget hotel. It is 100% prefabricated and has an infinite life cycle. The building captures solar thermal, solar photovoltaic, and geothermal energy. All of its components are demountable, reusable, and recoverable. It does not generate waste in any of its different configurations and has a green roof.

0512 

The Lliri Blau housing development is located in Valencia. It is Spain's first bioclimatic and sustainable housing development and consists of 129 houses of 17 different unit types. The complex is 50% prefabricated and consumes just 40% of the energy used by similar developments. The development recycles rainwater and only uses green, recyclable, non-polluting materials. Waste generation has been minimized. The complex captures solar energy to heat the water for the homes and swimming pool. The entire complex is covered with green roofs. And despite the high temperatures in the region, the houses do not need air conditioning systems.

0513

Casa Mariposa is located in Cali, Colombia. It has been constructed using green, recycled, recovered, and non-polluting materials and consumes only 10% of the energy used by a similar house. The dwelling has a bioclimatic design and self-regulating heating system that gives a steady temperature of 75ºF all year round, without the need for technology. The dwelling also has a green roof.

© Maite Piera

0514

The R4 House is a dwelling made only from recovered waste and recycled material. Its structure is made from disused shipping containers. The house has zero energy consumption and is equipped with solar thermal, solar photovoltaic and geothermal energy systems. Its bioclimatic design dispenses with the need to air conditioning systems. The house has an infinite lifespan, that it to say, it can last forever. It is demountable and transportable. No waste was generated during the construction process, and, since all its components are demountable, no waste is generated when it is re-assembled.

0515

Biopar is a housing development located in Montserrat, Valencia, consisting of 100% prefabricated houses arranged in pairs. Hardly any waste was generated during the construction stage, and the houses neither need heating nor air conditioning. Only green, recyclable, and non-polluting materials have been used in this project and the houses have green roofs. During the daytime, the houses do not need artificial lighting. At night, only LED lights are used. Each household consumes only 20% of the energy of a conventional home.

0516

The Casas del Río restaurant in Requena, Valencia, blends into the terrain by means of a green roof that extends the ground space. The restaurant is energetically self-sufficient, capturing solar thermal, solar photovoltaic and geothermal energy. The building is 100% prefabricated and demountable.

0517

The Miami skyscraper, USA, is prefabricated and demountable. All its components can easily be recovered and repaired, meaning the building has an infinite life cycle. Its bioclimatic design dispenses with the need for heating or air conditioning systems. The skyscraper's multimedia skin interacts with the environment, changing its appearance, lighting, and information. The tower has many different interior garden spaces.

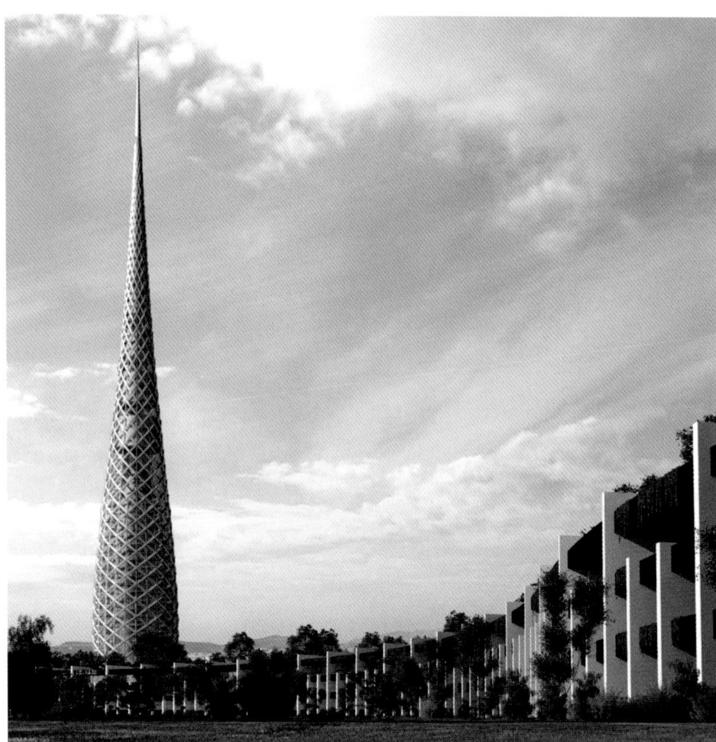

0518

The La Ilum complex (Ecópolis) is a recycling project in the city of Valencia. The volumes are concentrated in semi-buried buildings meaning that the roofs form part of the garden space. The project includes a 1,643-foot-high (500 m) bioclimatic skyscraper.

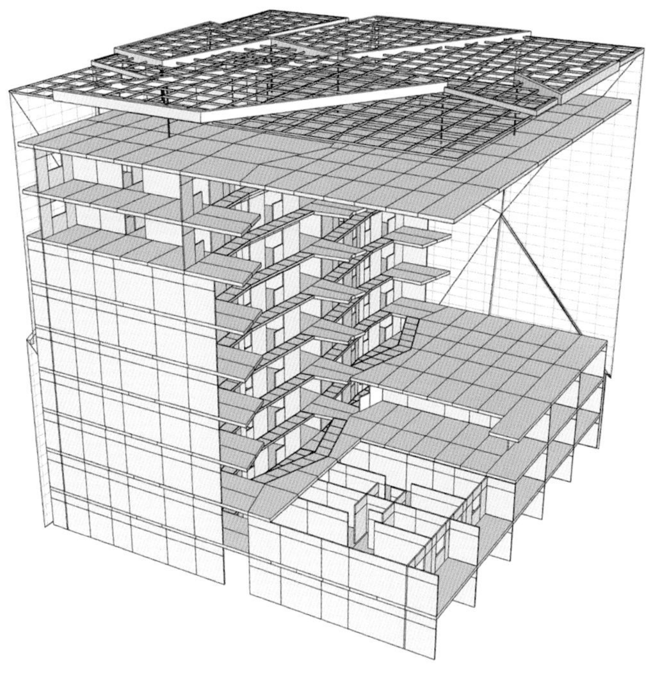

0519

These prefabricated and demountable public houses in Mondragón, the Basque country, have an infinite life cycle. All their components are recoverable and reusable. And they consume just 10% of the energy used by similar dwellings. Their bioclimatic design and glazed multimedia skin keep the internal temperatures at a steady level using only geothermal energy. All the roofs are landscaped and have a shell inset with solar thermal and photovoltaic collectors.

0520

The Berimbau wants to be the new symbol of Rio de Janeiro. The building has a double spherical glazed skin that automatically regulates the temperatures of the interior spaces. This double glazed skin is inset with solar thermal, photovoltaic collectors and interacts with its environment using multimedia techniques: changing its color, lighting, and the information conveyed.

Manuelle Gautrand

36, boulevard de la Bastille
75012 Paris, France
P.: (+33) 1-56-95-06-46
www.manuelle-gautrand.com

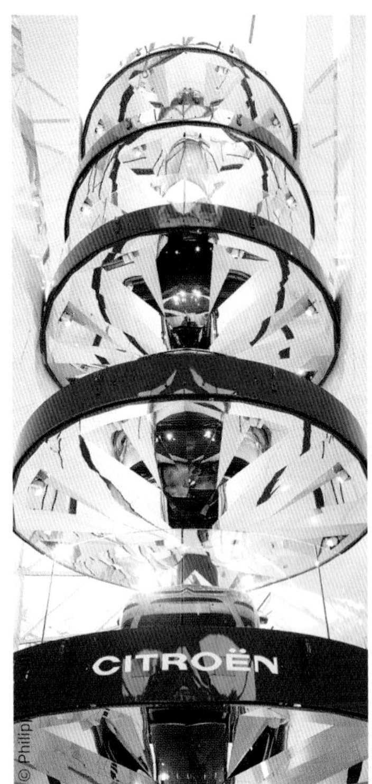

0521

For the C42 Citroen Showroom we developed a concept that would magnify their cars in a building that possessed a strong symbolic presence, a kind of corporate totem composed of eight vehicles stacked on plateaux, one on top of the other. The arrangement forms a gigantic vertical display around which visitors move in an ascending or descending spiral direction via flights of stairs and a series of landings. At the top, the sculptural structure affords superb views over the city.

0522

By concentrating floor space, high rise buildings limit distances and save space: the most precious raw materials in any city. They enable rational land use to control urban sprawl. The AVA Tower's architecture creeps under the circular boulevard and literally enfolds it, restyling the approaches and creating an arresting tableau in its own right.

0523

The concrete fan splay of the extension fits morphologically into the contour lines of the natural terrain, which is part of a nature reserve known as Heron Park. The perception of the surroundings from the exhibition galleries is one of the key features of the Modern Art Museum. But the inflow of daylight via these openings had to be carefully controlled: as every curator knows, strong light is harmful to works of art, and the *Art brut* collection is no exception.

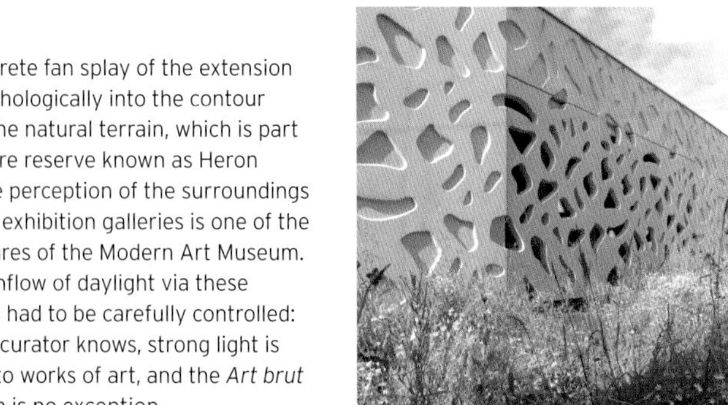

0524

The Business Centre Saint-Etienne project is like a large "Aztec serpent" rising from the lot. Its body has three identical outer faces, and an underside that is different: a skin of silvery transparent scales and a bright yellow "throat," shiny and opaque. The yellow marks out internal pedestrian movements with its rich luminous presence.

0525

In every city, housing occupies by far the majority of space. As it is the raw material of the urban fabric, architects have to be concerned with changing and reinventing the ways it is used, especially for social housing. A green approach is fundamental, it is not just about respect for nature but for the everyday environment where people live, in the light of new ideas of comfort and new user protocols.

0526

There is an exquisite subtlety in the Northern Lights, which many painters have captured so well. The façade, like a kaleidoscope, bringing transparencies and gold tinted reflections, diffuses these soft lights of the sky like something magic and the movement enhances this luminous effect. The complexity of this great glass sculpture is reminiscent of origami.

0527

Visual identity charts are necessary, but they should not prevent architecture from expressing things that are far more important. The idea behind Chaengwattana Shopping Mall in Bangkok was to create a place that has its own identity, over and above the label or the logo. Advertising and ornaments are never taboo in Asia; they escort the flow of people in the streets with entertainment and dynamism.

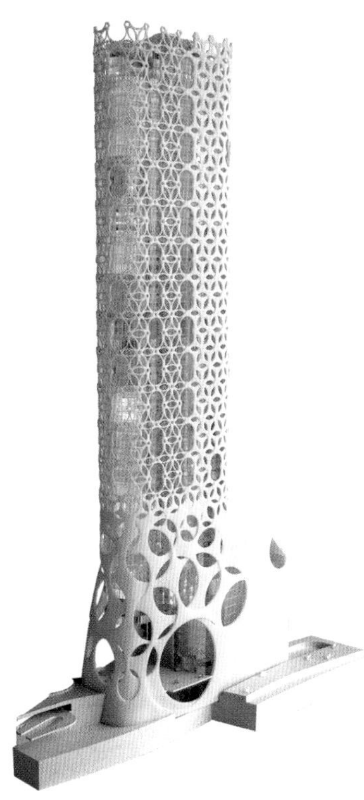

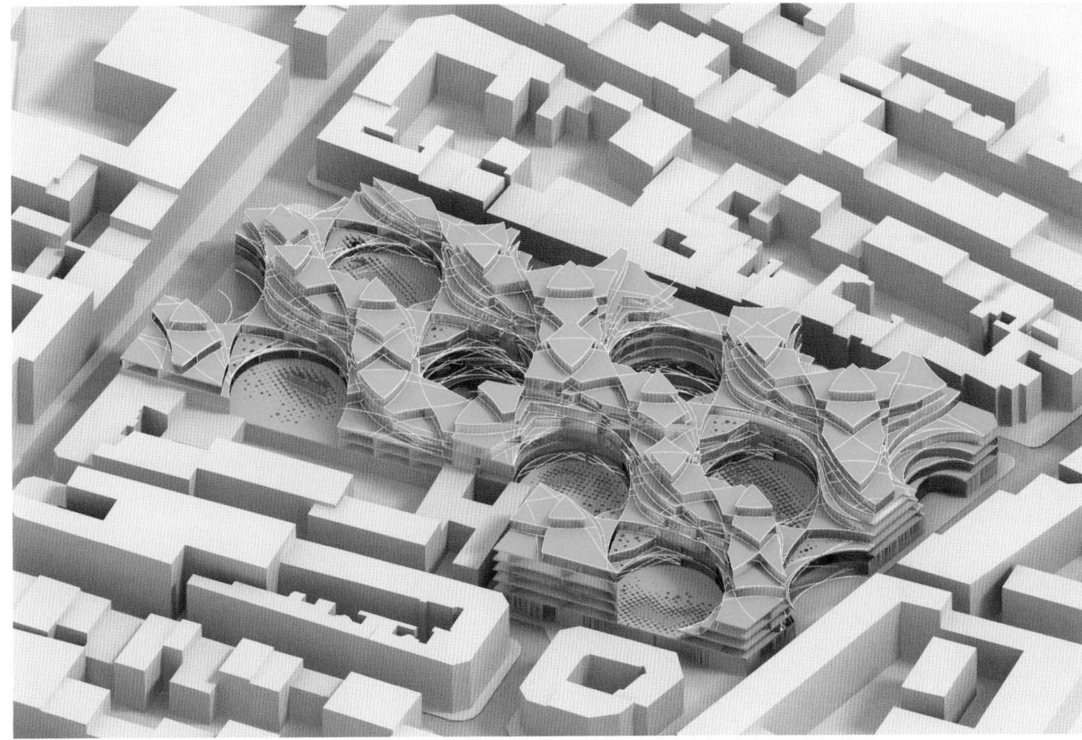

0528▲

The concept we are evolving has two aims: first, to express power in a high rise structure that is a communication device without precedents. Second, to create poetry by constructing a unique building the size of the Eiffel Tower. This structural skin soars a thousand feet upwards in graceful liberty, set free from the usual constraints that plague towers.

© Philippe Ruault

0529▲

It is not just greenery that is indispensable in a project, but the sequences and variety that come with an alternating arrangement of enclosed and open spaces, places that are dense and others that allow respiration, artificial lighting and daylighting, expansion and contraction. Contact with open air has to be sequential in order to create rhythms and enable people to get their bearings.

0530►

Every city needs shared facilities. These are the places that imbue a city with character, and they are often icons or landmarks in their own right. Architecture has also to express the spirit of a city in a contemporary, if not reinvented manner. In the Bethune Theatre project, this rich purple skin reinvents the traditional details seen on large brick expanses in northern countries.

Peter Barber Architects

173 King's Cross Road
London WC1X 9BZ, UK
P.: (+44) 207-833-4499
www.peterbarberarchitects.com

0531

I think the top of a building should be celebrated. High modernism was rubbish at doing the top of buildings.

0532

Architecture is easy. A piece of glass found on a skip balanced on three upturned traffic cones resulted in our Metachron B1 Table, designed in collaboration with Ben Stringer.

0533

I like conservative urbanism and racy architecture.

0534

Somebody said that this project is "souped-up minimalism," which is bit like David Green calling my friend Ben Stringer a "turbo-charged snail."

0535➤

Our architecture, carved out of a block.

0536▼

I like architecture that has been folded out of a flat plain like this south London homeless project.

0537▲

Pullens Building in Elephant and Castle is a cracker: a blighty-style toit jardin: garden gnomes, potting sheds and patios on top of a Victorian tenement—eat your heart out Corbu. In the eighties, residents saved the building with a rooftop protest when the housing association bulldozers arrived to clear the way for some dreary yellow brick housing; the powers that be said it did not meet modern standards. What do they know?

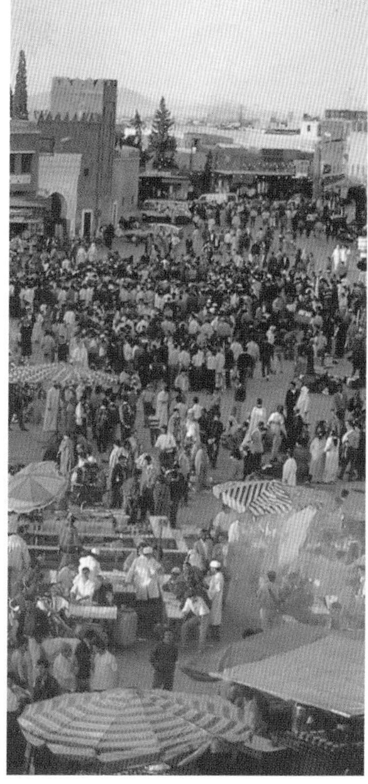

0538▲

Jema al Fna, or the *Mosque of Nothing* is my favorite public space: snake charmers, story tellers, musicians, acrobats, little bits of mobile architecture. I like the idea of public space belonging to everyone and no one, and of it being a *Mosque of Nothing*.

0539▼

Amazing what you can make out of a coat hanger.

0540➤

Top house this one. We should be doing everything we can to encourage people to build their own houses. Mass production could never achieve this.

Helliwell + Smith/ Blue Sky Architecture

4090 Bayridge Avenue, West Vancouver
British Columbia, V7V 3K1 Canada
P.: (+1) 604-921-8646
www.blueskyarchitecture.com

© Bo Helliwell

© Peter Powles

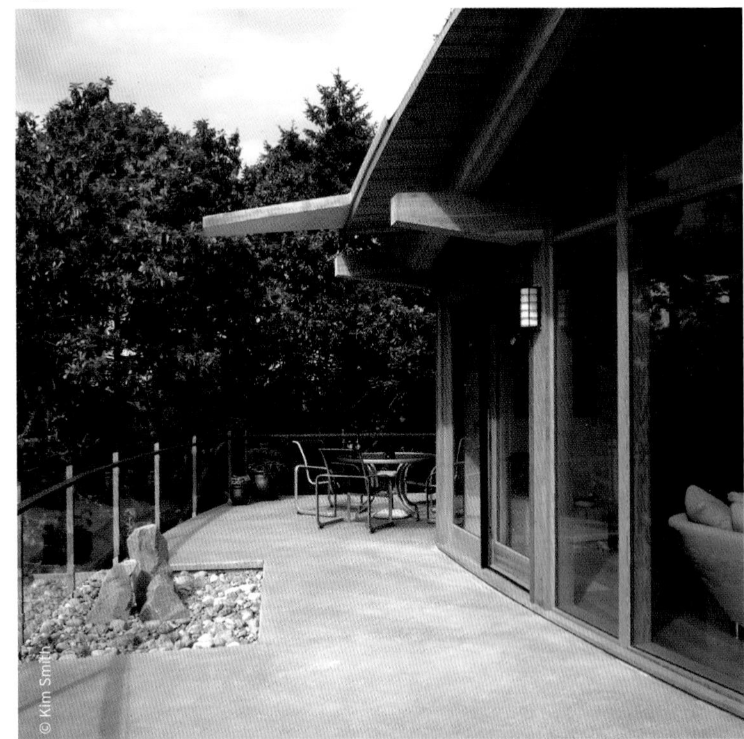

© Kim Smith

0541

Be guided by the site
Let the lines of the land guide the form of the building in plan and section. Do not fight topography; let buildings flex to follow the fluid lines of the landscape. Harbor House hugs a steep rock cliff and spreads out along its face in a sweeping fluid form.

0542

Celebrate the weather
In a rainforest climate we use large, simple sheltering roofs. We celebrate the rain and our roofs are formed in order to drain water for storage and reuse. On the Ridge House, the rainwater from the butterfly roof is channeled into an exaggerated scupper, which funnels the water into a pond that appears to float on the terrace roof. This pond is centered on the main hall which bisects the house and, when full of water, it acts as a small reflecting pond both terminating and extending the axis. The roof water is collected in cisterns and used for site irrigation.

0543

Capture light

Natural light animates, warms, and enlivens architecture. In the North West Pacific, a region with many days of grey skies, it is important to bring natural light into all spaces. Natural light acts as timekeeper in a building, connecting us to the time of day and season as well as the weather. Light should be balanced to avoid glare, to balance eastern light with western light, and northern light with southern light. An example of how we manage daylight is the Elma Bay House, where large north-facing windows overlook the sea. The natural light is balanced by clerestory windows that run the length of the south wall.

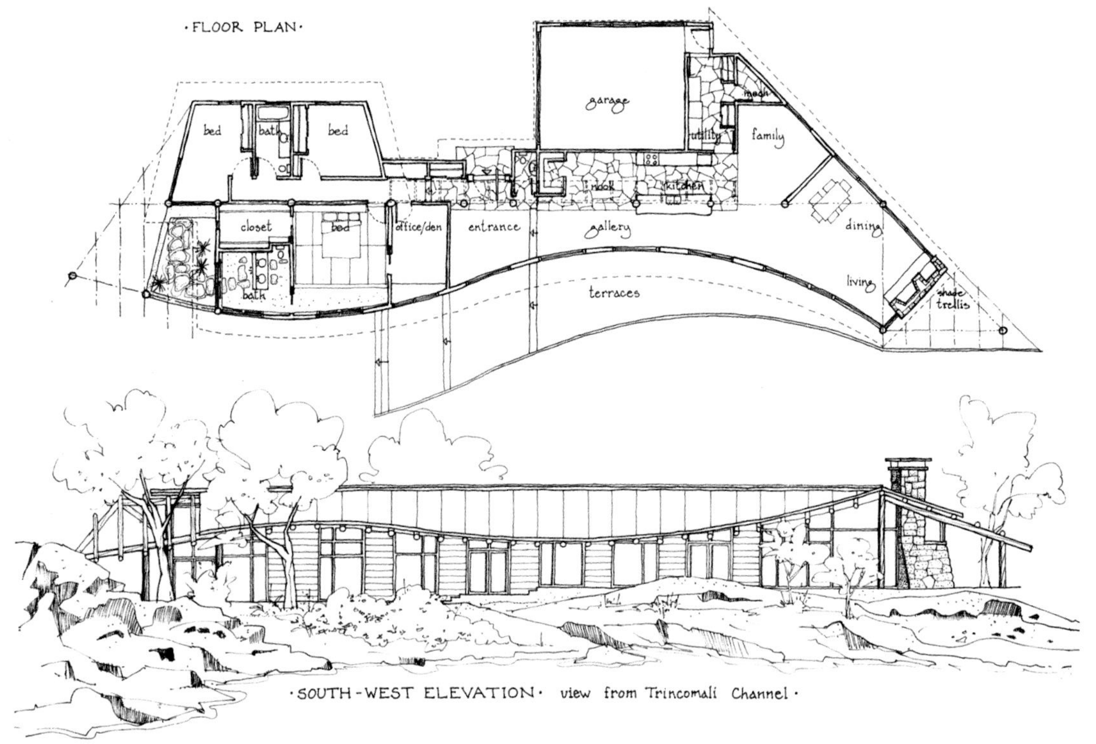

0544

Organic forms

There are very few cubes in nature. By designing with fluid and non-linear forms, our buildings fit with the landscape with sensual and embracing spaces. The undulating wall of Fishbones is inspired by the sensual, curving sandstone cliff bank it sits on.

0545▼

Structure and space

Exposed concrete fins act as columns and shear walls resolving the structural forces. Glulam beams curve through space and a rhythm of rafters lift up and down to form the sculptural roof. All key structural elements are exposed. What you see and feel is real.

0546▲

Provide shelter

With a temperate climate, outdoor rooms—large sheltered spaces—create year-round opportunities to be outside in comfortable, contemplative ways, sheltered from the rain, wind and sun.

0547►

Color and natural materials

We used a consistent palette of natural materials. The neutral and subtle quality of color in wood and stone give the buildings a warmth and connection to the place. An occasional staccato of color works as punctuation, emphasizing rhythm and texture in a playful way.

0548

Craft

Unique, finely crafted and skillfully made objects add a sense of value, care, and personality to a building. A pride in building through fine craftsmanship is a legacy that is felt in space.

© Peter Powles

0549

Wood

Wood is a natural building material in our region of British Columbia. With vast forests, a palette of Douglas fir and red cedar are used as building materials. Wood has a warm living tectonic quality that no synthetic material can emulate.

0550 

Spontaneous opportunities

Opportunities arise during the course of construction. A large 4.5 x 11.5 ft (1.4 x 3.5 m) sandstone slab was uncovered during site preparation. It was incorporated into the fireplace composition and is a stunning natural sculpture inside the home. It acts as a visual anchor to the flowing spaces and a close connection to raw nature.

© Kim Smith

© Peter Powles

Jakob + MacFarlane

13 rue des Petites Écuries
75010 Paris, France
P.: (+33) 1-44-79-05-72
www.jakobmacfarlane.com

0551

The best tips are the ones you give yourself for your own projects.

0552

First think about what has been there before you.
At Centre Pompidou it was at once the existing vocabulary and the geometries.

0553

A project is only rich in its presence through its accumulations.
Here the River Seine, the old Docks of Paris, the urban architecture of the 1980s, etc.

0554

We always think about the idea before deciding on the materials. . . but everyone has their own approach to tackling issues.
Maison Corsica was where we invented a non-existing material—somewhere between camouflage, moss and aluminum.

0555 

Sometimes it's about taking a background position.
Here we chose to be secondary to the car, which we wanted to be seen as the object of primary presence.

© Nicolas Borel

0556

Materials are paramount in the final interpretation but have to be related to the idea.
Here we deform the floor upwards into four volumes using aluminum as the best solution.

© Nicolas Borel

0557

Conceptual time in the studio is still where it all happens.
For FRAC ideas were paramount, as presented in the model.

0558

The details should be simple and always in relation to the bigger idea.
In the Herold project we wanted very simple details in order to see the bigger urban picture of the matrix.

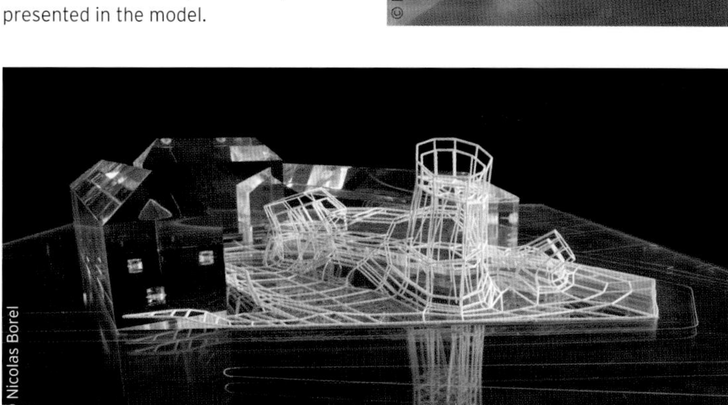

© Nicolas Borel

0559

Color should be primarily used to present the issues. However it's also about an emotional reading.
The green was the silk worm's cocoon and the red boxes, the tree branches.

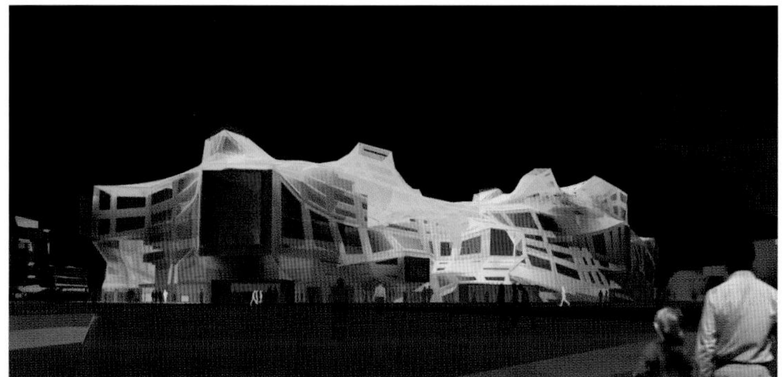

0560

Communication with all project agents is vital, even if it comes down to explaining things over and over.
At the SCI-Arc we built the *Breathing Wall* installation, a great school for communication.

Despang Architekten

Am Graswege 5
30169 Hanover, Germany
P.: (+49) 511-882-840
www.despangarchitekten.de

© Olaf Baumann

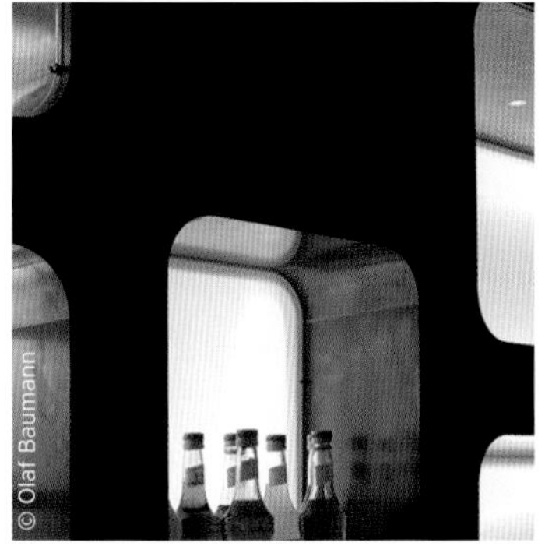

© Olaf Baumann

0561

Architecture is a gestural human activity which results in space. A simple walk through the street can end up stopping randomly for a coffee around the corner at the local café.

Architecture is about the little stuff that is not noticed immediately, but which cannot be ignored, and makes everyday life a little better.

© Olaf Baumann

0562

In the words of Wittgenstein, "architecture is a gesture, not every purposive movement of the human body is a gesture, and no more is every building designed for purpose architecture." The importance of bringing gestures back to everyday life is clear. Besides the special *haute couture* Sunday dress occasions, life needs architectural "prêt a porter," quality for the other six days of the week.

0563

Architecture needs to be reinserted into the most unlikely phenomenal spaces: providing moments of joy to a little child who only has money for one hot chocolate inside the materialistic, mega-structure urban malls. Architecture has the power to warm a space, and bring in the human element.

© Olaf Baumann

© Olaf Baumann

0564

On the other side, architecture must also delve into the opposite end of the spectrum, into the most remote areas of democratic dedication: being able to provide constitution-drafted soldiers with modern indoor and outdoor spaces as stimulation to become critical and sensitive citizens.

© Olaf Baumann

◄0565

An economically and ecologically challenging twenty-first century is reducing the horizons of travel for many. Therefore simple activities, such as walking to buy groceries in the neighborhood, take on a typologically increased relevance. These activities demand a new architectural rethinking: prefabrication, mass-customization and the sublimation of the ordinary are needed to provide affordability.

0566

Sustainability, being the agenda of the new millennium, means extending the life span of a product, such as a building, as long as possible. This becomes a fascinating challenge in transitioning domestic heritage architecture from the past into the future. Rural farm living, with its architectural manifestation of enclosed structural skinned space, can be transformed into a combination of light and bright vertically and horizontally liberated living.

© Olaf Baumann

© Olaf Baumann

0567

Socio-economic mechanisms change living patterns, and architecture evolutionarily adapts to it. By reducing a space and its essence down to the essentials of gravity and light, a calming, "temple-like" atmosphere is created. This creates a place of solace and relaxation the students who study in school all day long to prepare for a life of working all day long.

0568

The rediscovery of urban living results in a collaboration between the efficiency and socialization advantages of dense metropolitan housing types with the qualities of a rural/suburban natural setting. Living in bioclimatically engineered buildings with residential space in the upper floors, and ground floor working/retail space can embrace existing metropolitan density while also creating an urban treetop dwelling.

© Olaf Baumann

◄0569

Providing for all members of a society makes a society strong. Through a built abstraction of their favorite sense of place, a forest, mentally handicapped children are immersed in a comfortable environment. Composed of exposed solid wood louvers and customized cutting edge tectonics, such as UV light benefiting ETFE and a heat treated wood, this space provides a psychologically and physiologically healing environment.

0570▼

As the concluding tip indicates, we cannot invest enough in the future, which lies in the hands of our children. To encourage them as the generation p[ostfossil], we let them grow up in a synergistically eco- and archi-friendly environment, in which they can live and teach what they have been taught in a joyful way.

© Olaf Baumann

Gora art&landscape

Vilebovägen 4 A
21763 Malmö, Sweden
P.: (+46) 40-911-913
www.gora.se

0571

Develop your own ideas and design idiom through a succession of projects.
The Glass Bubble is a continuation of the spherical shape that originated in *A Drop of Light* but is modified for another purpose and made from totally different materials.

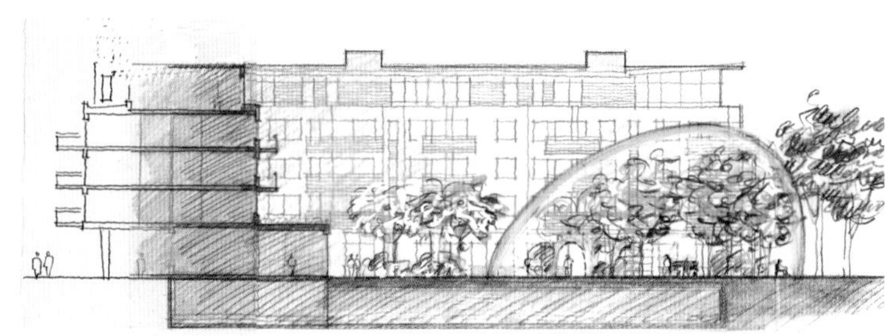

0572

Refine the concept. Allow yourself to be daring. Develop the essence of your idea.
A Drop of Light is based on the idea of creating a summer lighting experience during the darkest days of the year.

0573

Collaborate with the very best in each discipline.
The fragile and transparent impression of *The Glass Bubble* would be impossible to obtain without the close collaboration of highly skilled engineers and specialists.

0574

Use details to enhance the concept.
The *2 Piers* project is designed with a gap between the rails and pier, helping to dissolve the pier-railing connection. The result creates a special feeling of uncertainty when on the piers because the rails seem to be disconnected. This creates an illusion of insecurity in the piers, enhancing the pedestrian's sensation of being high above the landscape.

© Fredrik Karlsson

◄0575

Do not forget to use what is already in the space.

The project *Pat the Horse* emanated from the existing sculpture of the Swedish King Charles X in Stortorget Square in Malmö. *Pat the Horse* enabled the public to interact with the sculpture at close range, making it more accessible.

© Ursula Strine

0576►

Communicate the appreciation of beauty. Facilitate the enjoyment of a landscape, a place.

2 Piers involved the creation of a place to contemplate the landscape; this was achieved through intensifying the beauty of the landscape by creating a sensation of sailing through the air.

© Håkan Nordström

0577▲

Only create what you yourself want to experience.

Garden of Knowledge comes from a desire to create a garden where experience and knowledge go hand in hand.

0578 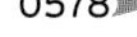

A low budget result in innovative uses for materials and exciting solutions.

The *Stensjö Planters* were the result of a budget cutback; later they were launched on the market as a commercial product.

© Fredrik Karlsson

0579▼

Mix challenge with consideration.

The Silver Tree is a landmark. It holds many symbolic meanings but it also serves as a pragmatic and functional meeting point.

© Per Mannberg

0580►

Find your own sources of inspiration. Look, travel, discuss.

Inspiration for *Jimmys* came from a formation called 'the Olgas' at Ayers Rock in Australia.

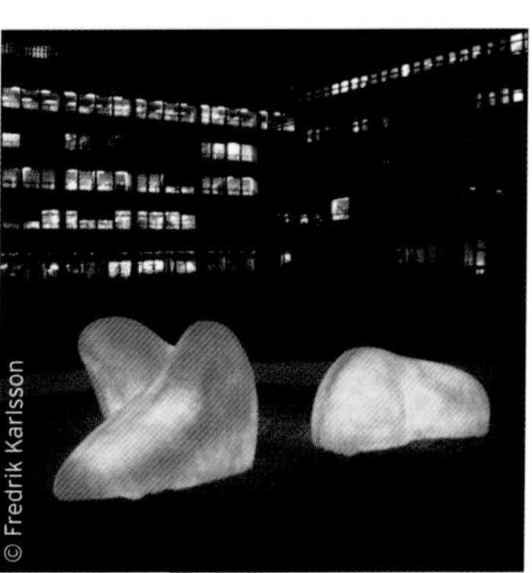

© Fredrik Karlsson

Ingarden & Ewy Architects

ul. Grabowskiego 5/3
31-126 Krakow, Poland
P.: (+48) 12-632-8010/12-425-0680
www.ingarden-ewy.com.pl

© Krzysztof Ingarden

0581

In the Polish Pavilion for the Expo 2005 in Aichi, Japan, the main theme "Nature's Wisdom" was interpreted in conjunction with the subtheme "Notice the Beauty." Our aim was to seek and apply a unique architectural vocabulary in order to create a metaphor of contemporary Poland as a country with a rich cultural and artistic heritage, and great natural beauty, while making reference to the concept of sustainability in modernization through the use of advanced technology.

0582

House B stands on the final lot near the edge of a forest with towering pine and birch trees, close to the city of Warsaw. The owners searched extensively for a unique and open space to locate their dwelling. Due to the tree shadows, however, the house has a moody location in the forest.

© Krzysztof Ingarden

0583

The traditional horizontal layout of bricks took on a vertical arrangement. These were mounted on steel rods by means of special elongated openings in each brick. We thus created a kind of external mobile curtain, almost like louvers constructed from brick "beads." We designed an outer layer of bricks, in which the position of each brick can be individually regulated, either opening or closing the layer, depending on the requirements at any one time.

© Krzysztof Ingarden

© Krzysztof Ingarden

0584

The Wyspianski 2000 Pavilion in Krakow has two main functions: providing information and exhibiting stained glass. Stained glass should be displayed in a high, calm, and dark space, whereas public informative spaces should be open, clear, and well-lit. We had to seek a solution for such contradictory requirements. We finally chose an elevation of a mobile nature: both transparent and enclosed.

0585

Wicker, a kind of willow *(Salix Sp.)* is the perfect material to be used to form dynamic, bi-directionally curved surfaces, since it is light, flexible, and semi-transparent. The high-tech, digitally generated form of the elevation helped to create a symbol of contemporary Poland as a country with burgeoning technological development. A contrast is formed by the white wicker mesh that is hand made in a low-tech process by Polish artisans.

© Bartosz Haduch

0586

The final building position was decided in relation to the layout of the trees on the site. Simple white forms create an interesting contrast to the natural environment. Walls have been bent to form a balcony, bench and dog kennel, all fully connected with the inside spaces. Key design concepts include connecting with nature and establishing a dialogue between the house and the garden and forest space. The design also took into account the needs of the two dogs and three cats residing in House B.

© Justyna Kosowicz

0587

The points of reference for the layout of the school building were decided in relation to its location. Its static, almost minimalist form has been adjusted in keeping with the gentle wave-like form of the center. The functional layout of the ground floor sets up a dialogue with the Tea Pavilion. The entrances of both buildings face each other, while combed plaster on the entry elevation of the school is echoed in the gravel garden of the pavilion.

© Krzysztof Ingarden

© Bartosz Haduch

0588

Each platform is finished with a different natural material that is recycled or reused, such as stone, gravel, sand, and wood. The platforms house different mobile and educational installations, based on experiences and experiments with optics, acoustics, etc.

◄0589

The landscape design of *Garden of Experience* is founded on the paths and trees that already existed on the site. The aim of the project was to infuse public park space with recreational and educational qualities. Leaf-shaped platforms were located alongside the paths; these are utilized for viewing and interacting with the mobile and educational installations placed around the garden.

0590►

The Japanese Language School building is an annex to Manggha Center of Japanese Art and Technology in Krakow. This add-on was constructed in order to transfer the educational functions from the main building.

The low budget school building was designed in the garden of the center, in immediate proximity of the main building and the Tea Pavilion—a location affording views of the garden and Wawel Castle.

Triptyque Architecture

Al. Gabriel Monteiro da Silva 484
01441-000 São Paulo, Brazil
P.: (+55) 11-3081-3565
http://www.triptyque.com

107 rue de Sévres
75007 Paris, France
P.: (+33) 9-70-44-66-00

© Beto Consorte

0591

When covering this building, we envisioned a hybrid space that stimulates coexistence. Instead of a simple roof, we created a wide deck that opens out onto the canopy of trees and transmutes into the building's fifth facade.

© Nelson Kon

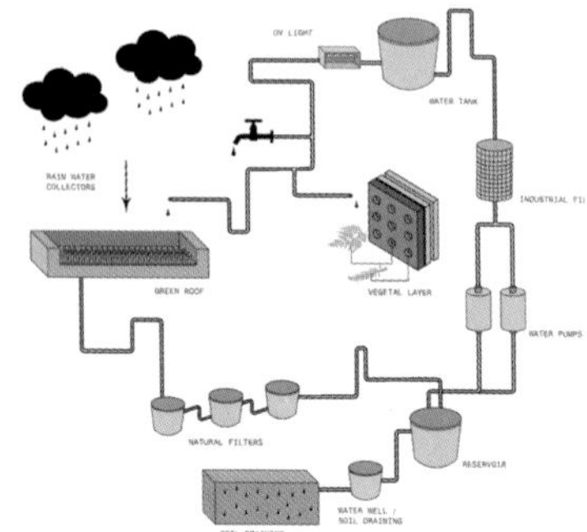

0592

A car park may be the first physical contact with a building. Thus, we pointed out the need for changes in architectural expression. In this space, we use a tri-tube lighting system, in green, yellow, and red colors, which merge together creating new hues.

0593 

In this project, water was an important element in the creative process. In a location with abundant precipitation, this building functions like a big machine: rainwater is drained, treated, and reused, forming a complex ecosystem that optimizes the building's impervious area.

0594

In this project, we wanted to create an infinite view over the deck. In order to form the solarium and establish a visual connection with the surroundings, the edges of the deck were tilted, eliminating visual barriers, avoiding railings, and creating a mine of illusions.

© Beto Consorte

© Nelson Kon

0595

We like to think up new possibilities for common architectural elements. In this project, the need for material in an anti-slip structure was the motto for its transformation into an area of expression. We created a form and from it, metallic prints in cement, increasing its visual appeal.

© Beto Consorte

0596

We believe in questioning the role of environments and creating other ways of understanding spaces. A commercial building may have a multifunctional spatial organization. In this project, a void integrates the interior and exterior of the building while also becoming a space for coexistence.

0597 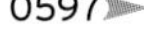

We used concrete because we strongly believe in the many possibilities of this amazing material and in its ability to create strong forms. In this project, the three floors are structured by a strong vertical element: a concrete staircase. Its folded geometry connects all the internal rooms, from the parking lot to the solarium.

© Beto Consorte

© Tryptique

0598

Another example of how we think in terms of space can be seen in this project, which has a body that extends into three separate volumes. The first levitates on concrete pillars arranged in an X-shape. The second has a garden that propagates along a vertical tower in an upward movement.
Thirdly, continuing into garden, the ground acts as a town square, returning space to the city.
This semi-public green space opens a gap and serves as a single place for the community and as a place for meetings and exchange.

© Beto Consorte

0599

Concrete is once again treated in a minimalist way, reflecting the full force of this material. The kitchen in this apartment is formed from a giant concrete block, from which the fire arises, standing in the center of the project. The stone, placed in the central position, is the component that brings together and articulates the entire structure. The aesthetic is a result of the process. The building has a primitive inelegance.

Estudio Mariani – Perez Maraviglia

Bernardo de Yrigoyen 3017
7600 Mar del Plata, Argentina
P.: (+754) 223-451-98-36/486-19-43
www.mpmarquitectos.com

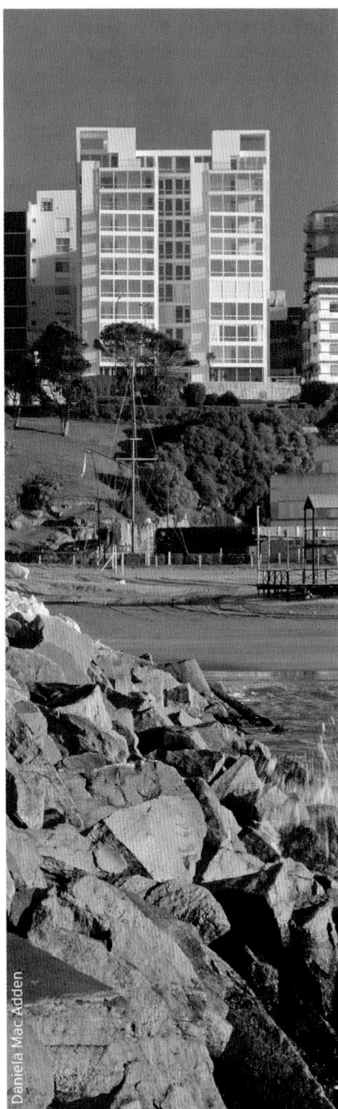

© Daniela Mac Adden

0600

Contextualize through extracting the data and key elements from the landscape. These buildings that absorb the landscape by adding an effective interface to resolve the relationship between proximity and farness.

0601

Sustainable activism through active and passive enables unique developments, forming a new and necessary relationship with the setting.

© Daniela Mac Adden

0602

Mechanisms of spatial and structural poetry are translated and communicated when realizing the project.

0603

Scale and proportion, perception and sensuality, entropy and serenity.

© Daniela Mac Adden

© Daniela Mac Adden

0604

Mass is connected to concealment, and transparency is related to immateriality.

0605

Local twinned with global. Build architecture that acknowledges the identity of the place.

© Daniela Mac Adden

0606

Textures can be used as sensory links to the theme. Tactile elements, visual features.

© Daniela Mac Adden

0607

Spatial devices, routes, transitions, meeting spaces.

0608

Use liquid functionality as flexibility expressed through contemporary logic.

0609

Use sensitivity in spatial and material matters. Be in a state of alert to the continually changing conditions that determine the way we work: technologies and techniques. Vernacular and foreign elements should be balanced from a social perspective.

© Edificio Normandina

Boora Architects

720 SW Washington, Suite 800
Portland, OR 97205, USA
P.: (+1) 503-226-1575
www.boora.com

© David Papazian

0610

When the delineation between interior and exterior is challenged in a performing arts building—as embodied in the University of California, Davis Mondavi Center for the Performing Arts—the environment surrounding can receive the energy and vitality of the event-going experience, a social format that continues to draw on human imagination, innovation, and investment.

0611

Adidas America's corporate headquarters house over 800 employees in five buildings. To ensure that this large population moves actively between locations and interacts among corporate departments, the design scatters shared amenities—such as the recreation center, the playing fields, and the dining commons—throughout the campus. This activates the outdoor plaza uniting the site, creating outdoor vitality as employees and guests move from place to place, and building a corporate community.

© Robert Canfield Photography

© Timothy Hursley

◄0612

Embracing the Mesa Arts Center's goal to immerse visitors in art and ideas, Boora Architects and Martha Schwartz Partners innovated the modernist "object in a landscape" paradigm by establishing a non-hierarchical relationship between architecture and landscape. When environment, landscape, and architecture are integrated on an equal, immersive level this creates a heightened sensual and intellectual experience for artists, audiences, and patrons.

Boora Architects were the design consultants for the executive architects DWL Architects +Planners.

© Sally Schoolmaster

0613►

The three pavilions housing the exhibition spaces of the National Underground Railroad Freedom Center (completed with Blackburn Architects) are clad in weathered copper, retaining color and texture deriving from the interaction of natural elements. Similarly, travertine stone defining the public passageways through the building is left roughly finished. The materials convey a rugged earthiness similar to the materials African slaves in the early United States would have experienced as they fled their captors over the landscape, largely at night and by foot.

© Farshid Assassi / Assassi Productions

0614?▲

When the Portland Institute for Contemporary Art asked Boora Architects to transform a warehouse into a theater, the firm proved that constraint is the mother of innovation. Boora placed the stage in one of the warehouse's structural bays, allowing the structural columns to define the performance area. In the bays surrounding the stage, Boora assembled 5-gallon plastic buckets and recycled carpet tiles into a bench seating system. This award-winning design was delivered for just $10,000.

© Timothy Hursley

© Timothy Hursley

0615

When designing The Metropolitan Condominiums, Boora Architects faced a decision that many teams confront when developing buildings for high-rise living: whether to vent the building's units horizontally or vertically. The resulting skin provided a watertight but visually unobtrusive venting system on the building's exterior, accommodating hundreds of exterior wall penetrations while preserving a sleek and clean curtain wall design.

0616

An architect's sensitivity to the environment surrounding a building is as important to the quality of an interior space as the choices made within the space.

The owners of this new residence in Portland, Oregon, Jan and Chris Kitchel, who are adventurers when on vacation, now find seclusion, quiet, and serenity at home. "It's so peaceful," they said and "it's been a little surprising to us how nice that is."

0617

Boora Architects's LEED Platinum Certified studio occupies the upper floor of the 19th-century Morgan Building in downtown Portland, Oregon. Placing team spaces at the center of the building's floor plate allows individual workstations—the most intensively occupied spaces in the studio—to enjoy extensive daylighting and natural ventilation by virtue of their close proximity to the building's exterior wall.

0618

Working with ethnographic researchers Point Forward, Boora clustered the social collaboration spaces in Stanford University's new Yang and Yamazaki Environment and Energy building around four atria, shortening the vertical and horizontal distance between collaborative spaces and infusing them with daylight.

0619

Located on a site in Oregon with expansive views over the Pacific Ocean—and a tangle of sensitive coastal plants at ground level—Boora architect Stan Boles and his artist wife, Wendy Kahle, placed living spaces on the upper floor of their retreat house rather than on the first floor, making the views optimally accessible to the living spaces that are used primarily during the daytime.

Blaine Brownell/Transstudio

740 Mississippi River Blvd S, Suite 16D
St. Paul, MN 55116, USA
info@transstudio.com

© Doug Ogle

0622

Study your local material ecology
What raw materials are harvested and processed where you live? What major material industries thrive nearby, regardless of where their products are typically used? Becoming an expert on local material flows will not only help you save on transportation costs, but may also increase your chances of creating innovative work by utilizing unexpected materials in building construction.

Image: Richlite, a compressed paper panel made for aerospace tooling, which demonstrated advantages when used as the skin of a local building.

0621

Adopt the process of active material seeking
Conventional practice reinforces a reactive attitude toward function, program, and material selection. However, successful design practice aligns its material research with its larger design mission. It is not enough to pursue materials for a current project; one must seek out materials for the project that does not yet exist.

Image: Disposable Office (PUSH>), recyclable office furniture originating from the paper used in the office, demonstrating enhanced closure of the material loop.

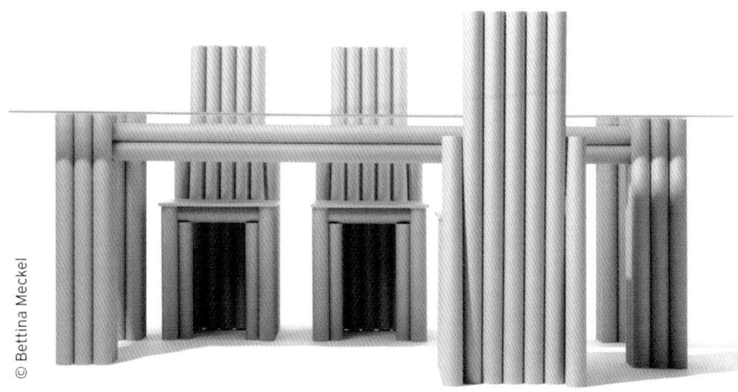

© Bettina Meckel

0620

Select simple material assemblies that satisfy complex functions, not the other way around
With a little extra effort, a simple assembly may be designed to satisfy the requirements for a building's structure, skin, and interior storage. Other functions might include power harvesting, storm water filtration, landscape growth, medium support, species habitat accommodation, and pollution reduction.

Image: GreenPix, a power-harvesting, self-illuminating media wall that doubles as a building skin.

© Simone Giostra

0623

Broaden your definition of sustainability

There is a lot of good green advice being passed around, but there is also a lot of green wash. Proscriptive models for green practice may also be easily misinterpreted, so look to performance-based models. Do not hesitate to propose your own solutions, even if they are not part of the mainstream design culture.

Image: Self-Healing Polymers, Beckman Institute, a polymer that injects healing agent into a rupture, thus prolonging the useful life of the material.

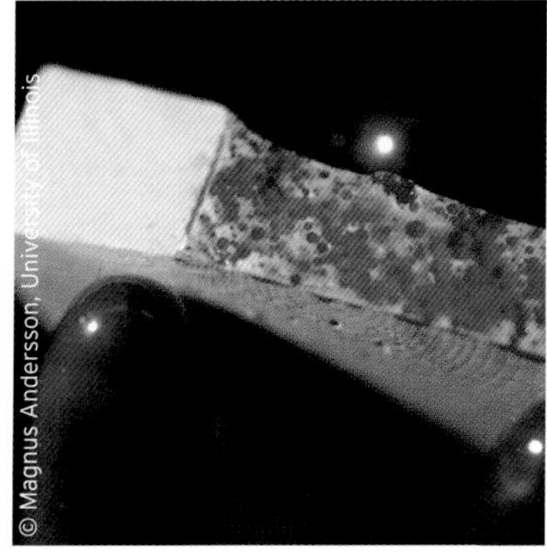

© Magnus Andersson, University of Illinois

© Texxus

0624

Increase material quality and decrease labor costs via prefabrication

In building construction, a little material premeditation goes a long way. Research the latest digital fabrication services in your area and explore what available technologies can achieve. Moreover, do-it-yourself solutions are on the rise, with expanding online services as well as architect-led design-fabrication business models.

Image: Texxus, a process that creates elaborate surface forms and textures in a variety of materials with precise control

0625

Seek treasure in trash

Not only are raw material harvesting, processing, and transporting energy-intensive, but also known supplies of many important materials used in building construction are approaching dangerously low levels. Study local waste stream operations and devise ways to redeem waste materials in new configurations.

Image: PET Wall, a programmable, illuminated surface that utilizes discarded beverage containers as aggregated lenses.

0626

Use sustainable materials that make an aesthetic contribution as well as a technical one

The surge of interest in green design provides an unprecedented opportunity for architecture to innovate in all areas. There is no reason to specify a green material that looks identical to a conventional, unsustainable one. Visitors to your building will never comprehend beneficial features if they are hidden.

Image: SuperAbsorber, a highway barrier that reduces noise, air and light pollution.

© The Living

0627

Deploy environment monitoring technologies

Studies show that people improve habits if given trustworthy, timely information. Integrate highly legible systems into your projects that actively monitor and display changing environmental factors, such as air quality, water quality, energy use, emissions and water use.

Image: River Glow, an intelligent, rapidly deployable archipelago of active monitors for urban waterways.

© field office

Michelle Kaufmann Designs

580 2nd Street, Suite 245
Oakland, CA 94607, USA
P.: (+1) 510-271-8015
www.mkd-arc.com

© John Swain

0628

Using less—design so that natural light is enough

We always aim to design our homes to minimize the need to turn lights on during the day. This is not about putting in a lot of windows, but rather being really smart about where we locate them in order to avoid hotspots, glare, and shadows. We place glass windows and doors to wash surfaces with light.

0629

Using less—use a smart window design: clerestory windows

Clerestory windows are my favorite privacy solution in areas where you want natural light, and views of the trees, not of the neighbors. They assist with natural cooling by drawing hot air up and out of the house, when the windows are open. Clerestory windows are ideal in urban environments where light, breeze, and privacy can be in short supply.

© John Swain

0630

Using less—rethink sun shading

In many of our Glidehouse® homes, we incorporate barn door tracks and slated wood sunshades that slide along the tracks, providing sunshading while still allowing breezes through. They can also slide out of the way when sunlight or views are desired, or both. This flexibility reduces the need for artificial heating and cooling.

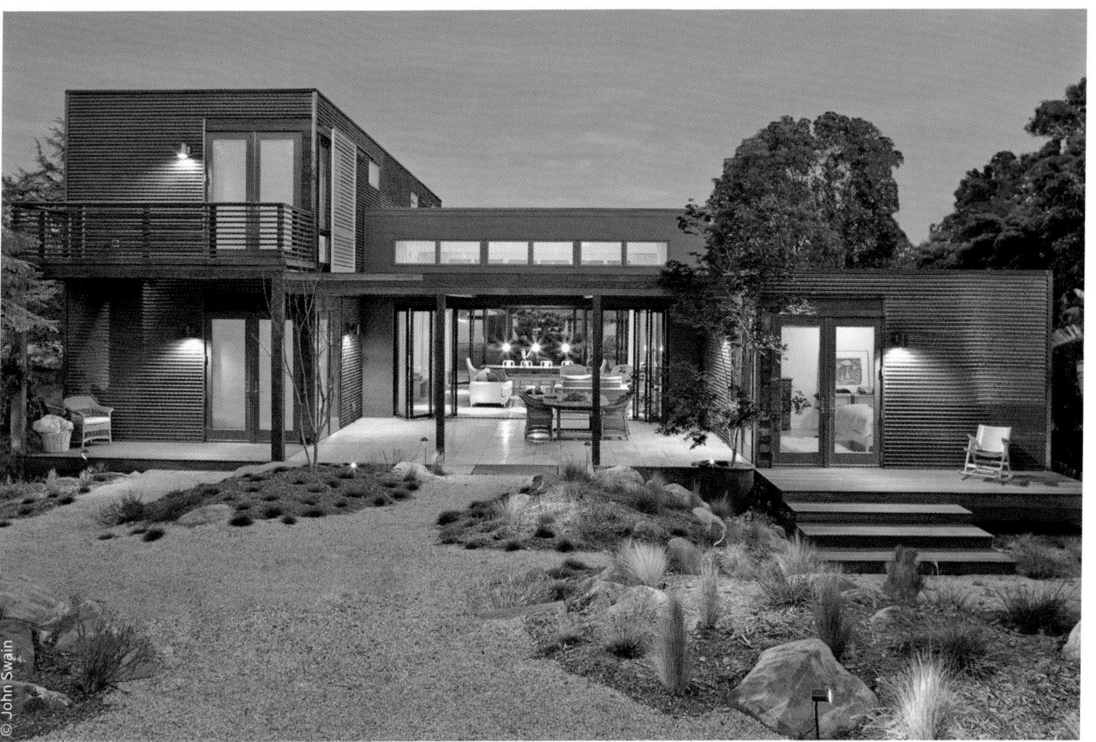

0631

Collaborating with the landscape—use what a site has to offer

At every turn, we strive to minimize the impact a home will have on the land; this includes collaborating with the natural elements found on and around the site. Instead of carting away the many rocks that were uncovered during the excavation of this home, we incorporated them into the landscape.

0632

Designing big, rather than building big—accordion glass doors

The more flexible a space is, the more useful it will be. Installing accordion glass doors that can be easily pushed to one side allows an interior space to open up completely to an outdoor room, drawing in natural light and breezes as well as extending the home's sense of space to make it feel larger.

0633

Using less—design outdoor rooms as much as indoor rooms

Another great way to build less while maintaining a home's spacious feel is to design outdoor rooms as much as indoor rooms, and to blur the boundary between interior and exterior. The interior living spaces of this Sunset® Breezehouse™ open onto an outdoor courtyard. Even in winter months when these outdoor rooms are not used they still visually extend the sense of space.

© John Swain

0634

Getting more out of less—utilize the roof

Roofs are typically underutilized spaces, serving no purpose other than providing cover for a home. We encourage the building of smaller homes that take advantage of all their space, including the roof, for additional functions like decks, which add living space; alternative energy systems, like photovoltaic panels; or green roofs, which reduce runoff, add insulation, and can even serve as vegetable gardens.

0635

Incorporating reclaimed materials—side table from logs

I love using materials that would normally end in the trash or landfills. For example, my husband and I made this side table from a tree that had fallen in our yard. We cut the trunk into pieces of equal height and wrapped them together with leather strips. It is now a beautiful, unique side table that brings the outdoors in.

0636

Getting more out of less—widen hallways and make them into rooms

I hate to see any space in a home go to waste, something that typically happens with hallways. This is why we take advantage of opportunities to widen hallways and design them as usable spaces, such as a small library, reading nook, or desk area.

0637

Using less—low maintenance materials

The idea of using less expensive materials to lower upfront costs can be enticing. However, such materials usually need to be replaced often or require constant maintenance and ultimately do not result in cost savings. We prefer to use materials that will last a long time, require little to no maintenance, and are stylistically timeless, such as Corten weathered steel siding.

© John Swain

© John Swain

nps tchoban voss

Tips: Sergei Tchoban

© Philipp Meuser

nps tchoban voss GmbH & Co. KG
Alf. M. Prasch Sergei Tchoban Ekkehard Voss
Rosenthaler Straße 40/41
10178 Berlin, Germany
P.: (+49) 30-28-39-20-0

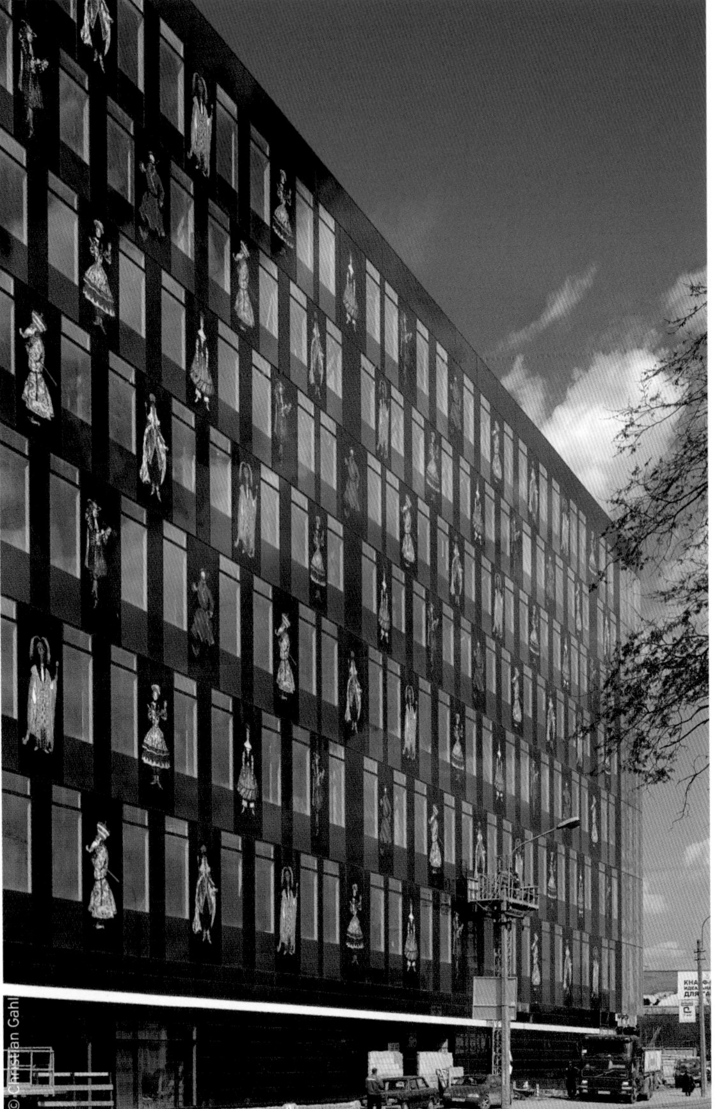
© Christian Gahl

0638

For Java-Turm in Hamburg, the central design idea for the old coffee roasting tower was to enclose its inner life, and several new features containing access facilities and lofts for living and working with different room heights, within a unitary, multi-layered cladding. Only the dynamic composition of the fenestration indicates the variety of uses and the internal tension, without infringing on the clarity of the cubic building.

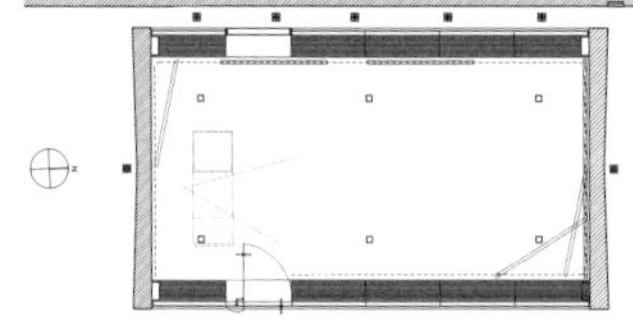

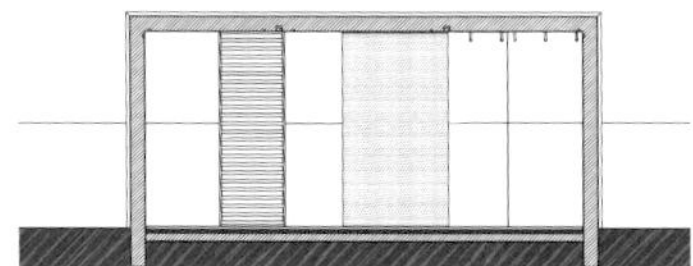

0639

During the times of the Russian Tsarina Catherine the Great, the site of Benois Business Center, St. Petersburg, was located in the park of Kuschelev-Bezborodko Manor, situated near the *datcha* of stage designer and author Alexandre Benois. Its modern glass façade is decorated with costume sketches of the famous Russian artist, whose Dyagilev seasons brought international fame to Russian art and culture.

0640

The interior of this art gallery (Galerie Arndt, Berlin) and former transformer station can be modified by a system of movable partitions in order to create different configurations for exhibitions. In resting position the wall elements hang like floating plaster in front of the massive walls. All installations are integrated into the raw structure in order to perpetuate the minimalist image as purely as possible.

0642▲

The courtyard of this 1960s Berlin building, located at 32-34 Unter den Linden, had to prevent shadows and moss infestation through traditional greenery. With its distinct black and gold coloring, the structure adapts to the new façade materials Nero Assoluto and brass-colored polished aluminum, evoking the floral brocade motifs and textile prints from the period when the boulevard was first built.

A modern coating system usually used for road markings was chosen for the façade, providing both longevity and the necessary slip resistance.

0643▲

The sliding elements made of perforated sheet metal serve both as sunscreens and blinds in the courtyard of the Kronprinzenkarree building in Berlin. During midsummer, residents can place them individually sideways, thus creating a Moorish-style shadow effect through the hole patterns. This way the apartment is naturally ventilated, sufficiently lit, and at the same time secluded from the public.

◄0641

Right from the first sketches of the aquarium with the integrated elevator, the concept combined two of the main design ideas of the DomAquarée complex in Berlin: bringing the river from the outside into the interior, and allowing the entire development to be vertically accessible. Starting out as a rather crazy idea, this rough concept turned out to be a technical masterpiece through cooperation with a large group of experts and professionals.

0645►

The façade of this residential complex, called House by the Sea, combines modern style with historical architectural elements of St. Petersburg. The traditionally stringent and sleek style of precise lines and logically proportioned tectonics achieve a modern look through adding a limestone cladding with a special finish—sanded, embossed, and profiled. The details of the ornaments, borrowed from the blinds and shutters of French and Italian architecture, are long-standing traditional St. Petersburg design features.

0644►

The synagogue of the Chabad Center in Berlin is a tall, self-contained space that is the spiritual and cultural heart of the complex of this remodeled transformer station. Its character is determined by the dark, room-high walnut planking, which appears to be compact, despite its horizontal, flowing layout. The tilted ladies' gallery was configured in suitable distance from the column and walls in order to avoid the effect of horizontally cutting the room.

© Julia Jungfer

◄0646

The Cubix cinema in Berlin rose to the challenge of the urban limits of the location through playing with spatial density: the structural design enables all nine theaters to be stacked on four levels above a base area of 120 x 150 ft (36.5 x 45.7 m). Being Germany's largest cinema at the time of its construction, the formation ensures a rigorous, compact hall layout, creating a unique entranceway.

Bruno Stagno Architects

PO box 680-1007, San José, Costa Rica
P.: (+506) 2233-9084
www.brunostagno.info

© Jimena Ugarte

© Jimena Ugarte

0647

The dematerialized façade

In tropical latitudes, insulating buildings by sealing their façades to isolate them from the surrounding area is a bad architectural practice. Our solution in this case was to create a dematerialized façade. This is deconstructed into different elements in order to keep the direct sunlight away from the glass surfaces, directing the breeze toward the interior spaces and protecting the building through the creation of shaded spaces. Eaves block some of the sunlight and parasols moderate the high temperatures. The "ears" or fins help to channel breeze toward interior spaces, enhancing cross ventilation.

0648

Materials and technological prudence

In countries where advanced technologies are very pricey, we only resort to this solution when natural resources are insufficient or non-existent. We choose simple materials produced by local, small-scale industry and employ the skills of the local labor force. In this project, we opted for metal tubes for the lightweight structures and blocks of cement for the exposed surfaces. Corrugated zinc sheet metal was chosen for the roof and eaves. Vegetation and trees were employed as a climate control system. In our use of glass, we offset the higher costs of this material by using economical panes that we designed ourselves.

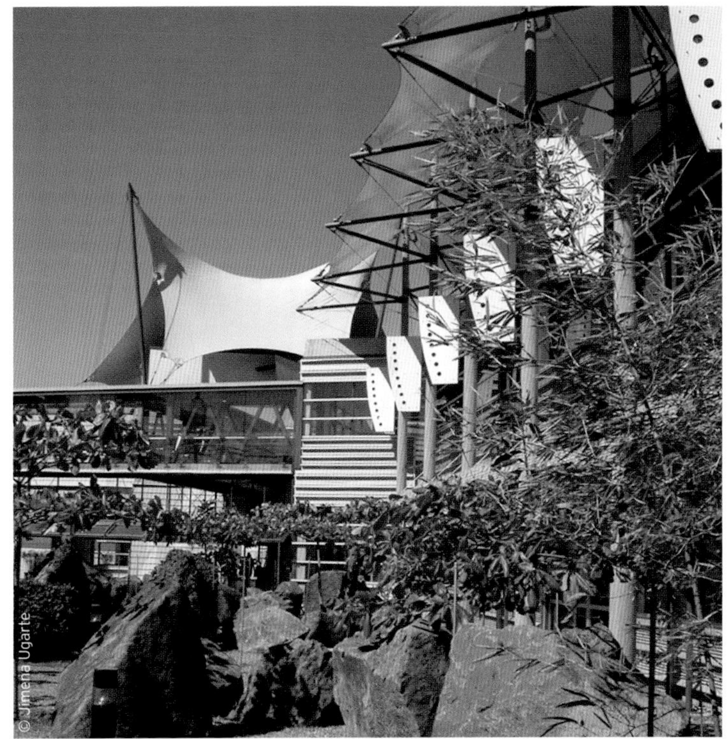

© Jimena Ugarte

0649

Architecture in the light of shade

In tropical latitudes the sun is strong. In the same way that optimizing passive heat from the sun is a central design objective in colder climates, shade is an important design element in the tropics, where the emphasis is on creating shade and coolness.

Gloominess is not a lack of lighting or a state of confusion. It is a state of fertile clarity, because it allows the perception of both light and darkness.

0650

Passive buildings for active people

In regions where the climate has a relatively small thermal differential and the environment is healthy, buildings can be passive, thus exploiting renewable resources. We design passive buildings for active people. Our aim is to reduce energy consumption through user interaction with the environment to harness passive, renewable energy.

0651 

Elevated buildings, freed space

Separating buildings from the ground is an environmentally friendly construction technique since it eliminates the need for earth-moving. This freed space means free flowing air and water, the liberty of a protected space, unobstructed views, a play space for children, a direct relationship with vegetation, the conservation of flora, and no walls. The *piano nobile* of Palladio was a solid pedestal of this mass architecture. In contrast, the freed space is the empty pedestal that symbolizes the freedom of tropical architecture.

0652

The tropical "span" roof

It is easy to understand how tropical rain is an important factor in the design of roofs in this region. The "span" roof has perforations and is broken down into different sections. It is a clear contribution of tropical architecture since it adapts to the climate. We have evolved a pyramidal or gable roof to bestow it with new functions, such as ventilation, illumination, shading and shelter.

0653

Tropical bioclimatic architecture

The tropics have special conditions that require special solutions. And what could be better than using renewable resources to find these solutions? Adapting architecture to meet the special requirements of tropical environments will bring about a positive impact on climate change. Of the 192 UN member countries, 108 are fully or partly in areas with tropical or subtropical climates. These countries account for 35% of the Earth's surface area and 40% of its population. Moreover, it is precisely these areas where demographic growth is strongest.

© Jimena Ugarte

0654

The tropical space
In tropical architecture, the interior space lies beneath a roof characterized by strong slopes. This provides a high zone close to the roof and another horizontal zone with a stronger relationship to exterior spaces. It is a very different spatial composition to that of Mies van der Rohe in which space slides unhindered smoothly outwards between the horizontal planes of the floor and the roof, since the beams, columns, and walls are well concealed.

0655

Sustainable architecture = replicability
Sustainable architecture that is reliant on expensive equipment, materials, and maintenance processes cannot reduce energy consumption on a global scale, because it cannot be replicated on a large scale. For architecture to be labeled as "sustainable" it must have the potential to be easily replicated. This is the only way to reduce our planet's energy consumption.

© Jimena Ugarte

0656

Tropical landscaping
The vegetation is abundant and grows quickly in the tropics. We use it as both a vertical and horizontal element in architecture. As well as being an important universally accessible resource, vegetation is a low-cost architectural material with huge potential. The idea is to employ vegetation to reduce pollution and radiation, to absorb CO_2, and to create a microclimate.

David Baker + Partners, Architects

461 Second Street, Loft c127
San Francisco, CA 94107, USA
P.: (+1) 415-896-6700
www.dbarchitect.com

Ten simple things by David Baker:
In architecture, there is a tendency to try to do something very complicated, which by nature is half-understood. In that confusion, people tend to leave out the simple things. Do ten simple things, and then if you can also be brilliant, all the better. That way, if the brilliance does not work, at least the building does.

0657

Better living through density
Reduce carbon footprints through thoughtfully designing dense, service-rich buildings. This 100% affordable building will feature 300 units per acre, multiple outdoor rooftop "yards," and a neighborhood-serving grocery store.

© Cesar Rubio

0658

Street-level residential entries
Adding porosity puts people on the street, as can be seen in Mabuhay Court.

0659

Feng shui compliance
Decompression gardens add a touch of green and respite, and create a transitional oasis between the dwellings and a gritty urban exterior.

0660

Mixed-use retail under housing
Ground-level retail makes for an active street edge and brings in services for tenants as well as other shoppers, while the housing guarantees a base population to support the retail.

© Brian Rose

© Brian Rose

© Cesar Rubio

0661

Green stairs

A beautiful open-air staircase tempts residents away from the elevator.

© Brittany McCall

0662

Bike parking

Making it safe and easy to ride and store bikes helps people choose to cycle rather than drive.

0663 

Urban agriculture

Small allotment garden lots allow residents in dense parts of the city to grow their own food and get their hands dirty.

© Marion Brenner

0664

Active solar

Generating renewable green energy on site helps this public affordable housing use 60% less energy than a typical apartment building, while saving the low-income tenants money on utility bills every month.

© Brian Rose

0665

Think outside the property box

Addressing context in an active way integrates a building into the community. The design of Daggett Place's breaks boundaries by turning the street into a half-acre public park.

0666

No parking

Each structured parking space adds at least $30,000 to the cost of the building, and means extra congestion in the neighborhood. Buildings in transit-rich areas can forgo parking garages in favor of additional units or common space.

Sebastián Irarrázaval Arquitectos

O'Brien 2458
7630368 Vitacura, Santiago, Chile
P.: (+56) 2-245-6252
www.sebastianirarrazaval.com

© Juan Purcell

0667

Context can define architecture, not just in relation with the notion of creating a "sense of place" but as an extra component or element, as used in this house built close to the Andes, where the nearby mountains function as walls "limiting" the space.

Sebastián Irarrázaval Arquitectos with Ximena García-Huidobro and Guillermo Acuña.

© Carlos Eguiguren

0668

Very banal elements can be used as sculptural units. In this house, prefabricated sanitary tubes are used as skylights.

0669

Structure is something that cannot be taken away if the budget does not suit later on in the project. It therefore becomes an intrinsic part of architecture: its very soul.

Structure not only gives our creation stability against wind, earthquakes, or snow, it also defines space. In this house, vertical structural elements, round and V-shaped columns, are randomly placed in order to create an interior "landscape," and are strategically located to receive shadows cast by the roof, creating an interplay of shade and light, and a three-dimensional effect.

© Carlos Eguiguren

0670

In order to emphasize the corners, angles, and sharp geometry of this house, we used steel profiles that correct the concrete construction errors.

0671

Placing a deck over a roof is a complex process. Prevent rainwater from entering a house by creating a supporting structure that rests on the roof with no pillars penetrating the cover, thereby avoiding the associated risks.
Sebastián Irarrázaval Arquitectos with Guillermo Acuña.

© Cristobal Palma

0672

In this exhibition created using shipping containers, I solved two simple problems that helped me later on when designing other projects. The first was how to create natural ventilation and the second was how to avoid claustrophobic feelings. The same simple strategy worked for both problems: placing a simple fenestration at the far end of the container.

© Alberto Piovano

0676

Vertical transit spaces can be used to achieve variety through employing alternating ramps and staircases. This is the design technique we used in the Indigo Patagonia Hotel in order to create an alternating effect that allows softer climbs in small spaces where a full ramp cannot be built.

Sebastián Irarrázaval architects with Ximena García Huidobro.

0674

In general, wood reacts very badly when it is left unpainted and exposed to the elements. If you want to avoid painting and the associated denaturalization of texture and color, the dimensions of the pieces of wood and the way in which they are arranged can be used to extend their lifetime. In this showroom, designed for the firm Moro, we proposed a façade consisting of 30-ft-long (9-m) strips of laminated wood. These were left unpainted but were treated with oil. The horizontal pattern and the profile of each piece of timber help to prevent water from entering the slats and rotting the wood, although façade maintenance work must be carried out every five years.

© Cristobal Palma

0673

Cube spaces can have poor acoustics. We address echoing through the use of interior wood cladding laid over insulating material. The wood strips are placed 0.4 inches (1 cm) apart from each other.

Exterior steel finishing can be used to help avoid overheating. This may sound unusual, but if steel plates are placed 2.8 inches (7 cm) apart, with openings in the top and base, air will be able to move through the inner void created.

Sebastián Irarrázaval Arquitectos with Andrea Von Chrismar.

© CarlosEguiguren

0675

Small modifications to construction techniques can sometimes make all the difference. In this house, built with very economical and everyday Canadian construction methods (OSB panels and imitation wood plastic siding), we decided to use real wood in the areas that are within hands reach, enabling an authentic tactile experience, while we maintained imitation wood in the rest of the construction.

Sebastián Irarrázaval Arquitectos with Guillermo Acuña.

© Guy Wenborne

Balmori Associates

833 Washington Street
New York, NY 10014, USA
P.: (+1) 212-431-9191
www.balmori.com

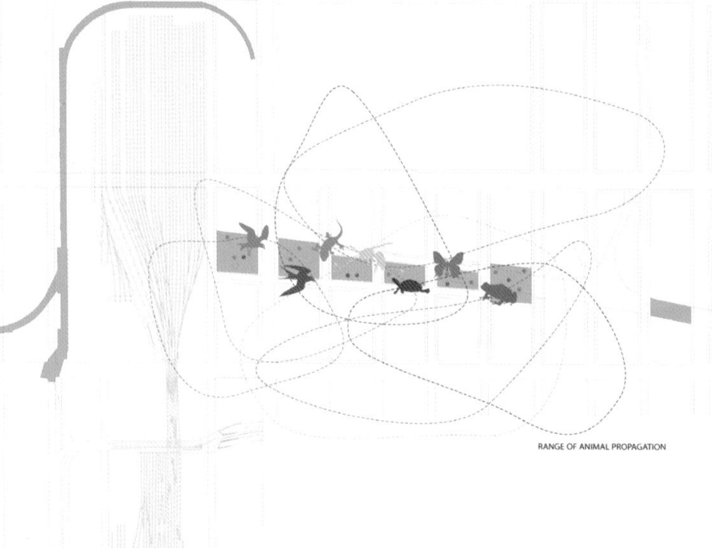

0677

Nature is the flow of change within which humans exist. Evolution is the history of these changes. Ecology is our understanding of the present phase.

0678

New landscape types can become niches for species forced out of their original environments.

0679

Landscapes—through new cityscapes—enter the city and modify our ways of interacting with it.

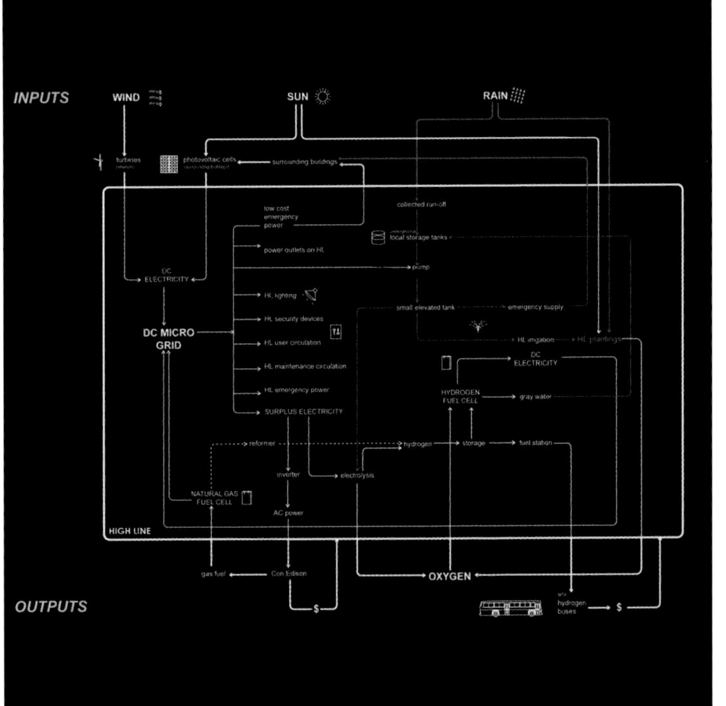

0680

A landscape, like a moment, never happens twice. This lack of fixity is landscape's asset.

0681

Nostalgic images of nature are readily accepted, but they are like stage scenery for the wrong setting.

◄0682

We can heighten the desire for new interactions between humans and nature where it is least expected, such as in derelict spaces.

0683▲

Landscape can bridge the distance between us and other natural elements, between ourselves and a river.

0684▼

Once just background scenery, landscape is becoming the main actor on the urban stage, a mobilizer and carrier, not just a destination.

><

0685

The edge between architecture and landscape can be porous.

0686

Rather than putting nature in the city, we must put the twenty-first century city in nature; this will involve utilizing engineered systems that function like those in nature and which derive from natural forms.

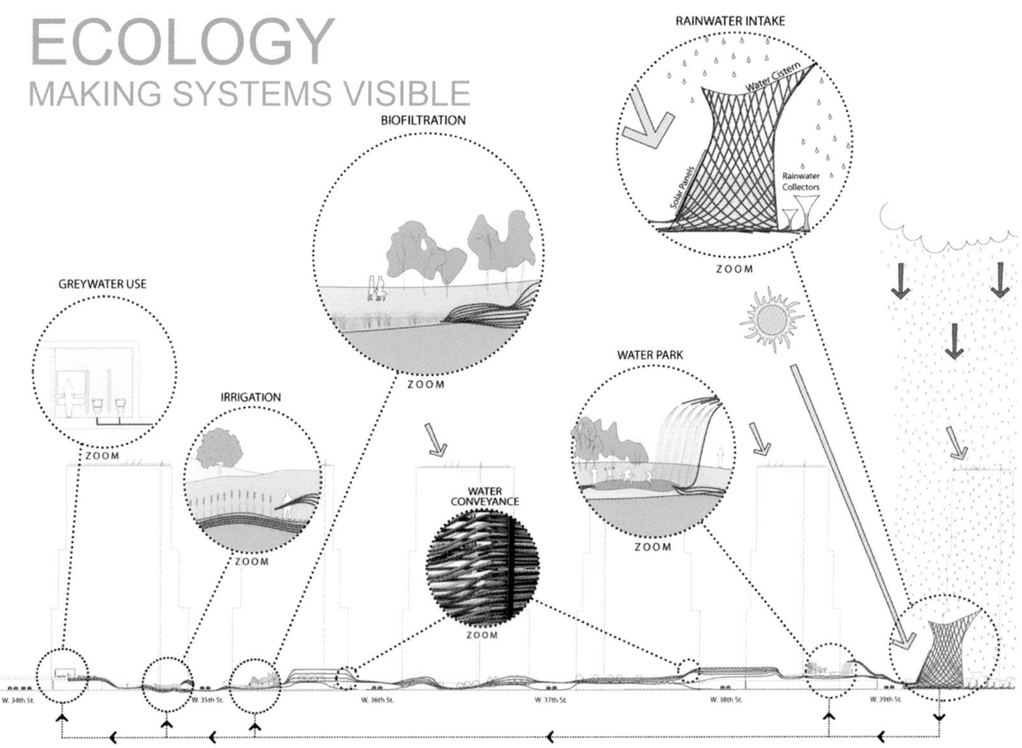

Reiko Miyamoto/Curiosity

2-13-16 Tomigaya, Shibuya
Tokyo 151-0063, Japan
P.: (+81) 3-5452-0095
www.curiosity.jp

© Daici Ano

0687

Abstraction
The first impression of a design triggers curiosity. Is this a house?

0688

Perception
Architecture plays with reality and the perception of reality. Where is this perspective going?

© Daici Ano

© Daici Ano

0689

Disappear
The elements disappear to reveal the essential; the floor thickness is just a visual line. Is this person flying?

0690

Movement
The user moves between sequences in a continuous flow, the building is merely a stage.

© Daici Ano

© Gwenael Nicolas

0691

Surprise
A house is a unique experience that reveals itself step by step. Where is the kitchen?

0692

Respect
A house is a ship that lands delicately on a piece of land.

0693

Discovery
The interior reveals its secrets from all angles, even under the tables.

0694 

Mystery
The entrance inspires a shift into a different dimension.

© Gwenael Nicolas

0695

Light
Light is a stroke of life on bare walls.

0696 

Scale
The scale is only revealed by the objects. A small space can appear huge if all the information is removed or redesigned.

AMP Arquitectos

Tips: Felipe Artengo Rufino
José Mª Rodríguez-Pastrana Malagón

Bethencourt Alfonso 2, ático
38002 Santa Cruz de Tenerife, Spain
P.: (+34) 922 24-51-49 / 24-40-33
www.amparquitectos.com

0697

The volcanic stone slopes surrounding the Tincer Stadium were designed to shelter the athletes from the northerly trade winds. This new enclosed sports competition facility was created from stone mined from the site itself.

0698

The indoor space created underneath the roof of the Tincer Stadium enjoys natural lighting and ventilation. The events room forms an aperture in the main façades, allowing the athletes to be observed and providing a space for learning about the sports activity.

0700

The service areas, changing rooms, and gym are located under the stadium's bleachers. These spaces are all naturally lit and ventilated. The building is covered with greenhouse fabric, enabling light and air to permeate. The slats of the front closures create the illusion of forming part of the prefabricated bleachers, providing optimal continuity between the façade and roof.

0701

The floating pool on the River Spree in Berlin has been recycled from an industrial barge that used to work this river. This intervention enables swimmers to bathe 20 inches (51 cm) above the river waterline, giving a remarkable sensation of swimming in water on water. The project re-integrates the riverbank with the city while forming a great floating light on the Spree.

© Uwe Walter

0699

The façade of Bouza Apartments was conceived as undulating horizontal bands of blue-stained concrete that contain the ventilation openings of the residential units. The wood shutters are made from vertical slats of plywood, in various shades of blue. They have been cut in a similar way to the formwork in order to create vertical continuity in the façade.

© José Oller

0702

In the Drago de Icod de los Vinos Visitors' Center the semi-buried concrete structure blends with the natural rocky setting. The slits of light that creep in between the beams, pillars, and the ground fuse the architecture into the surrounding landscape.

0703

The interior spaces of the San Agustín Halls of Residence reflect the tectonic and material character of the building through the textures of materials: stone, concrete, and wood. Natural light plays a central role. It is introduced in a zenith-like way to some of the interior spaces to enhance this expressive value of the materials.

0704 

In the larger spaces of the Canary Island Government Headquarters building, light plays a leading role. The natural light is strategically filtered through wooden roofs hanging from the building structure. The luminosity is reflected by the handles carved in the side of the solid white mulberry wooden door jambs.

0705

The Magma Convention Center design stems from a study of the landscape. It extends the protruding rocks in order to form spaces to accommodate the structure's different uses. The faults have been configured to favor the flow of the roof. The roof is envisaged as a liquid in motion that demarcates the space in all directions, producing natural lighting and ventilation apertures that enhance the interior sensation of lightness created by the undulating surfaces.

0706

The Parque de Vallehermoso Visitors' Center in La Gomera was designed to be just another natural topographic occurrence in the landscape. The concrete blocks were colored with a black additive to enhance the building's connection with the volcanic rocky site. The building incorporates one of the rocky outcrops and blends in as if it were part of the ravine.

0707

The concrete finish of this school, located in the town of La Orotava in the north of the island of Tenerife, has been produced through velatures in different hues. The urban center of La Orotava lies to one side of the school; the other side faces southeast toward a more natural, rural setting. The building has an important colorful nature both inside and outside, reflecting its educational function.

© Miguel de Guzmán

Caramel architekten

Schottenfeldgasse 60/36
1070 Vienna, Austria
P.: (+43) 1-596-34-90
www.caramel.at

© Hertha Hurnaus

0708

During the construction period, the use of prefabricated concrete components enabled onlookers to see the house taking shape very quickly. The contrast of large-scale glazing and closed walls creates lookout points where concrete blinkers orient the views while creating retreats; expanses of glass merge continuously into the glazing in the roof above, intensifying the sensation of complete openness.

© Hertha Hurnaus

0709

The house seems to have only one level as its main entrance is on the second floor. The backbone-like longitudinal axis passes the garage and the terrace into the interior, through the living-kitchen and staircase, ending opposite the glazed façade of the living room that affords breathtaking views over the valley.

0710

To prevent onlookers, the building has a hermetic appearance on its north and east façades, whereas it opens up toward the south and west with two completely glazed façades.

The house is made from prefabricated high performance structural insulated panels, which were mounted onto the concrete floor slab in just a few hours. An externally mounted textile curtain blocks out excessive sunlight and heat.

© Hertha Hurnaus

0711

The lower garden level seemingly grows out of the terrain and contains the more private and peaceful areas such as the bedrooms and bathrooms. On the west side, a small studio opens up onto the garden, terrace, and pool. Opposite the studio, on the other side of the terrace, the basement merges into the slope above the garage. The east-side, facing the neighbor's house, is completely enclosed.

© Otto Hainzl / Augment

© Otto Hainzl / Augment

0712

The south façade retreats from the edge of the cube in a free form, producing a covered terrace area. The west side of the building offers a magnificent view of the Danube Valley and is bathed in sunlight until late in the evening. Moving inwards from southwest, the open plan kitchen-dining-living space faces the swimming pool; the private bedroom units lie to the northeast.

© Dietmar Tollerian

0713

The task of converting two lengthwise adjacent, 150-ft-long (46-meter) gymnasiums into a fully functional triple gymnasium was a real feat of structural engineering. The engineers accomplished this by using only a 6-ft-high (1.8-meter) prestressed reinforced steel girder that absorbs the loads of both the existing gyms and the new extension.

© Dietmar Tollerian

0714

In keeping with the strict budget for the gym, but also with the intention of clearly articulating the newly built extension, a light frame construction method with a high proportion of prefabricated components was chosen. Reinforced concrete ribs measuring just 6.4-inches-thick (16 cm) were used to support prefabricated wooden panels.

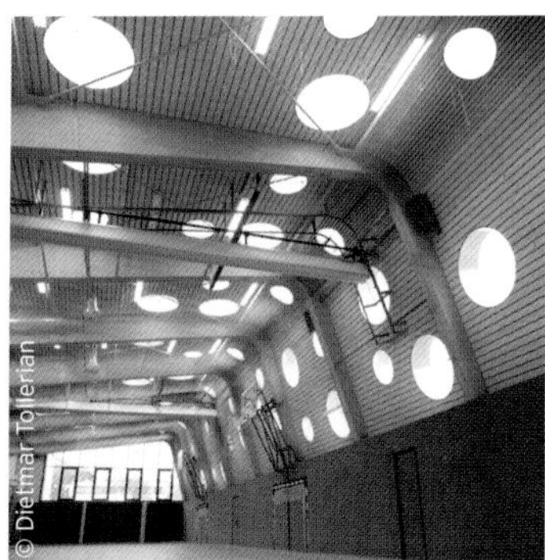

© Dietmar Tollerian

0715

Standard synthetic domes arranged in a seemingly random order were a low cost solution for natural lighting in the sports hall, also providing views of the outside. Like a bulge in the ground, the gym rises as a hull with no differentiation between roof and wall. The two fully glazed narrow sides appear to be wide open.

© Dietmar Tollerian

0716

The main objective was to visually integrate the inner and outer areas. For this reason, both the indoor and outdoor flooring is painted in a pink and white checkered design. To defend against the elements and minimize costs, the ideal coating choice was polyurethane, which is used to cover the walls and the furniture.

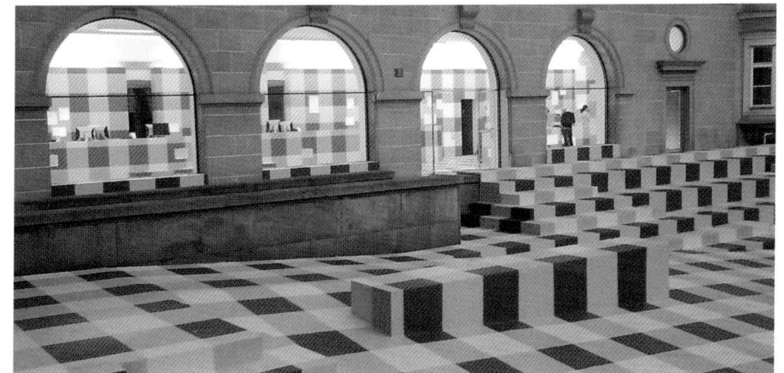

0717

Indoor checkered painted furniture and shelves seem to grow out of the floor. The raised structures, made from oriented strand board (OSB), are also covered with polyurethane coating. The public floor also has a raised floor structure made from OSB to preserve the original flooring, which can be removed in the future without destroying the old paving.

ECDM Architectes

7 Passage Turquetil
75011 Paris, France
P.: (33)1-44-93-20-60
www.ecdm.fr

© Gaston Bergeret

0718

Create a never-ending summer with colored glass.

© Benoit Fougeirol

0719

Enlarge your living space: detach your bedroom from the floor and suspend it from the ceiling.

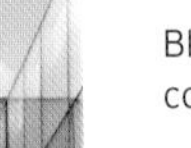

0720

Blend your building into the territory; continue the façade on the floor.

© Benoit Fougeirol

0721

Make your living space seem larger by utilizing two circulations and open space.

© Gaston Bergeret

0722

Transform concrete into gold by creating a soft texture using glossy color.

0723

For student housing, design a Tetris game garden.

0724

Make social housing chic.

0725 

Instead of creating heavy infrastructure, put the car park on the ground floor and design it as a playground and garden.

0726

Transform a residence entrance into a playground.

0727 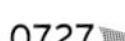

Make it nice for the street kids: let them play basketball under a golden translucent roof.

Saunders Architecture

© Bent René Synnevåg

Vestretorggaten 22
5015 Bergen, Norway
P.: (+47) 97-52-57-61
www.saunders.no

© Michael Permutter

© Michael Permutter

0728

Create shelter

The climate on the west coast of Norway can vary greatly and the designs for my houses have to take this into consideration. I often integrate covered outside spaces into my houses. These enable occupants to still enjoy the outdoors if the weather takes a turn for the worse. Such spaces offer protection from the elements and inevitably extend the house's usable space. The house truly acts as a shelter.

0729

Collaborate with enthusiastic builders

The recipe for a great project has three essential ingredients. The first is obviously a good architect; the second a challenging client; and the third, builders that enjoy their work. For my practice, I always work with the same two or three construction companies because they enjoy my projects and construct my buildings better than I could ever imagine. *Villa G* was a project where I spent plenty of time on site watching the house being built. We improved upon the details while on site, learned from one another, and we continue to collaborate on other projects. A solution-orientated attitude will make the process of building better for all those involved. Conversely, an unengaged builder will inevitably ruin any good project.

© Jan Lillebø

© Saunders & Wilhelmsen

© Saunders & Wilhelmsen

0730

Equate architecture with furniture
Your body integrates intimately with chairs and other furniture, and it should be intimate with the buildings that architects design. Architecture is often composed of simple elements that include floors, walls, and roofs. I often attempt to find ways to utilize all these elements in a twofold manner. The Summer House in Finland is a good example: the roof is used as an evening sitting area, the long edge of the front floor of the building is always used as a bench, and the open space between the two elements is a great place to lie outside on sunny days.

0731

Know the site intimately
Many of the sites I work with are extremely beautiful. To get a thorough understanding of them I always get a surveyor who makes me a detailed map with 10-inch (25-cm) contours (3.3-feet or 1-meter contours are standard). These maps also show the location of trees and other natural amenities on the site. From this detailed map, I make a physical model of the site and a 3D digital model; this enables me to ensure that the designs I propose match the site exactly. When creating a design I visit the site a number of times and make 1:1 building footprints there in order to get a *real* feeling of how the project will sit in its natural environment.

© Bent René Synnevåg

© Nils Vik

0732

Improve upon, but respect the past

How do you extend a house form that is 100 years old? This was a question I was asked when designing the Halvorsen Hansen extension. I decided to do something completely different with the form, so that the extension did not compete with the proportions of the existing building. While the form is different from the main house, the materials and finishes are nearly identical in order to visually tie the two components together. This project tells a really clear story. In a hundred years from now, people will be able to see that the addition is definitively from our era.

For me, as an architect, it is a pleasure to look for inspiration in the past, but find new ways for building in the present.

© Hy Rosenberg

0733

Experiment with Simplicity

The *blueskymod* summerhouse is designed as a building that will be prefabricated in a factory, then sent to the site and set up in just a few days. This is the first time that I have worked on such a project, but I found it had similarities to the way that Ikea has been successful in developing its products. Like Ikea products, this project had to be simple in form, function, and assembly. This exercise in simplifying all the parts of the project challenged me immensely. Experimenting with simplicity has helped me to make better designs since completing this project; I now often eliminate common, redundant elements.

0734

Leave some spaces undefined

Children often create their own imaginative worlds when playing and the same can stand true for adults. I often leave plenty of rooms for space that has no immediate function or is not always used. What will happen in this room? This question fascinates me. Not controlling every space enables surprises, changes, and gives a piece of architecture the chance to evolve in its own way over time.

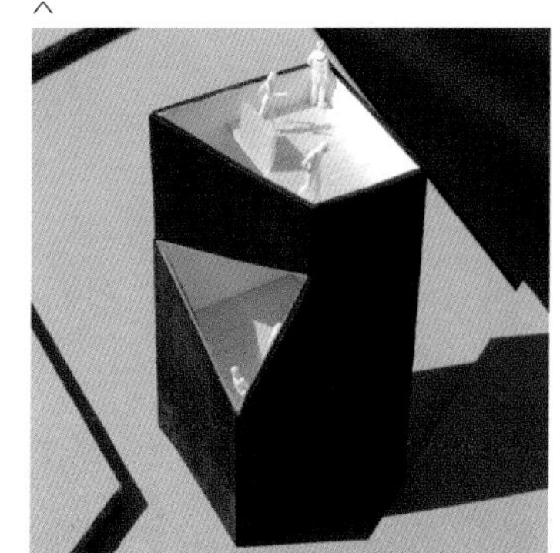

0735

Use physical models as the ultimate design tool
My studio is a digital office, yet we build physical models to test our design ideas. I can stop at any time to study them, to discuss them with colleagues, or to be reminded of the building's appearance. Another advantage of physical models is that they can be viewed from all sides and angles, giving the opportunity to consider changes that can be made before the final building is constructed. I am so convinced of the benefits of models that I have become superstitious and often tell people that if a project does not have a physical model, it will never get built.

0736

Form, then detail
Focus on the larger form first and then on the details. The composition of a piece of architecture is most powerful when it has a strong shape and clear identity. Reducing the importance of details allows a project to survive unforeseen situations that may arise on site. This was a rule of thumb I used when I first started practicing, even though, over time, my interest and ability to make good details has improved.

© Jan Lillebø

© Michael Permutter

0737

Make windows into pictures
As many of my projects are located in pristine sites, framing views is essential to making a building that is right for the site and its inhabitants. Openings in architectural structures connect the inside to the outside. Views can be framed up to the sky, over the fjord, or even of a forest, giving the chance to experience and contemplate the natural landscape.

TOPOTEK 1

Gesellschaft von Landschaftsarchitekten GmbH
Sophienstraße 18
10178 Berlin, Germany
P.: (+49) 30-24-62-58-0
www.topotek1.de

◄0738

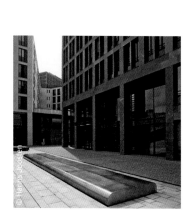

Tear things out of their context.

0739▲

Surprise with the ordinary.

0740▲

KPM-Quarter Berlin: use gold if you build for dentists.

◄0741

Enlarge things to BIGGER THAN LIFE.

◄0742

Use guerrilla tactics: be effective and surprise.

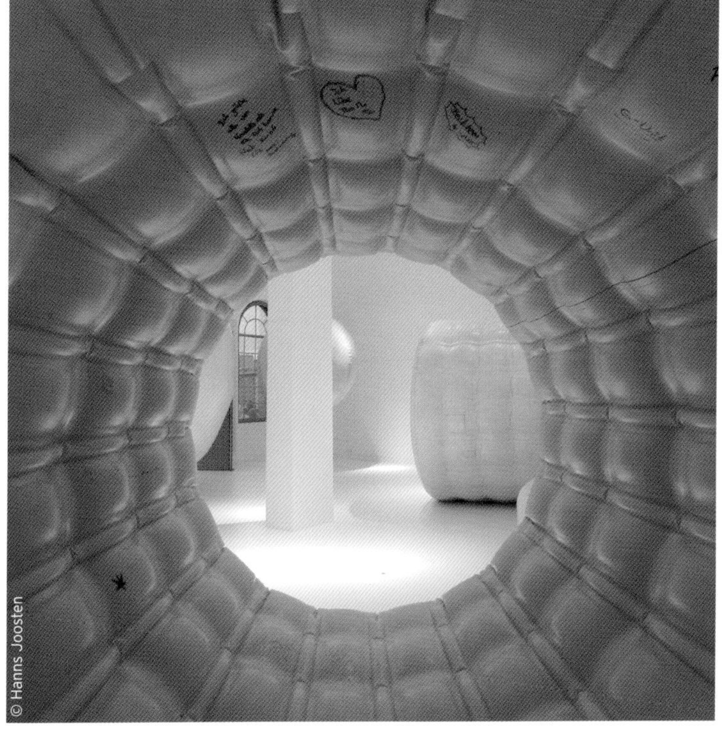

0743

Luoghi e non luoghi. Bologna Fair 2008/Cold war Biennale Venice 2008: Translate your strategies.

0744

Cultivate conflict.

0745

Be sexy.

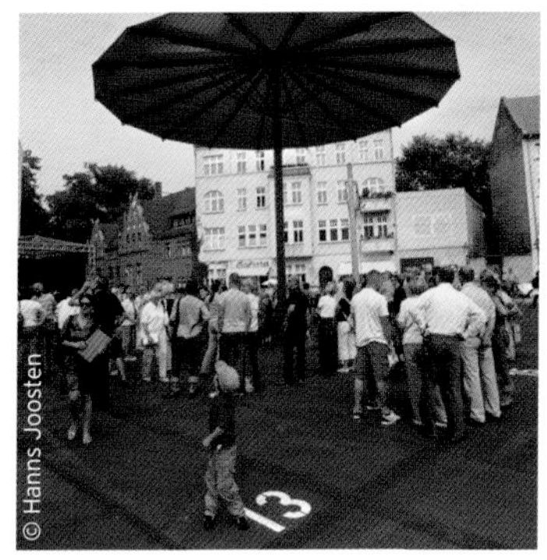

0747

Be visible.

0746

Think of the dialectic between destruction and creation.

Atelier Werner Schmidt

Mag. Arch./SIA/Visarte/IASS
Areal Fabrica 117
7166 Camorino, Switzerland
P.: (+41) 81-943-25-28
www.atelierwernerschmidt.ch

0748

Through a small interference a sad situation can easily turn into a happy walk.

0749

From old to new, without destroying the classical barn, that was my mission. With a consistent intervention I breathed new life into the old barn.

0750

Through the appropriate design and construction, a toilet can become a functioning, sensual illuminated object.

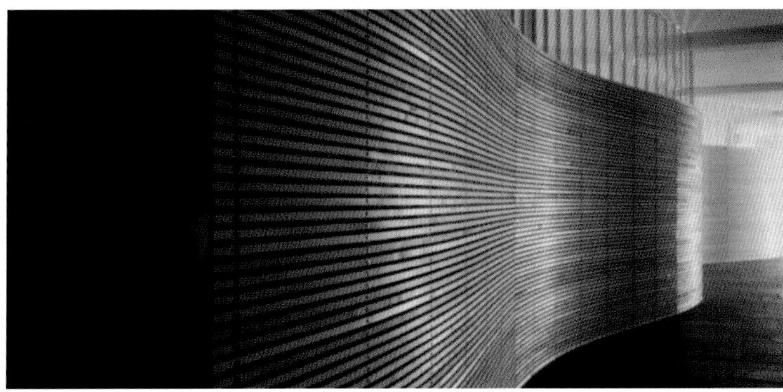

0751

With the pragmatic claim to improve the acoustics of a passage, a sensual experience can be created.

0752

The task was to create 36 student rooms in the old building of the monastery. The existing school is a rigorous, rectangular concrete vision of the 1970s. The idea was, after a day in a rectangular school, students should have the opportunity to move into another world. Their minds will be refreshed and reopened once more.

0753

Other forms and, accordingly, other areas can help people to liberate themselves from established schemes. Winston Churchill once said, "we shape our buildings and afterwards our buildings shape us."

0754

Using load-bearing straw bale construction methods ecology, economics and sensuality be brought together.

0755

The consistent implementation of a straw casing with high-tech glass, allows a life at 6230 feet (1,899 m) above sea level without heating. A house without heating needs to be thickly insulated. Insulating a house with a conventional insulating material would be far too expensive. When using straw as an insulation material, 13.8 or 47 inches (35 or 119 cm), price is no consideration.

0756

If you were sitting inside this building, you would not believe that it is constructed with straw. You would only feel it. A properly constructed straw bale house will save you from a hefty heating bill in the spring. It is rumored that people living in a straw bale house instead of a conventional house, will live ten years longer.

0757

A building can also be like a space station, underground, made of wood and straw.

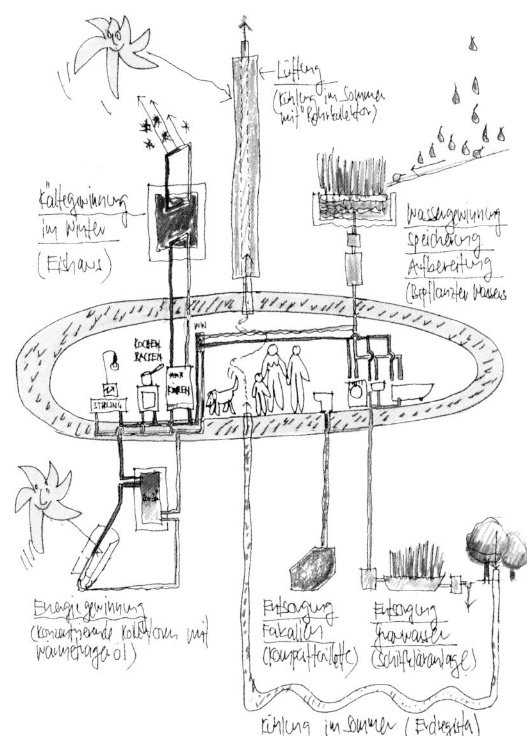

0758

Nowadays, the money for energy is floating in the Arab states, Russia, energy companies, etc. It is time to end this dependence or better this blackmail. Future buildings and regions must become self-sufficient. This keeps money and work in the regions. People win back a bit of freedom, there are fewer wars, and the environmental burden is lessened.

0759

Round multifamily houses can also be constructed out of wood and straw.

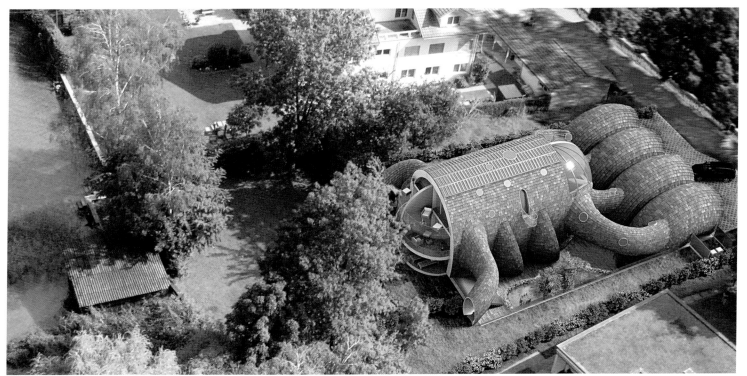

Jürgen Mayer H. Architects

Bleibtreustraße 54
10623 Berlin
P.: (+49) 30-31-50-61-17
www.jmayerh.de

© Dirk Fellenberg

© David Franck

0760

The double façade of the ADA 1 office complex was designed as a necessary climate-control device and noise buffer. It gives the building a striking visual identity even from afar. Alternated glazed strips and stucco panels create an impression of a flowing movement that glides around the building and across its surfaces as a metaphor for the nearby river and the surrounding traffic flows.

0761

The building's articulation is guided by the volumes set like individual boxes within the plan, housing its various functions. The intermediate zones lying between them serve as public transit areas. The structure's gentle slant is also perceptible on the large staircase, although here the incline is spatially set into the transverse axis. The main stairs can be seen as an internal connector for the openings formed by incisions in the shell.

© Schaulin

0762

The interior is laid out on a flexible grid structure that can be reconfigured as needed. The rear ventilation of the double façade and the concrete core for storing both heat and cold eliminates the need for air conditioning system. Inside, the "eyes" of the façade, boasting spectacular views over Alster Lake, can be used as VIP conference rooms or executive offices.

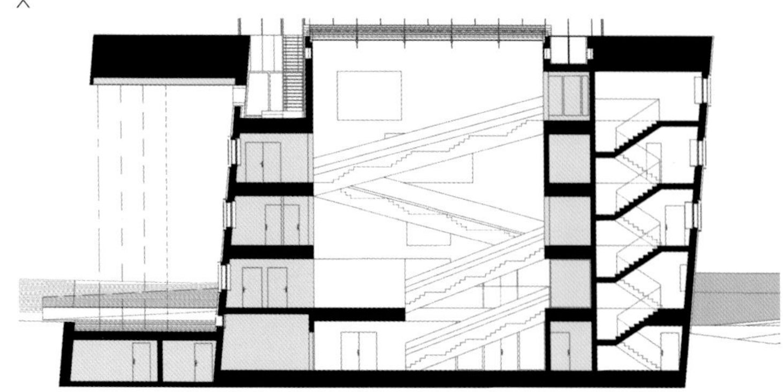

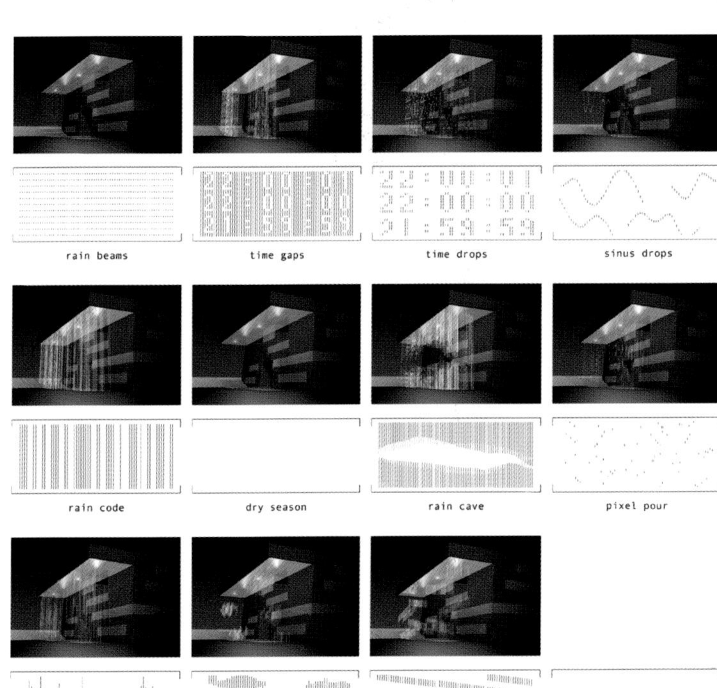

0763

Pitter-patterns emblematize the possibility of radically novel approaches to designing such buildings. With its computer animated rain curtain and the *Wind.Light installation*, the exterior of the town hall also represents a new approach to the insertion of public buildings into public spaces.

0764

The structure's dynamic character is emphasized by flowing transitions between supports and walls, and by the rounded windows which protrude from the plane of the wall. As an organic and replenishable material, wood proved to be the most sustainable option. Polyurethane coating provides the timber with long-term protection against weathering.

0765

The design of the Mensa Moltke building uses the largest possible construction surface: a skewed rectangle topped by a roof with identical dimensions. In the design process, the ground plane and roof were pulled away from one another, as if a viscous mass had generated vectors of force to join these two levels. The structure conveys an image of movement and immobility, visualizing nonlinear fields of energy.

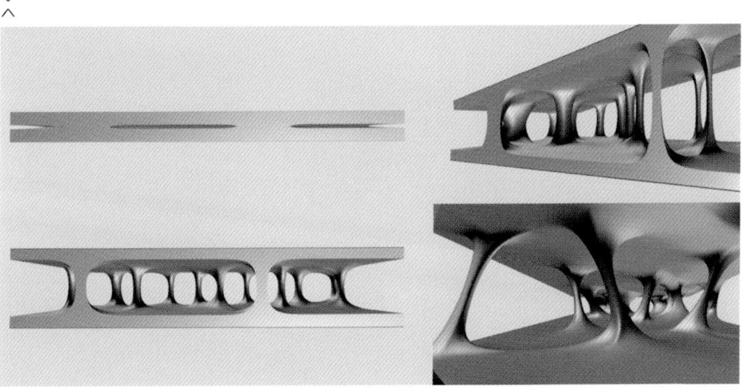

0766

The multifunctional Townhall Scharnhauser Park has been slanted backwards by a few degrees, just enough to generate a mild sense of unease, and to endow its seemingly orthogonal volume with aesthetic tension. The color scheme of the external cladding—with its stepwise progression from a pale strip below to a dark one above—runs counter to expectations, heightening the sensation of defamiliarization. The ribbon windows run around the building like stripes, without exposing the structure's internal subdivisions.

© David Franck

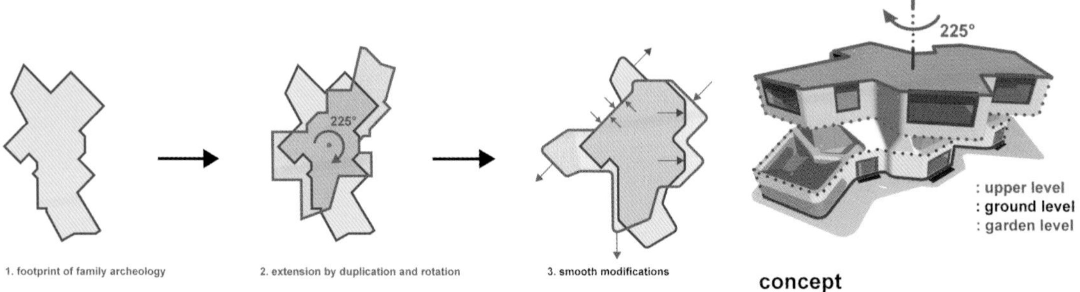

0767

The geometry of Dupli.Casa is based on the unique outline of the house that formerly occupied the site, which was built in 1984 and underwent many extensions and modifications. This "footprint of family archeology" and the new building recalls the lot's history by duplicating and rotating the footprint. Lifted up, the structure creates a semi-public space on the ground level, set between two layers of discretion.

© David Franck

0768

The interior is much quieter than the outer sculptural appearance; it guarantees a long-lasting comfortable living system based on customized programmatic spaces to accommodate the users and their lifestyles. The whole upper floor is rotated to offer spectacular views toward Marbach historic city center, while the rear of the building provides privacy and intimacy.

0769

The building was constructed using a brand new thermal insulation composite system in order to shape its smooth geometry and create the partial polyurethane coating details, as carried out earlier in the Mensa Moltke project in Karlsruhe. The results are homogeneous transitions and a powerful sculptural expression.

© David Franck

© David Franck

Art & Build Architect

Art & Build—from master planning to interior design, a humanistic approach to architecture

Brussels, Paris, Luxembourg, Toulouse
255/8 chaussée de Waterloo
1060 Brussels, Belgium
P.: (+32) 2-538-72-71
www.artbuild.eu

◄0770

The Agora Building in Strasbourg considers both urban and natural existing fabrics; it is the missing link that fosters the European district's town-countryside relationship. The concept maximizes the potential offered by microclimates, sun, wind, water, greenery, and underground conditions in order to increase comfort while reducing energy consumption and maintenance requirements. Atria, internal streets and generous staircases are used to give the complex both conviviality and radical contact with its surroundings.

0771►

The project's creators adopted a very bold approach to the competition, seeking to develop the principles of a hyper-ecological architecture with the least possible impact on the site and to incorporate water recovery and natural climate control. Designed like trees, the buildings absorb geothermal energy from the ground, and solar and wind power from the canopy.

0772

Textile solar chimneys aid natural ventilation by increasing both stack and venturi effects in a response to Strasbourg's climate.

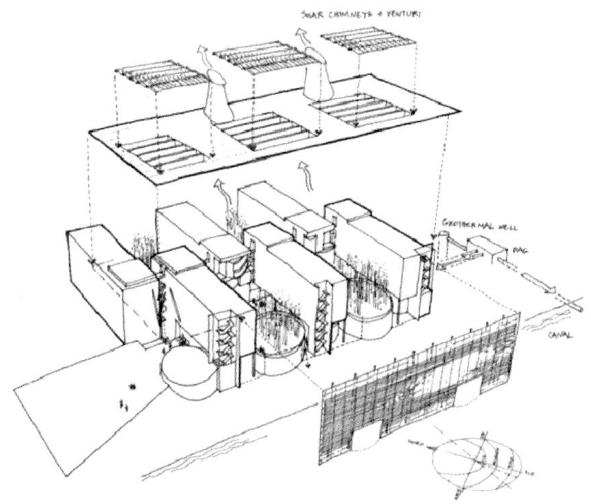

© S. Brison

© M. Detiffe

0773

Internal spaces help to connect office spaces, conference facilities, and restaurants. The results create a convivial environment where European Nations representatives can meet and work.

0774

The workplace as living space: the creation of complementary office and social spaces provides the flexibility to meet the varied demands of the market, and also has the potential to bring the concept of 'city living' into the workplace. The office building becomes an integral part of the neighborhood; its corridors are like streets, it communal areas like plazas. Vertical transit spaces are areas for meeting and interaction; all in contact with the external environment.

© M. Detiffe

0775

The glass roof covering the interior street gives a view of the reception area that is planted with trees, offering a pleasant yet magisterial environment and incorporating a water purification process that recycles into the sanitary system.

© S. Brison

0776

Natural light and visual contact promote conviviality and efficiency, while providing additional working and meeting spaces around a building's circulations.

0777 

The interior garden providing natural light in the heart of the project provides an optimal working environment with its dense and architectural varied green spaces, and integrated islands of greenery and mineral elements.

© S. Brison

0778

Preliminary studies for the project focused on the subtle nuances needed to create an individual identity that would also blend in with the tone of this business district. Attention was also paid to the forms and materials of an elliptical hall standing at the corner of a central roundabout, marking the center of the Brussels North District, which functions as an entrance zone and deconstructs the rigorous lines of the surrounding buildings.

© M. Detiffe

0779

Set in a park dominated by truly remarkable conserved trees, the Agora Building's day care nursery is dedicated to the little ones.

© S. Brison

0780

Art & Build Brussels studio: this 26,909-sq-ft (2,500-sq-meter) space, treated as landscape, offers a very user-friendly atmosphere for the 130 Art & Build collaborators.

atelierworkshop

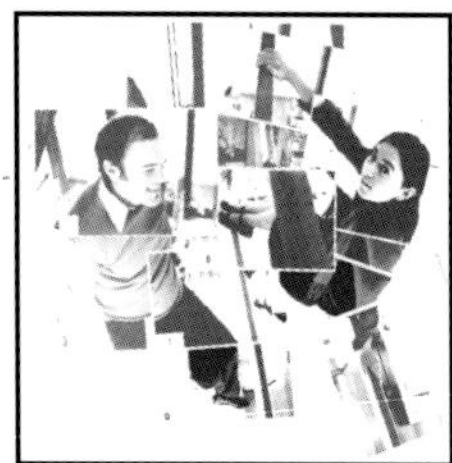

212 Taranaki Street, Te Aro
Wellington 6011, New Zealand
P.: (+61) 644-384-6688
www.atelierworkshop.com

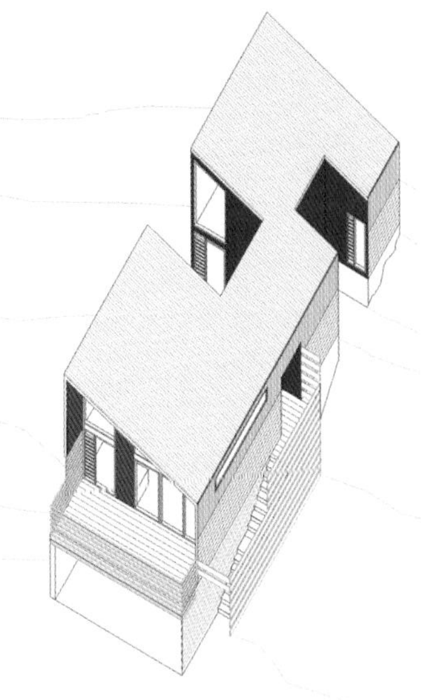

0781

Transforming the complexity of the elements contained in a client's brief and site into a simple form is the core of our work.

For this house on a tight urban site, this resulted in a mono pitch volume raised high on the site to avoid excavation and to take advantage of the view of the distant mountains. Courtyard spaces were carved into the volume, giving all rooms direct sunlight, and a view to the exterior without looking directly into the neighboring houses.

0784

We attempt to embrace the history of a site in order to create an imaginary geography based on the inherent qualities of the site; this is a revealing process.

In this urban square project, the line of the imaginary riverbank—surveyed from an original early settlement map—runs along the length of the new square. The riverbed is made of printed glass that folds at the edge, creating an illuminated riverbank bench. A promenade stretches along the length of this elongated piece of urban furniture.

The same material and pattern is echoed in the skin of the neighboring building, offering a silhouette of a canopy of native pohutukawa trees.

0782

In every project, we seek passive solar solutions adapted to the site, brief, and budget. In this project, a 20 ft-long (6 m) gallery space was created following the principals of a Trombe Wall, linking the main volume of the house and the guest wing.

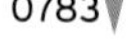

0783

The 26 sq ft (2.4-sq-meter) footprint of this house is inserted into an existing orchard grid. The top of the volume is shaped as a square pyramid with an off-center apex popping up above the foliage and conversing with the profile of the surrounding hills.

0785

Bathing the internal space with zenithal light introduces the scale of the cosmos, as a point of reference for everyday life. In this project, strips of glass run the full width of the building and are repeated following the regular landscape pattern, creating a rhythm of sunlight throughout the house.

0786

The use of passive solar energy, in this case, was enhanced by automatic sensor controlled louvers. The system "wakes up" in the morning using a light sensor. During the day, it operates on thermostats to retain a preset temperature or can be manually controlled by the occupant. At night, or on a cold sunless days, the system closes to form a highly insulated building envelope.

0787

Our projects are developed from our quest to create a structure that becomes one with the site. The long asymmetric gabled roof of this concrete block house stretches east to west along the soft undulations formed by the natural contours of the site. The building is immersed within a regular grid of white birch conceived as part of the design process. The grid is brought into the house by intrusive gardens bordered by skylights.

0788

The relation of the house to the site generates dimensions, characteristics, and materiality as a multiplicity of variations on a theme.

The ground floor works within the microcosm of the orchard with two sliding doors on the eastern and western sides, calibrated to the distance between trees and the height of the foliage. The courtyard space mirrors the living area in its dimension and details, providing an important extension of the living space of this small 260 sq ft (24-sq-meter) house nestled in the midst of the apple trees.

0789

The use of a limited palette of raw materials gives clarity, simplicity, and unity to a project. This galley kitchen sits centered under a mezzanine floor and its staircase, screened by slats of Gaboon plywood. This same material is used for the woodwork throughout the house and in the wall cladding up to a datum of 7.9 ft (2.4 m). The cladding above this line is in blond Italian poplar plywood, meeting the client's brief to avoid using plasterboard.

0790

The port-a-bach is an ongoing project that acts for us as a laboratory to test, at a micro-scale, solutions to larger general issues of energy production and sustainability.

It takes as its basis a 20-ft (6 m) shipping container in order to produce a minimum living unit, which is recyclable, mobile, and cost effective, yet well designed and comfortable.

EAA-Emre Arolat Architects

Tips: Kerem Piker

Nispetiye Cad. 112/2
34337 Etiler, Istanbul, Turkey
P.: (+90) 212-265-0714
www.emrearolat.com

© Thomas Mayer

0791

Dalaman International Airport Terminal in Muğla, Turkey, strives to tackle the boredom and feeling of emptiness of terminal buildings and the conventions of international airport buildings. The main inputs were the region's rich landscape, climatic characteristics, and differentiating features of its tourism activities. A simple shading instrument, which is quite common in vernacular architecture in the region, was used as a secondary roof in order to create a holistic serenity through its regular repetition along the fragmented masses.

© Ali Bekman

0792

Constructed on the outskirts of Edirne, the main inputs of the factory building were the technical descriptions of the cyclic relations of production, the limited size of the lot, service and main road connections, and local building techniques.

0793

The objective behind the Kağıthane office project was to avoid a generic *tabula rasa* building, created without taking into account the location and its relationship to social and physical structures. The aim was to create a building that emphasizes its context, taking into account the other buildings in the area as architectural reference points as well as exploiting regional publicity opportunities, while satisfying capitalist expectations.

© Thomas Mayer.

0794

This high-rise building, designed to be located on one of the most crowded housing zones in Istanbul, aimed to reinterpret the customary living conditions in tower-residences by proposing a rationale for a type of vertical city. The building establishes its relationship with the surrounding built environment through references to the mass fragmentation of the scales of those buildings. It vertically echoes the horizontal relationships between the existing buildings by means of inner voids and terraces.

0795

Instead of dispersed units, a large mass was formed, housing both production and administration functions. Linear gardens were placed between the production and administration spaces, as spaces to be used by the staff during breaks.

0796

As a high-rise building experiment enriched by inner voids and vertical gardens, the Maslak No.1 office building is a kind of reaction to the current custom of building towers defined as standard office spaces, planned around a rational core and glazed facade systems. The building was designed taking into account how it will be experienced from inside and how it is perceived from outside, Maslak No. 1 awaits the day it will be built on the most crowded business axis of Istanbul.

0797

All of the apartments were fronted toward the Bosphorous panorama. Their northern façades are celestial gardens protected by means of vertical and horizontal circulations; sunlight and fresh air enter in a controlled manner and each mass has its own unique character.

0798

In the design process of this cultural center building, which will be built in Yalova city, the aim was to establish a relationship between the building and the city while avoiding a deductive and instructive design tendency that can appear at any moment and in any place, as an easy contemporary architectural trap to fall into.

◄0799

The voids between the masses and the promenade are designed to form part of the city's social life, providing "indoor streets" where passersby can view digital media exhibitions that change every three months and which are displayed on the surfaces of the interior masses, and to create café and restaurant spaces. In this way the builder has aimed to avoid telling users how to absorb the culture through the structure he placed in "this" setting.

0800►

During the renovation of old Silahtaraga Power Plant, a typical modern industrial setting formed between 1910s and 1950s, two large boiler houses were demolished and rebuilt on the footprints of former buildings as a contemporary art center. The most prevalent design principle was to integrate them into the setting without engaging them with a specific time segment, in contrast to habitual aim to create contemporary structure, containing only the current architectural specifications while being disconnected from the historical context.

Saia Barbarese Topouzanov Architectes

339 est, rue Saint-Paul
Vieux-Montréal, H2Y 1H3 Québec, Canada
P.: (+1) 514-866-2085
www.sbt.qc.ca

0801

This central spine, the main pedestrian path, facilitates campus access, while clarifying and uniting two sectors.

© Marc Cramer

0802

The new field characterizes a renewed notion of campus interlaced by a continuous flow of gardens and pathways, where green voids and erected structures are architectural equals.

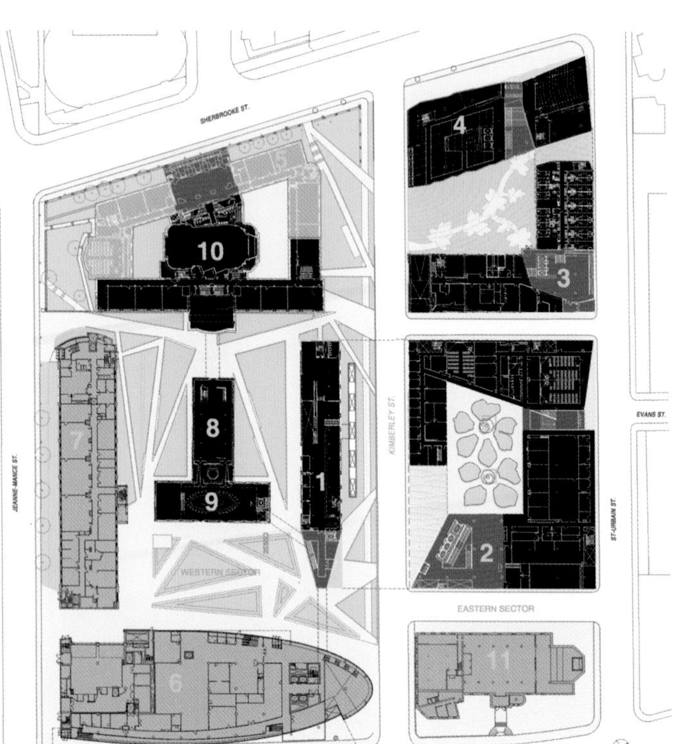

0803

The transformation of the existing buildings into a three-story library integrates the campus within its broader community.

© Marc Cramer

0804

DNA patterns spiral upwardly, unraveling across the façades.

© Marc Cramer

0805

This L-shaped student residence, identified by the "swallow's nest hatch" weave pattern, alluding to a hive, folds one wing inward to protect an inner courtyard.

0806

A "city forest" containing five special tree species and more than 160 trees recalls the site's historical use as a botanical garden.

© Alain Laforest

0807

The court-facing façade of the TELUQ building evokes the image of tree trunks, inspired by the site's garden history.

0808

Campus life permeates its environment thanks to luminous, glazed entry portals bathed in a bright yellow hue.

0809

The most public corner of the campus exposes an undulating veil of glass faceted surfaces. This façade acts as a screen on which a composition of textures from surrounding urban structures is reflected and "printed" onto the building face.

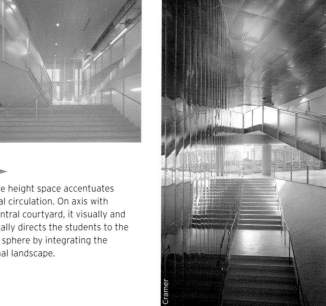

0810

A triple height space accentuates vertical circulation. On axis with the central courtyard, it visually and physically directs the students to the public sphere by integrating the external landscape.

Vetsch Architektur

Lättenstrasse 23
8953 Dietikon, Switzerland
P.: (+41) 44-741-07-10
www.vetsch.ch

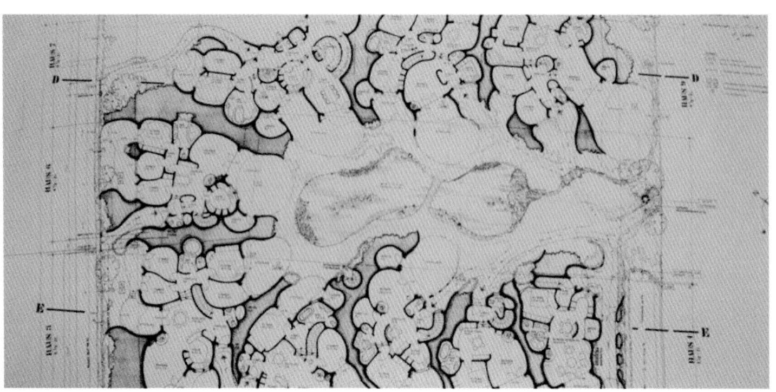

0811

The basic concept of these nine earth houses with ceiling and the biotope in the courtyards is to construct a closed area. The earth covered roofs can be walked on, and can be used as gardens and verandas. The earth covering and the ground pump heating, minimizes the need for heating energy. In the summer heat, these houses provide optimal living conditions.

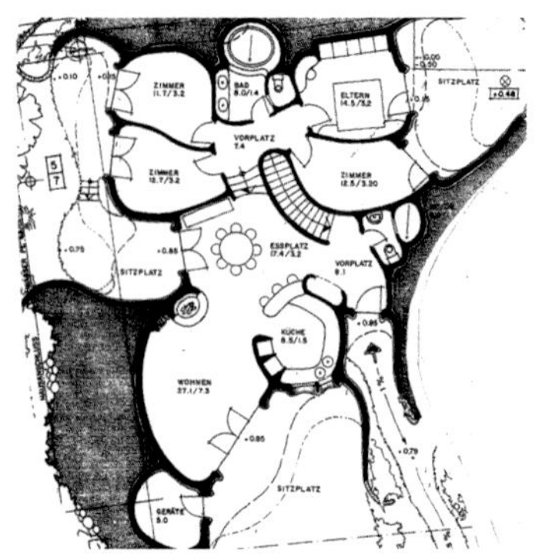

0812

This floor plan belongs to one of the nine earth houses in this settlement.

0813

The living room opens south toward the veranda with biotope and private waterfall.

0814

The dining area is adjacent to the kitchen with dining bar and has a separate east-facing sitting area.

◄0815

The bathroom with separate shower and whirlpool affords a special view of the inner biotope.

0817▼

The master bedroom has a special tube in the wall through which occupants can throw used clothes directly into the laundry room on the floor below.

◄0816

This sitting area on the eastern side on the dining room enables inhabitants to enjoy the evening sun.

0818▼

The earth houses are horseshoe-shaped, arranged around an inner biotope. This creates an intimate atmosphere and blocks out external pollutants.

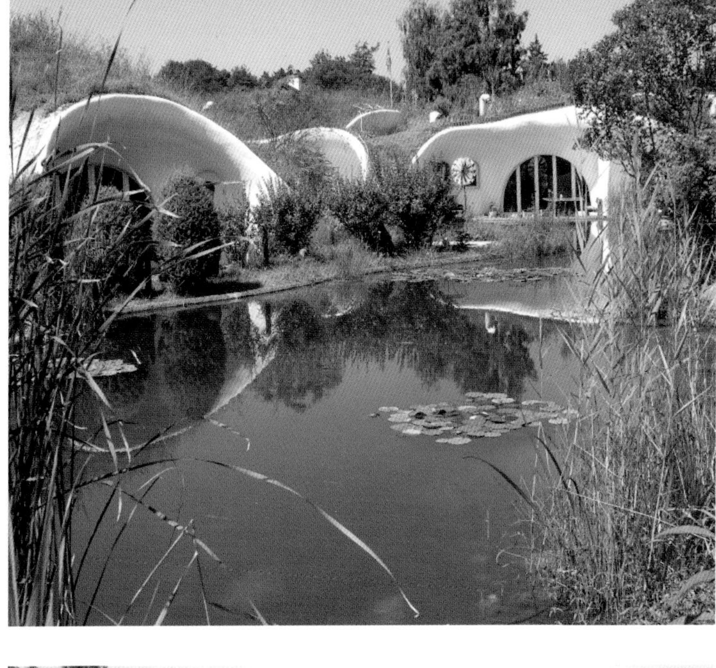

0819▼

In this kitchen, all appliances are integrated. From here, the earth house entry way is visible.

0820►

The idea of the overall concept was based on minimizing the impact to the natural setting by using earth to cover the roof. This high density sustainable concept was developed as a result of expensive land prices. All nine earth houses have ceilings and access to underground parking with 27 parking lots. The biotope is located over the garage. It is essential to return green spaces back to nature through green roofs and minimal energy consumption.

Architectenbureau Paul de Ruiter

Leidsestraat 8-10
1017 Amsterdam, The Netherlands
P.: (+31) 20-626-32-44
www.paulderuiter.nl

0821

The clients of Villa Röling are passionate art collectors. Their main wish for their new dwelling was that it should do greatest justice to their collection of paintings and sculptures. However, the location of their house, at the edge of Lake Westeinderplas, is so splendid that it was not an option to make an enclosed volume that would have large wall surfaces for hanging paintings but would limit the view of the surroundings. The view of the lake and the garden had to be optimal. Architectenbureau Paul de Ruiter therefore decided to design two contrasting volumes, a transparent glass volume overlooking the lake and the garden, and a wooden box "floating" on top of it for the works of art.

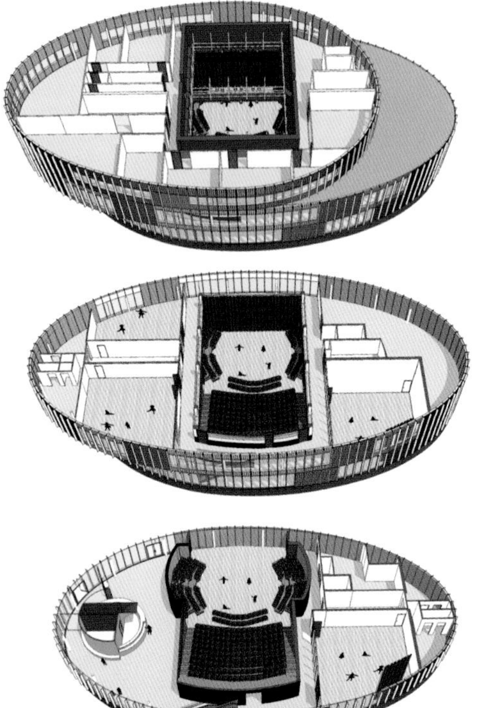

0822

One requirement for this theater was the need for daylight in the main auditorium. Lessons and rehearsals would take place here during the day, and a good level of daylighting is very important for the atmosphere and sense of orientation. At the same time daylight is deliberately blocked for performances. For this reason, a glass gallery was created on the first floor surrounding the main auditorium. This gallery not only allows maximum amounts of light to enter, it also enables parents, and others who may be interested, to unobtrusively watch lessons and rehearsals. The windows can be darkened to block out the light when performances are held.

0823

In order to create the simultaneously dynamic and clear image that Paul de Ruiter had in mind for this car park—both from the inside and the outside—great attention was paid to the details and materials of the façade design. The façade of the Veranda multi-story car park is composed of horizontal strips of aluminum, alternated with small strips of mirrored glass. To combine plasticity and transparency in the façade, Paul de Ruiter himself developed the perforated and folded deep drawn aluminum panels.

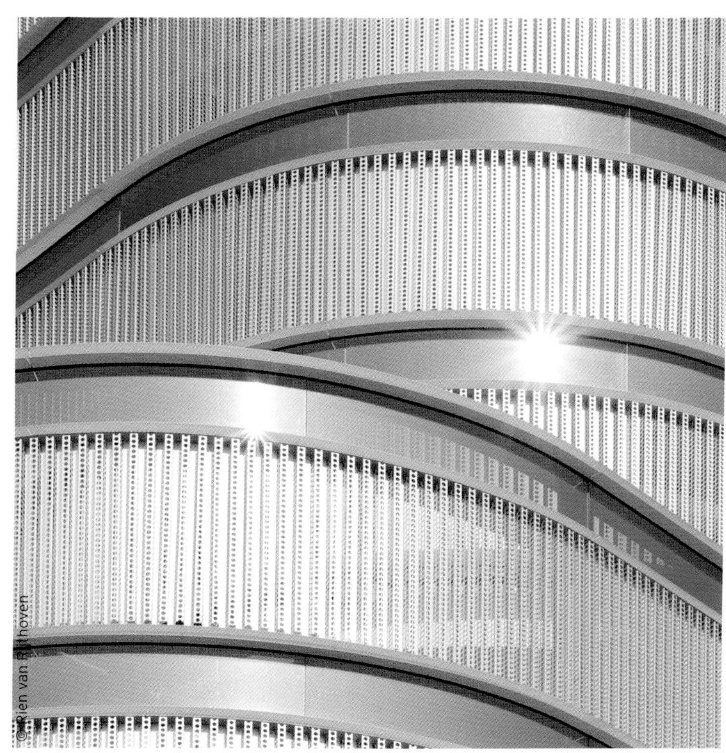

© Rien van Rijthoven

0824

Although Villa Deys is a house for senior citizens, there is nothing in the outward appearance of the villa that hints at this. Architecture can cater in many ways to the wishes and the infirmities of people who are growing older, without sacrificing modernity and appearance. Villa Deys is all on one floor without thresholds and is almost completely electronically functional, but this is not the main feature that makes this villa such a pleasurable residence: daylight plays the leading role here.

0825

Sliding glass and aluminum doors run along the entire length of the southern façade of this villa. To keep out excessive heat and sunlight, a sunblind was developed consisting of ten panels with horizontal wooden slats, made of western red cedar to blend in with the farm outbuildings that are scattered in the surrounding landscape. To adjust the sunblind, the whole panels move, rather than the individual slats. Each of the ten panels consists of two sections with a horizontal joint in the middle. When they are opened, either manually or automatically, the panel is lifted to form a porch above the glass door. When the panels are closed, they are automatically secured at the bottom.

© Rien van Rijthoven

© Rien van Rijthoven

0826

The water in the swimming pool of this villa has a constant temperature of 81ºF (27ºC), which of course consumes energy and costs money. However, by linking the pool heating system with the low temperature heating system of the house, in combination with a water pump, the pool area re-emits the energy it has absorbed and becomes part of the house's energy saving climate system. The swimming pool therefore helps to achieve the maximum yield from the energy available.

0827

The presence of daylight in living and working areas is crucially important for the "feel-good factor" of the working and living environment and also for the health of the user. Daylight gives energy, generates happiness and stimulates productivity. It is like the inspiration created by a pleasant, peaceful, and natural environment. The client's express wish for a transparent building therefore resulted in the use of glass almost everywhere. The southern façade consists of 50% glass, while the northern façade is 100%. The glass façades not only have a high aesthetic value, they also admit a large quantity of daylight and provide superb views.

0828

One of the client's requirements for this office building was to create a flexible layout allowing flexible utilization of the new office. Paul de Ruiter's design satisfied this requirement in two ways. First, the flexible construction, both structural and in relation to utility systems, means that the building can be divided up in many different ways and can be split into large units that can be rented out. Second, it was possible to provide all the 450 employees—who often spend a great deal of time working in the field—with their *own* workplace by means of flexible workstations.

© Rob't Hart

◄0829

To keep a building cool in the summer and warm in the winter, cooled or heated air is generally blown into it. However, this uses a great deal of energy, and often leads to complaints about draughts. In the RWS office building, use has been made of active concrete, in combination with underground cold/heat storage. This makes it possible to create a constant and comfortable working climate and to achieve an energy saving of 40 to 50 percent over traditional cooling and heating methods.

0830▼

To create openness and lightness and to give the residents the sensation of living outside in the green, this house is entirely oriented to a south-facing secluded garden. Because three of the four façades are glazed, every room in the villa looks directly out on to this garden. The spacious wooden terrace forms an outdoors room, partly covered by a wooden awning supported by steel brackets that taper upwards. This gives it the appearance of floating above the ground. Ponds have been laid on both sides of the villa, so that the house here, too, appears to be raised above ground level, emphasizing the lightness of the building.

© Pieter Kers

R&Sie(n)

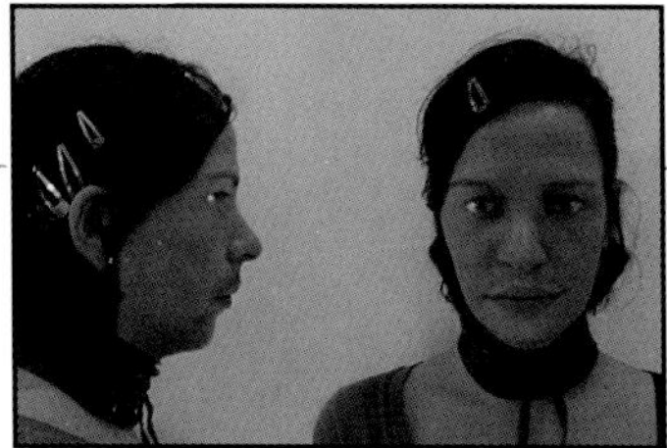

24 rue des Maronites
75020 Paris, France
P.: (+33) 1-42-06-06-69
www.new-territories.com

0832▲

Some 300 beakers are arranged as "glass blown" components to enable bacterial culture or extra light through refraction. Rear windows negotiate with the opposite neighborhood, offering views over an enclosed courtyard.

0833▼

1,200 hydroponic ferns are a key design feature.

0831▼

The structure combines devil's rock emergences (*Close Encounters of the Third Kind*) with nature (ferns) from the Devonian dinosaur period. These elements are technologically domesticated to come back in today's regressive French period.

0834▲

Rainwater is captured for watering plants with a mechanical drop-by-drop system incorporating nutrient addition controls.

0835 

This is a private laboratory designed as a camouflaged duck cabana. (*i'mlostinParis*, Paris, 2008)

0836

Hollows in this volume have been scooped out as if it was an ice cavity, but in this case the structure is from wood and it has been hollowed using a 5-blade drill machine.

0838

Digitization of the envelope of a traditional habitat. (Design of a building for an art museum/alpine ice research station; Water Flux, Évolène, 2005-09)

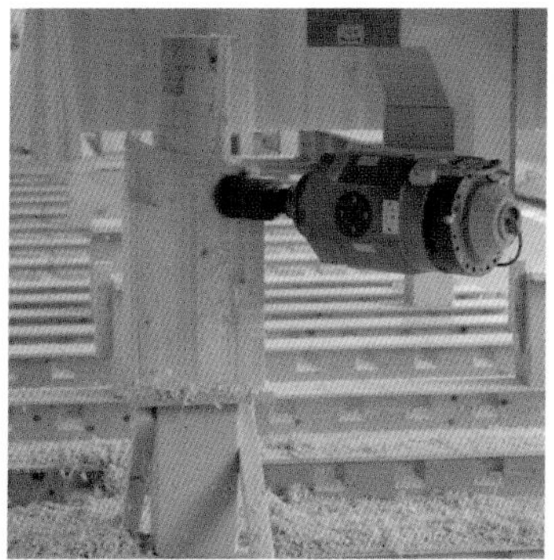

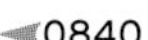0840

Water stagnates and flows and varies according to the seasons. Ice flows and freezes. In this structure, ice façades freeze and melt, forming a pond in front of the building.

0837

The winter climate has been highlighted through the use of artificial snow (17,657 cubic ft [500 cubic m]).

0839

The project was constructed using CNC machine processing, five blades, 100 percent wood (70,630 cubic ft [2,000 cubic m] and 1000 trees) and reassembling the 180 prefabricated pieces on site.

RAU

KNSM-Laan 65
1019 Amsterdam, The Netherlands
P.: (+31) 20-419-02-02
www.rau.eu

0841

Footprint

Use urban infrastructure as building ground. In many cities, infrastructure, such as railways and roads constitutes an unnatural and almost unbridgeable pit in urban development. The efficient use of sparse inner city space plays a key role in the way these areas are experienced. Green Office 2015 mixes and stacks functions, thus affording a sevenfold activation of a single footprint. This project is a flexible building that is capable of fulfilling various functions over the years.

0842

Color

Light can only be seen as color, and color only exists through light. For this project, sunshades and colors are combined in order to emphasize color in all its facets.

0843

Mimicry

Translate nature's designs into buildings. The Institute for Movement Sciences is interpreted as a gesture of frozen movement. Like muscles wrapped around joints and bones, the golden, double-curved aluminum skin flows around the body of the building in a continuous line. The structure was designed in co-operation with a ship builder.

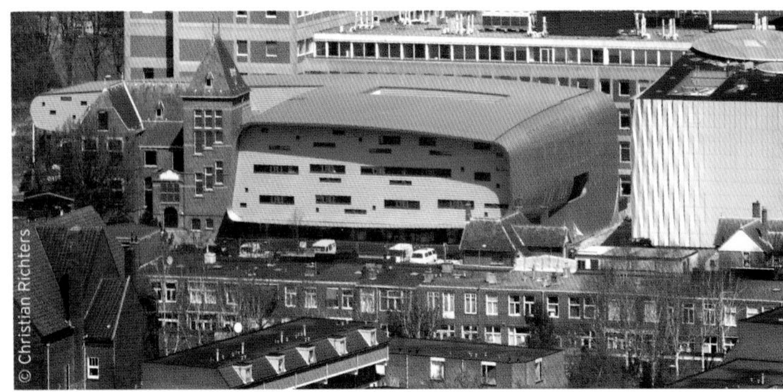

© Christian Richters

© Christian Richters

0844

Reception

Treat pupils as future prime ministers. The staircase leading to the Piter Jelles YnSicht school's main entrance is painted red. By rolling out this red carpet, pupils are given a feeling of importance. This helps to stimulate social integration and a feeling of acceptance among pupils.

0845

Preservation

Relate to historic surroundings. This school is located at an important junction on a former brown site that is currently being redeveloped into a residential area. Since the 19th century, industry of the area has grown in regional importance mainly due to its positioning in key transport axes, like the River Ijssel, roads, and railway lines. While the infrastructure might change during the redevelopment, the historic traffic network will be preserved in the façade of the school.

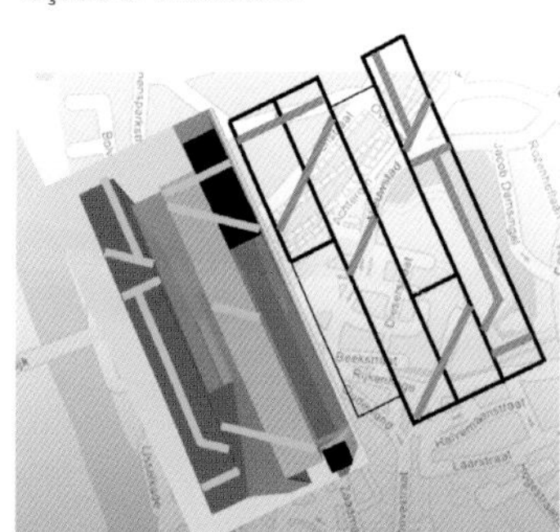

0846

Density

At Community College Leiden stacking building volumes, like stacking boxes on tables, frees up outdoor space for squares and parks. This "vertical city" brings pupils, teachers, and visitors closer together. A series of interior courtyards amid the classrooms, library, gym, and shops, serve as market-like platforms where individual paths intersect. The density of the design thus creates a variety of indoor and outdoor meeting spaces.

0847

Security

Situated between anonymous housing estates, the school's old building had become unfit for use due to repeated vandalism. In order to stimulate intimacy, the new building was designed in a more protective manner. Threefold structuring principles are reflected in three basic colors, three spatial orientations and three building materials. The rolled up building floats above a glass pediment floor, and embodies the linguistic metaphor of a cocoon that shields itself against hostile surroundings. Inside, a process of growth takes place that, through intellectual and practical education, resembles the transformation of a caterpillar into a butterfly. The multicolored glass sidewalls evoke the beautiful colors of a butterfly that unfolds from its cocoon.

0848

H2O

The fuel cell was invented in the 19th century, but wider commercial use of the technology has begun only in recent years. In the H2Otel, cutting edge water-driven technology is used for heating, cooling, cooking, and generating electrical power. The building is CO_2 neutral and entirely self-sufficient. Drinking water consumption is reduced by reusing gray water in the heating/cooling-circuits before flushing toilets, using the swimming pool as a heat storage mechanism, and irrigating with rainwater.

© Christian Richters

0849

Kinetic energy

Visitors to the Natuurcafé La Porte café generate the energy needed to make their cup of coffee by entering through the world's first energy-generating revolving door.

© Boon Edam

0850

Reincarnation

Recognize the value of existing structures. The concrete skeleton of an abandoned 1950s agricultural laboratory served as a valuable starting point. Through combining energy efficient technologies with natural materials—such as clay, wood, reused bricks, and other recycled materials—the WWF Netherlands complex was transformed into a CO_2 neutral, self-sufficient office building.

© Kusters fotografie

querkraft architekten zt gmbh

© Hertha Hurnaus

dunkl, erhartt, sapp (and zinner–2004)
mariahilfer strasse 51
1060 Vienna, Austria
P.: (+43) 1-548-7711
www.querkraft.at

0851

Never try to carry out a task without first challenging it. We were asked for a spectacular building but now the biggest part is hidden. The elongated structure became an icon while building and operating costs were minimized.

© Hertha Hurnaus

0852

When the site is extremely small, try floating your building. This house cantilevers over two thirds of its volume, providing a wonderful space to play table tennis underneath a protective shelter.

© Lisa Rastl

0853

To make an economical façade, try this: we called numerous glazing companies and asked for reject glass panels. One manufacturer sold us 58 double-glazed panels that had been duplicated in the production run by mistake. For the cost of cardboard we bought a fully glazed façade.

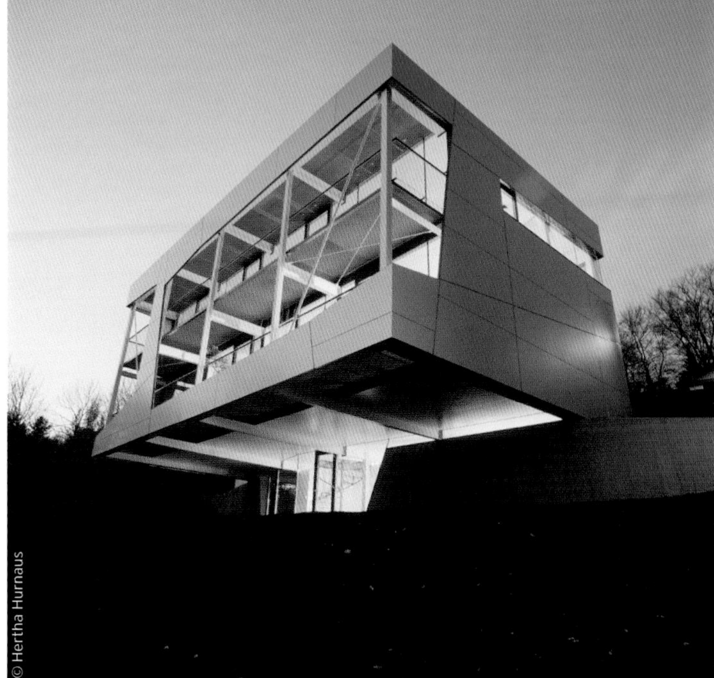
© Hertha Hurnaus

0854

Do not feel frustrated when your project is used by its end-users. Feel happy because this is what it was built for.

© Patrizia Gapp

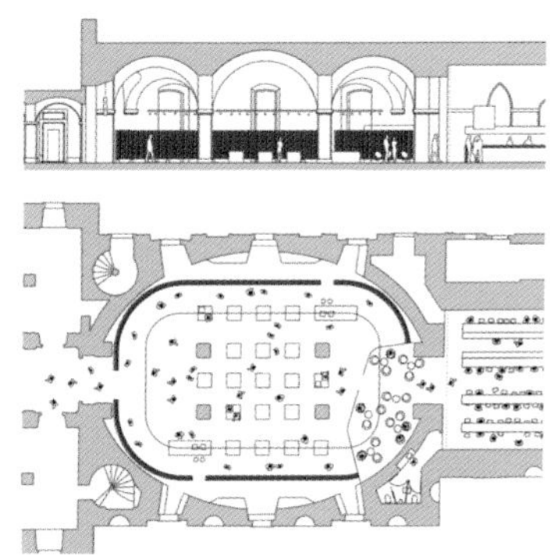

◄0855

Present the same project again with a better line of argument if you are truly convinced of your idea. We won a two-stage competition for a bookstore in a listed historic hall despite the fact that two weeks earlier the jury told us that our idea was absolutely unbearable.

© Manfred Seidl

◄0856

If you wear a t-shirt with the slogan "nothing is impossible" for the key presentation, a client who asks again and again for a suspended ceiling might be persuaded against it if you tell them about the beauty of exposing a Harley Davidson engine block.

0857►

Never act against your ideals. A client wanted a detached office, just for himself, on the top of his premises. As this demonstrates excessive hierarchy we refused this feature, offering instead a smart office annex at the side of the building on the same level with his staff.

© Hertha Hurnaus

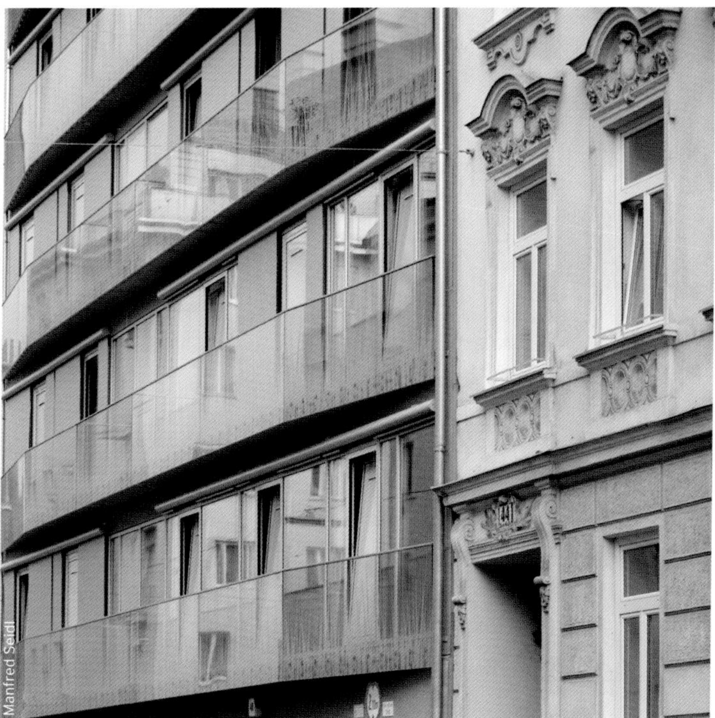

© Manfred Seidl

0858►

Why not open up elements of the building that were enclosed obeying the physics of construction? As a result, the whole exterior wall can become transparent.

◄0859

If regulations prohibit balconies, ask if decorative elements as featured on neighboring buildings are allowed. When the answer is yes, ask if an ornament can have a railing. You might eventually win a small balcony for your building.

© Manfred Seidl

Paolo Bürgi

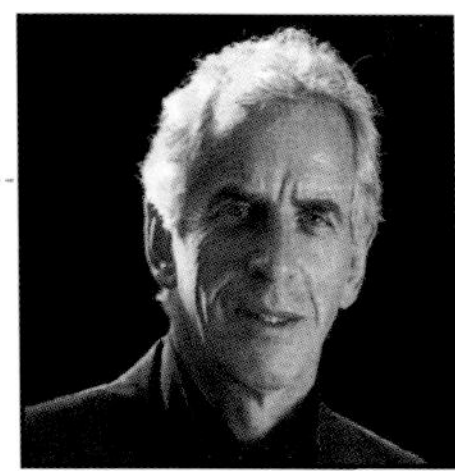

6528 Camorino, Switzerland
P.: (+41) 91-857-27-29
www.burgi.ch

0860

High above on Cimetta-Cardada, the geological observatory enters into a dialogue with the horizon, inviting visitors to approach the hidden dimensions of geological times. Past and present intermingle from this mountain-top view.

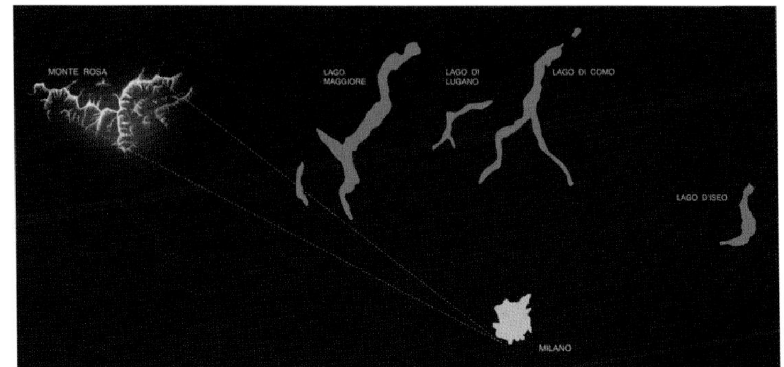

0861

On the Cardada promontory, suspended over a unique panorama of woods and lakes, the observer enters into a relationship with the surrounding landscape. Chronological scales play an important role while pictograms inset in the floor show the development of life on earth. These backgrounds provoke thoughts about the caducity of human existence.

0862

Through a shortened perspective, the Monte Rosa Massif is integrated in the skyline view of this Memory Park close to Milan, and becomes a central element in the landscape composition: a new scenery evolves. The appearance of this mountain towering in the distance can give a feeling of reassurance or temporary rest.

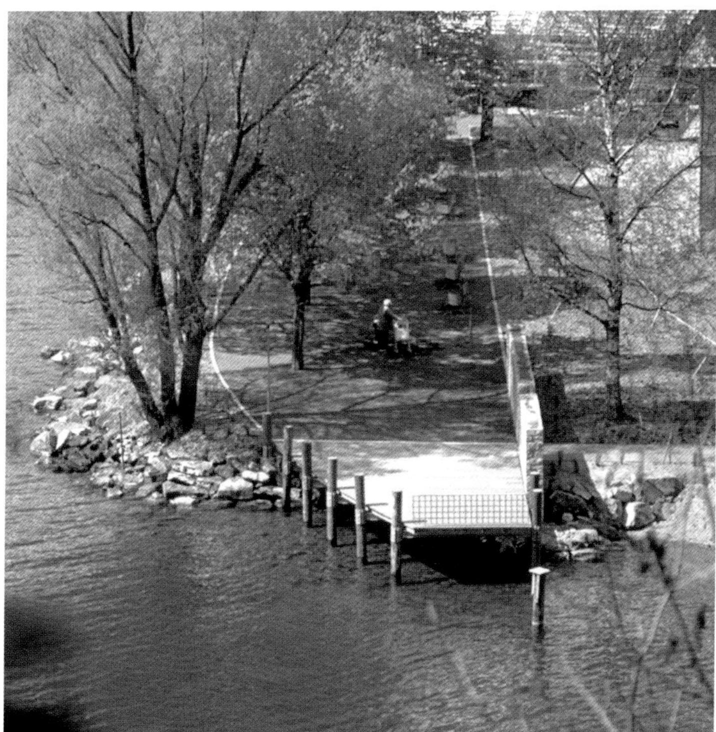

◄0863

The tracks and movements on the Lake Vierwaldstaettersee are visually connected to the historical Axenstrasse situated overhead, a symbolic image of the village of Sisikon. As you walk under the leafy canopies of a line of trees, this dialogue is unexpectedly revealed, arousing your curiosity.

0864▼

The harbor plaza project in Kreuzlingen represents the connection of a city, as a landscape of works, and the lake, as a platform where visitors may arrive. The spectator, sitting on concrete seats, close to the water's edge and looking to the lake horizon, becomes an active observer, experiencing the fascination of this context of transitions.

0865►

This project relates indigenous vegetation to art, living organisms to architecture, and the infinitive to the definitive. A window in a courtyard wall frames natural elements in a cultural and typically Cypriot landscape, contrasting the expressive forms of the cactus in a precise rectangular shape thereby connecting the observer to the landscape.

0866

This small terrace floats over the boundaries between a garden and a wild forest, entering into it with a respectful gesture. Approaching the wilderness this way allows the observer to partake in a strong conversation with the environment, without intervening in it. This enables a direct encounter with nature and the experience of being amongst it.

0867

A slightly curved bamboo path running along the border of a garden allows visitors to become immersed in dense vegetation, leading them on to an end point that takes some of them by surprise: a lookout boasting spectacular views across a deep, inaccessible, and unexpected ravine.

0868

The hidden ichthyic fauna living in Lake Maggiore, just below the terrace is themed in this private garden by means of engravings in the stone pavement surrounding the swimming pool. This echo emphasizes the identity of the location and creates an interrelation on many levels with the nearby lake.

0869

The idea for this campus in Lugano originates from the observation of how, after finishing their studies in the University, the students will spread their knowledge and know-how around the world, like seeds scattered by the wind, floating on water, sticking to fur, or flying with birds. . .until one day they finally grow and become a new generation of plants (or know-how) somewhere else in the world.

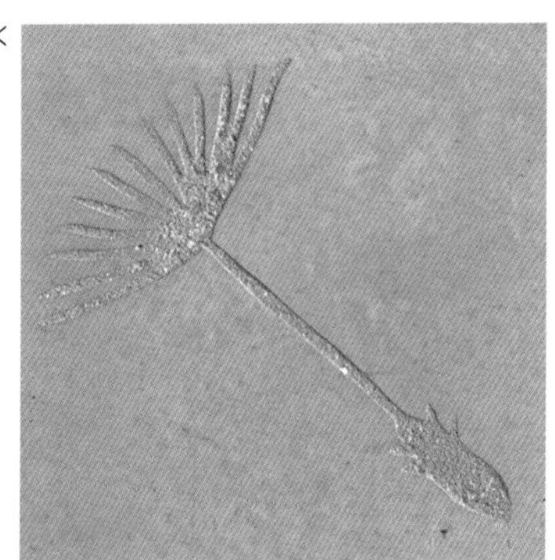

Drozdov & Partners

31 Darwin Str., office 1
Kharkov 61002, Ukraine
P.: (+380) 57-758-76-90
www.drozdov-partners.com

◄0870

The new building facilitates the client's business activity and philanthropic programs by means of a new concert venue on the open street front terraces and a public courtyard for hosting sculpture exhibitions.

© Andrey Avdeenko

0871►

Energy efficiency principles can become a key architectural feature in the building. This was the case for this office center with an auto supermarket.

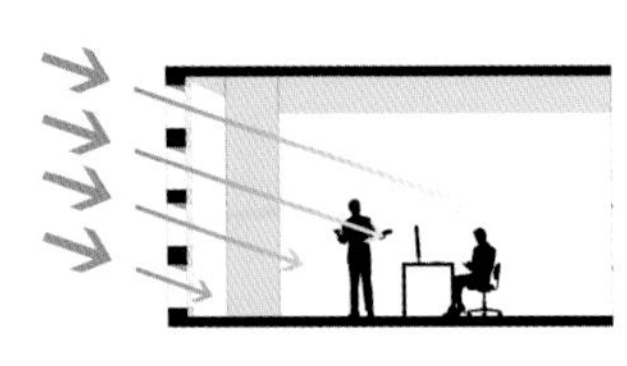

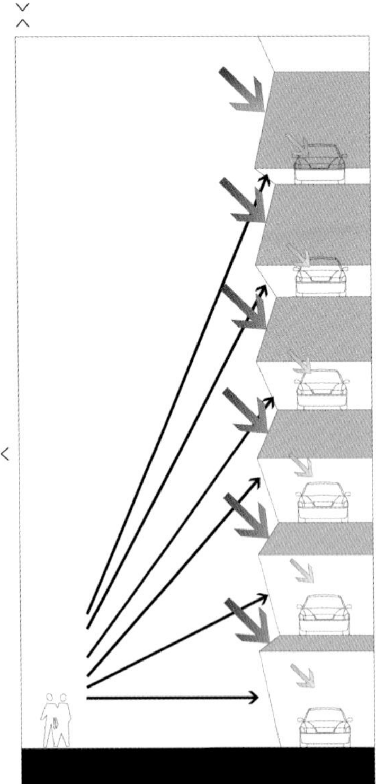

© Igor Lyalyuk

0872▲

Despite the client's apprehensions, the loose border between the interior and exterior on the intersection of two busy pedestrian flows leads to total visitor satisfaction.

◄0873

The dialogue between the horizontal "bridges" and the vertical lines of trees introduces a new spatial perception of the park.

0874

Using landscape dialogue rather than architectural language can lead to surprising results.

0875

The visual proximity of the sea is enhanced by the two mirror-like swimming pools—inside and outside the house—that are interconnected via a lock gate in summer.

0876

Each story of the house is marked with a narrow strip of glazing that provides 360-degree openness of the interior space. After a bit of practice, you can tell the time by the angle of the sun's rays penetrating into the house.

0877

The combination of stone terraces and volumes unifies the garden and house in a single structure, accentuating the dynamic terrain.

0878

The internal space of the house is organized around a patio in the winter garden, with all the lines of vision between different zones passing through it.

0879

The tower-volume implanted within the atrium forms the core of the building and culminates in a roof garden. It plays a number of roles: enriching the interior space of the trading floors and creating a piece of nature to marvel at from the offices on the upper floors.

ONL [Oosterhuis_Lénárd]

From Personal Universe towards Customized Building Body
© 10 Tips from Kas Oosterhuis/ONL [Oosterhuis_Lénárd]

Essenburgsingel 94c
3022 Rotterdam, The Netherlands
P.: (+31) 10-244-70-39
www.oosterhuis.nl

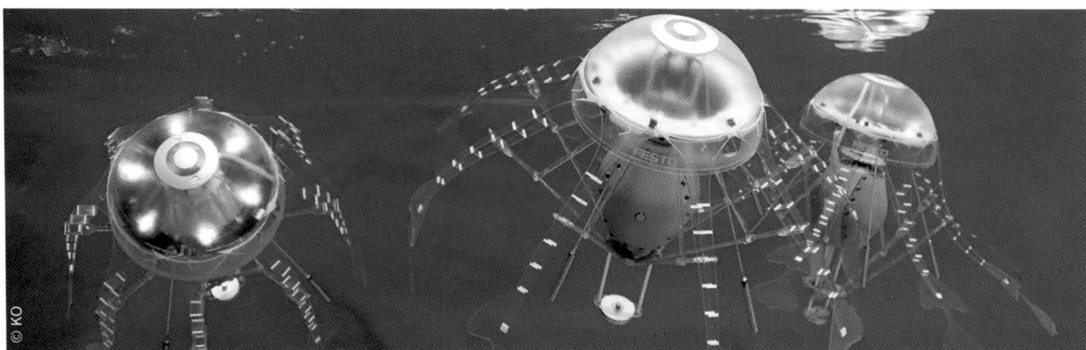
© KO

0880

Define Internal Drive
Impose an internal drive in your Personal Universe. Inform the individual Points with a simple behavior. Write scripts to enable them to communicate with their neighbors. Let them execute the behavioral program and follow their genetic instinct. Let the members of the Point Cloud swarm interact to configure your unique architectural concept. Let them work for you, let them play your game, but take care that they play by the rules. Architecture is a rule-based game.

0881

Shape your Building Body
A set of Powerlines organize the positions of the main nodal points of the structure, like birds on a wire, representing a special configuration of the swarm. Typically we advise you use Powerlines as folds in your Building Body. The most simple form to create the fold is to span the linear surfaces between the Powerlines. But we often use more complex outwardly bulging double curved surfaces. Look at a car's bodywork design in order to understand the communicative power of the Powerlines. Traffic jams will never again be boring.

© ONL - KO

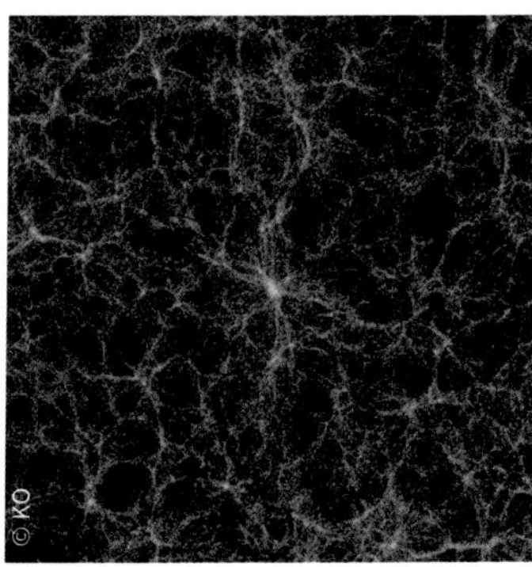
© KO

0883

Start with a Point Cloud

Start by imagining your Personal Universe of free-floating immaterial dots in endless space. The immaterial points of the Point Cloud form your basic design material. Your brain will make connections between the points. Some of these connections will be strong, whereas others will be connected by weak forces. Some will form tight clusters, others will be much more loosely related. Everything is constructed from this endless, shapeless, meaningless, and dimensionless Personal Universe. It contains all the necessary substance for the imagination and evolution of conceptual ideas.

0882

Create Powerlines

Place attractors and repellents in and around your swarm of behavioral points. These attractors/repellents can be points, splines, or surfaces. We call the linear attractors Powerlines. The attractors attract the points of the Point Cloud to populate the lines or surfaces. These points can be further used to form the nodes of a tessellation, for the structure or for the skin, or both. Repellents can chase away points in order to clear the space from points, leaving room for maneuvering between the swarm of points. These areas can be later used as functional space, for linear spaces (passages) and enclosed spaces (rooms).

0884

Define External Forces

Each Point Cloud is a temporary and local densification related to other Point Clouds or Universes. For each new design project your Personal Universe is affected by external forces, redirecting the size, position, shape, and meaning of the points in the Point Cloud. The External Forces represent the climatic and physical context in which your Personal Universe is embedded. The interaction between external and internal forces acting on the swarm of points in the Point Cloud forms the basis for the evolution of the architectural concept.

© KO

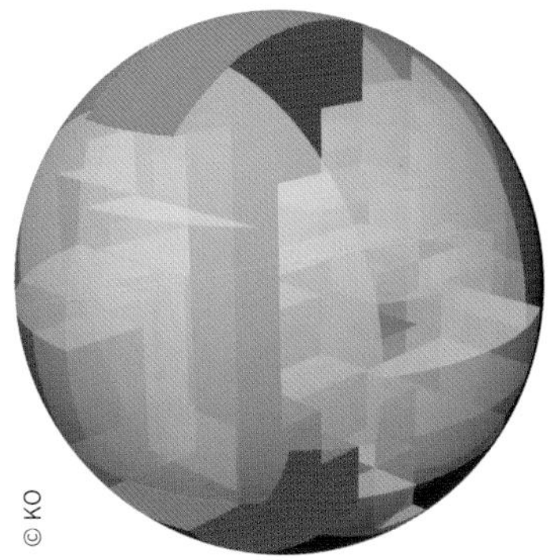

0885

Specify Body Parts

Each Body Plan evolves through a process called specification. Certain parts of the Building Body specialize to be the structure, other parts specialize to be the skin, again others the internal empty spaces, others become the arteries/MEP installations. There is a specific instruction in the evolution of the genes for the Body Plan for each of those functions. At the same time all points/cells of the system continually communicate as members in a swarm. They become members of a specialized sub-swarm.

0886

Develop Parametric Detail

Develop each specialized swarm of nodes of the structure or the internal or external skin, either enveloping spaces or enclosing gas, water, electricity, or air systems, with parametric detail. Make all details one big family, where all family members share the same detail in principle, but with local and temporal differences. They share the same formula, but have point-to-point changing parameter values. Aim at limiting the number of different parametric details; try to integrate as many details into one complex system of Parametric Detail. One building, one detail.

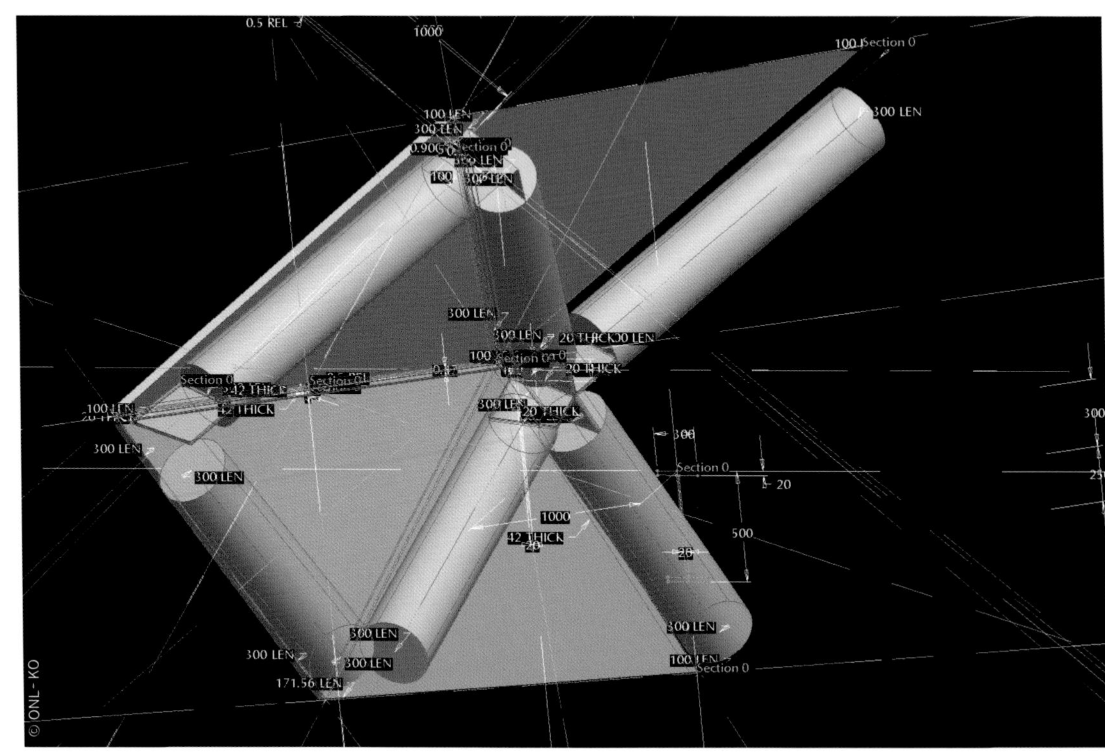

0887

Build your personal BIM
Build your personal Building Information Model. Do not import doors and windows and such from a library. Develop your own library. Reinvent all parametric details from scratch, based on the availability of basic materials. Create your own added value to the basic materials, do not accept added value as an element created by others. Create your own component-building families and inform them with great exactness. Your personal BIM labels should have, in painstakingly precise detail, the information needed to build your design. You must communicate this information directly with the manufacturer, not the contractor.

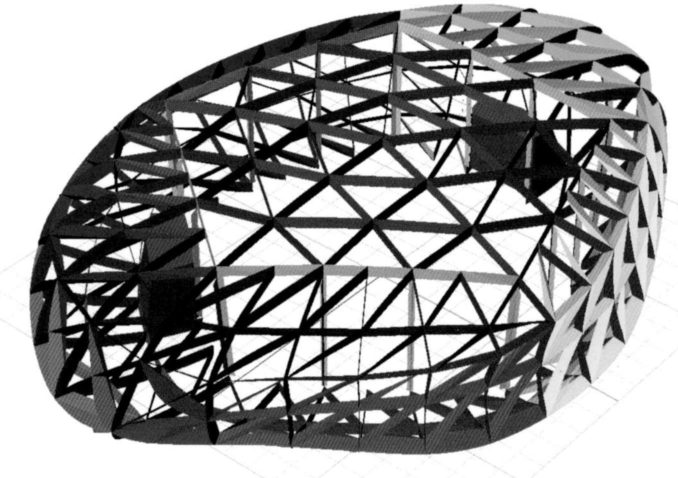

© ONL - KO

© KO

0888

Assemble the Body Parts
Finally, customize your Body Parts in order to complete the three-dimensional puzzle of your Building Body. Assemble them following the principle of dry construction, perhaps using bolts, or even assembling your structure without them. Prepare your components to avoid the need for local on-site adjustments. Do not use molds, scaffolding or other temporary support structures. Build your building only once. Make sure it can be dismantled after its purpose has been fulfilled. Design your personal building components to be recyclable or to be used as basic material for other designs. Think C2C.

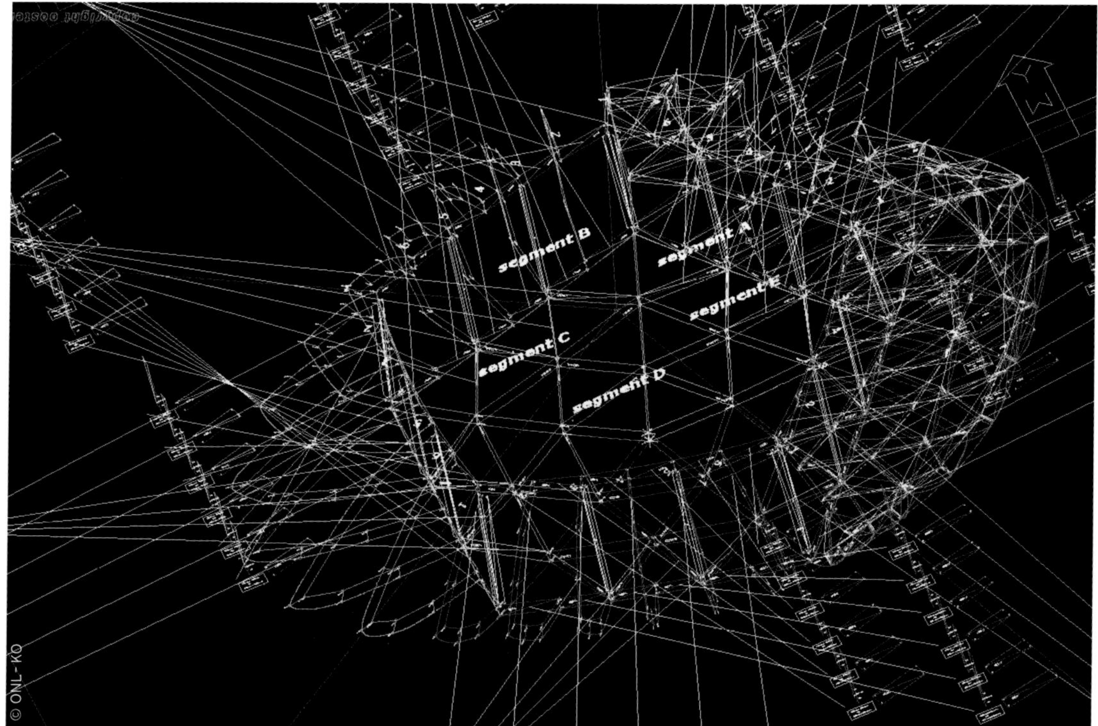

© ONL - KO

0889

Write scripts for CNC Fabrication
To ensure a direct relation between your BIM and the actual manufacturing, you must write your own scripts to link your machine to their machine, this is called machine to machine (M2M) communication and file to factory (F2F) manufacturing. Design components to be produced only by CNC (computer numerical control) machines. Avoid bypasses, but make sure the manufacturer imports your data directly, without rebuilding three-dimensional models and rewriting scripts. Talk with the manufacturers and prepare your data in such a way that it can be used unconditionally.

Ofis Arhitekti

Kongresni trg 3
1000 Ljubljana, Slovenia
P.: (+386) 1-426-0085/426-0084
www.ofis-a.si

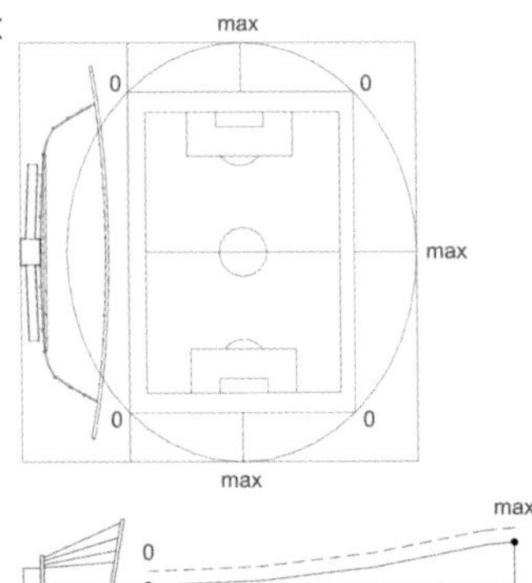

◄0890

Use relevant concepts

This is what we did for this football stadium extension. The visibility diagram (best views in most seats) also becomes a formal design concept.

0891►

Use traditional local typography elements

0892

Use a low budget to your advantage
Complete the missing façade by filling 30% of it with cut-outs of the new skin.

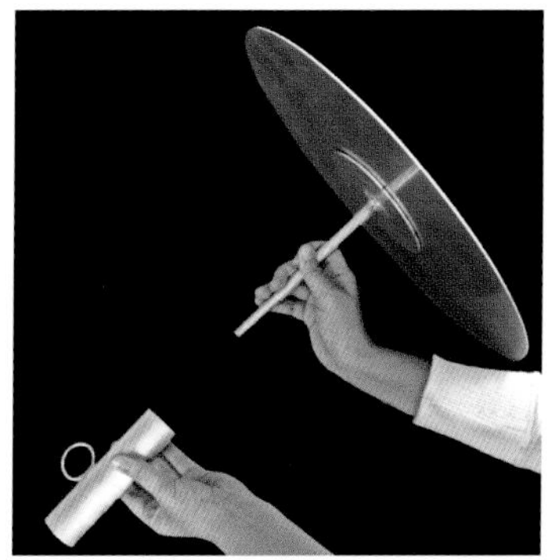

0893

Use logical solutions in the design process
For this museum extension, the visitors' walkway becomes a structural element through the building.

0894

Use the way nature builds as inspiration for a social apartment environment

© Tomaz Gregoric

0895

Take your inspiration from everywhere. A leaflet from the street becomes the front elevation of 650 apartments.

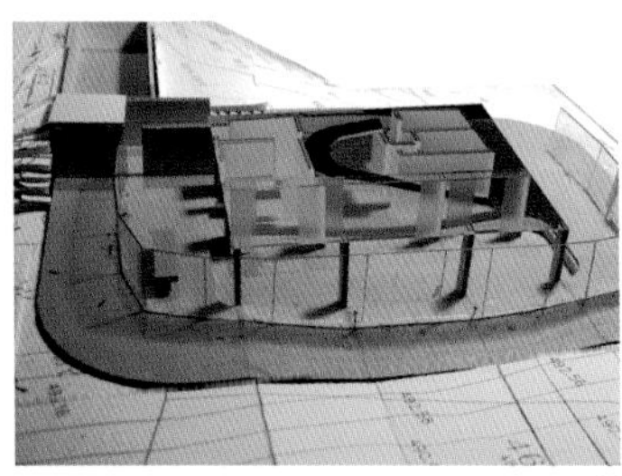

0896

Use the specific topography of a site to your advantage This extension was made underneath the existing villa.

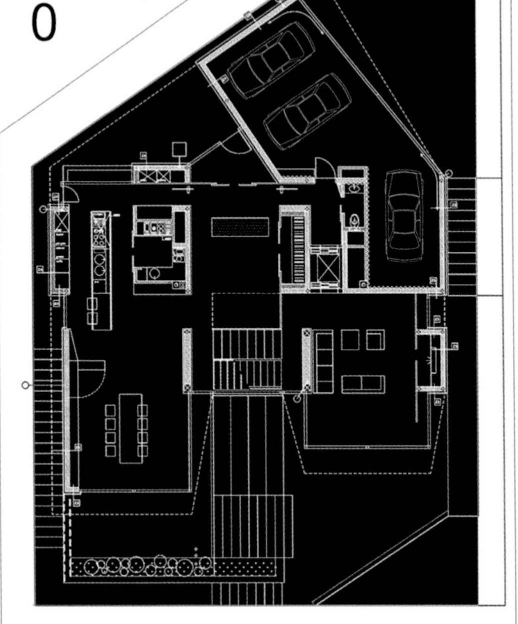

Offset 4 m the plot border

0897

Use a given lot to create a new form A 13-ft (4-meter) offset from the site border becomes a plan and a new shape for the house.

Next:

Level: 4

Lines: 11
-1

Left arrow-move left
Right arrow-move right
Down arrow-drop fast
Up arrow-instant drop
Spacebar, X-rotate right
Z-rotate left

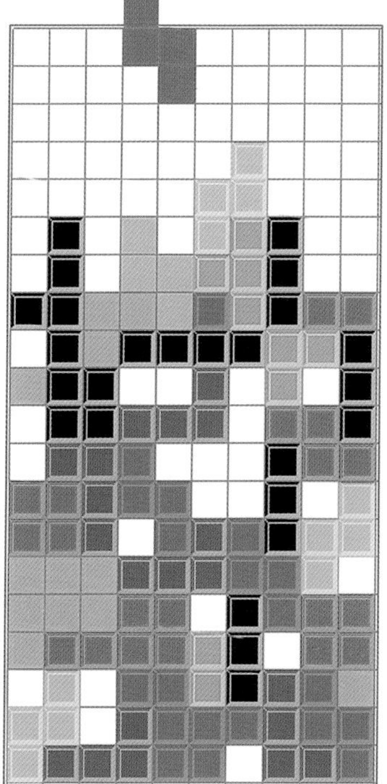

0899

Use associations
For example, from your favorite game.

0898

Use existing space as a resource.
The roof of this mall creates an ideal location to site a new building.

Mokhtar MIMOUN

Rue Goethe, residence Jade 5
Tangier, Morocco
P.: (+212) 539-93-52-66/539-32-24-74
www.mimoun.com

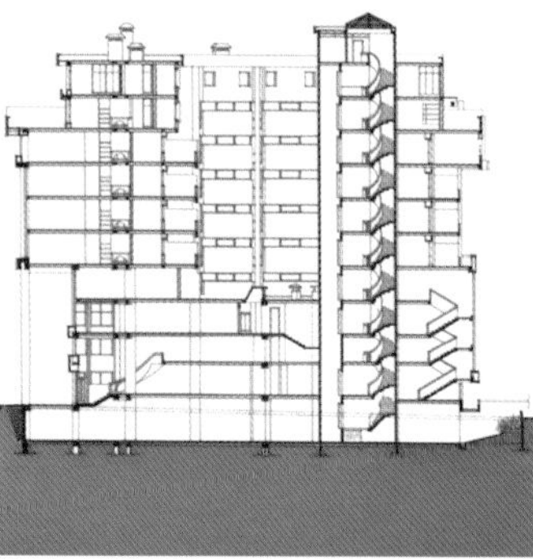

0900
This section shows how different activities are organized into "layers," grouping together the floors.

0901
The opposite side of this building is mainly residential and unified though symmetry and scale.

0902
In this nine-story multifunctional building, the commercial, business, and residential activities are given specific design treatment. Doing this introduces a scale quite different from the story scale. Unity is kept by the curved floor design and the structural elements.

0903
In this project, every shape shows its use through primary volumes but there is also a hierarchy that we can refer to as "mother to child" between the larger building that houses the communications hardware and the smaller one that is used for power supply.

◄0904

This Health Center was built on the site of a former Spanish colonial residence that architecturally was not worth preserving. The new building fits between ancient trees that were conserved and evokes colonial architecture using contemporary vocabulary.

0905▲

This residential building finds its unity in the way every story is exposed regardless of the topography. Balconies and large glazed windows are designed in the same horizontal stripe that gives unity to the whole, regardless of the site characteristics.

0906►

This project uses the ancient Roman and Arabs technique of placing water flows inside family houses to provide natural cooling on hot summer days.

0907►

Different shapes are a reflection of different uses.

In this project we have bathrooms and toilets. The natural red tiles protecting these humid rooms are an evocation of natural spaces.

◄0908

In the process of renovating the ancient Dar Boukhari in the Kasbah Museum of Tangier we followed the rules of modern archeological restoration. Instead of replacing an ancient and valuable, but damaged, mosaic star pattern in a patio floor, we chose to protect the original pattern with a layer of sand and make an exact replica over the original. This way, historic strata are preserved for future generations.

◄0909

This glazed door uses a modern pattern inspired by ancient tiling.

Nabil Gholam

15 Nasra Street, Beydoun building, 5th Floor
Achrafieh 2062 5303, Beirut, Lebanon
P.: (+961) 1-219-037
www.ngarchitecture.com

Montserrat 64
08950 Esplugues del Llobregat
Barcelona, Spain
P.: (+34) 933-72-26-60

© Pascal Vacher

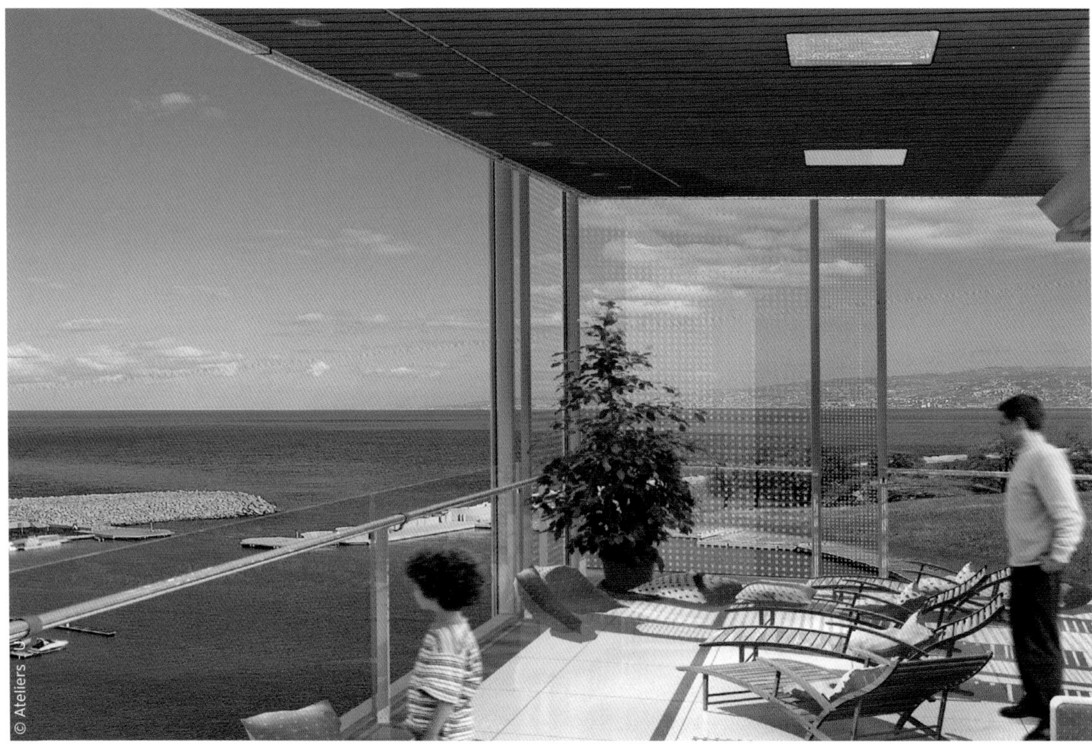

© Ateliers 7/J

◄0910

The Platinum Tower was commissioned to be the most exclusive building on the Beirut coast seafront; an area that is fast becoming a collection of uneven large-scale architectural gestures contrasting against the cluttered backdrop of the city. With a geometry of four stacked cubes to create a 537-ft-high (164 m) tower, the tower offers a sober, poised formal solution to the problem of a luxury high-rise building in an urban context marked by excess.

0911▲

A closer look at this all glass luxury high-rise building reveals a revisited setting for a Mediterranean lifestyle at its simplest. Large loggia-like urban balconies overlooking the sea are reminiscent of large outdoor Levantine living rooms, screened from the sun and protected from the wind through partial enclosures of frit glass.

Nabil Gholam with Ricardo Bofill Taller of Arquitectura.

0912

Along with the usage of local stone from the site, the house is topped with a series of green roofs, blending it even more into its green backdrop. The rainwater collected throughout is recycled for irrigation and feeds the ponds that are located at different levels in the house.

© ngap

0913

The layout of this high-density chalet compound raised the challenge of dealing with a substantial project mass in a natural setting. To camouflage part of the large volumes, we borrowed the ancestral language of local cascading stone terraces to make use of sloping agricultural land. This ashlar rock base, built with masonry walls and construction techniques, houses the night spaces within the solid terraces and smaller openings. The day spaces are houses in wooden volumes scattered over the landscape.

© Richard Saad

© Richard Saad

0914

The aesthetics of managing a series of walls in a natural landscape was developed here in order to define a house on a hilltop 3,930 feet (1,198 m) above sea level with extraordinary vistas. The visitor is presented with a mute succession of stone walls with occasional vertical slits and trees peeking from behind, hinting furtively at the private world beyond. It is a façade that plays hide-and-seek, creating a sense of subtle mystery that enhances the client's desire for discretion while expressing a calm opulence, in addition to providing a safe haven for the family.

© ngap

0915

To emerge safe and to reclaim an icon from the Lebanese civil war, where occupation, torture, and death were a cruel reality, requires plenty of positive vigor and contemplation from both the client and the architect. The nostalgia of the childhood house and its memories of safety and joy led to the respectful preservation of the old shell. Once gutted, it was reinvested by nature and cleansed. The new rusty occupant is then carefully inserted and extended discretely into the forest.

© Richard Saad

0916

The characteristic thick wall houses created by old stone construction techniques were echoed here and revisited to create "intelligent walls." By thickening the masonry shell, space was made against the outer wall to accommodate all the structural and technical networks of the house, freeing the internal spaces that are easily accessible through a second layer of storage spaces facing the interior. (Shelves, closets, etc.). The tapering walls range from 23 to 39 inches (58 to 99 cm) as they rise.

0917

A retractable fabric cover system shades the connecting space between the two wings of the house. This cover provides the flexibility needed in using this inside/outside space almost nine months of the year, diffusing or letting in the desired amounts of sunlight. The fabric opens and closes with the sun. It retracts if strong wind is detected.

© Ateliers - U

© Ateliers - U

0918

Located in quaint traditional district with strict zoning guidelines, the building laws for this lot required a minimum of 60 percent stone coverage on the façade. This contradicted the building program, which was to create spectacular views towards the sea and the old crusader castle opposite. Bringing together both these aspects, the solution was to introduce massive stone stacked panels on the façade in tune with the historical, prevalent surrounding materials, but louvered to maintain maximum transparency of views. This allowed light and air where one expects to find massive concrete and stone walls.

Nabil Gholam with VVD.

0919

The logic of the outdoor fabric covers can be repeated inside, where, mounted on tensed stainless steel cables, they serve many purposes in an office space. They are excellent light diffusers for working environments and they dampen down the reflected sound or noise generated by a multitude of users in a high ceiling space. This economical solution, with its soft light, very low maintenance, and easy access, ensures a unified and elegant appearance.

© Richard Saad

0920

Located in the extremely hot environment of Doha Qatar, a comfortable climate in this state-of-the-art mall, called Doha Souks, is achieved through a sustainable system combining façade shielding, artificial air conditioning, and a natural passive system relying on radiant cooling and air stratification. Water walls flanking lush greenery facilitate vaporization and condensation, and carefully placed openings channel the strong southern winds into the mall, and help preserve a layer of cooler air close to the level of the shoppers. Humidity can be condensed over the inner gardens into an indoor rain shower over the landscaped atrium.

© ngap

© ngap

ARX Portugal Arquitectos

Largo de Santos, 4-1
1200-808 Lisbon, Portugal
P.: (+351) 21-391-8110
www.arx.pt

0921
Have a concept

©João Simões, ARX Portugal

©João Simões, ARX Portugal

©João Simões, ARX Portugal

0922
Live your time

© FG+SG

0923
Global vs local

© FG+SG

0924
Tectonics vs. durability

© FG+SG

0925
Timeless vs. oddity

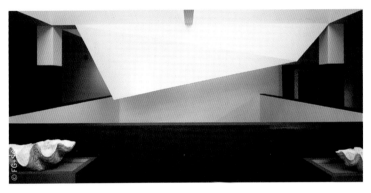

0926
Specificity

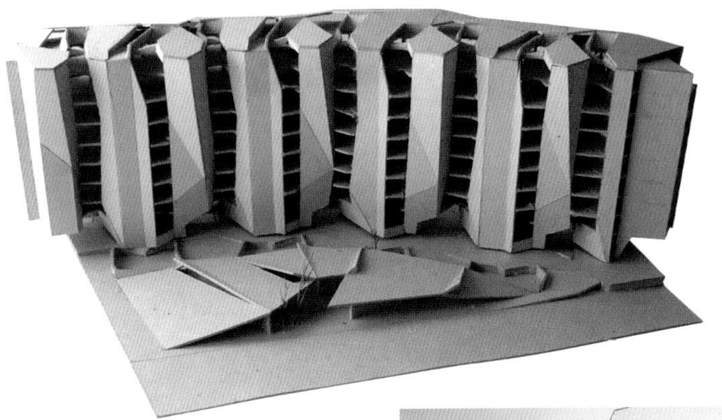

0927
Light

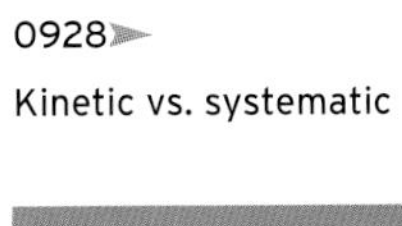

0928
Kinetic vs. systematic

0929
Public presence

0930
Ludic, poetic and critical

Makoto Sei Watanabe

1-23- 30- 2806, Azumabashi, Sumida-ku
Tokyo 130- 0001 Japan
P.: (+81) 3-3829-3221
www.makoto-architect.com

0931

The solution was to "layer" the garden and the interior. A total of five 15-ft-wide (4.5 m) units were arranged in a linear form: two internally and three externally. When the glass screens at the boundaries are all opened, the entire sequence becomes one.

0932

In traditional Japanese houses, the rooms are divided by sliding paper doors called *fusuma* and sliding outer doors are called *shoji*. Traditional western hinged doors are still visible when opened, whereas sliding doors disappear. The difference between "On" and "Off" is unmistakable.

0933

When the screens are all shut, it becomes a five-layer sandwich of interior and exterior with a multitude of possible combinations and layouts. The idea is to enable occupants to enjoy life among these altered spatial variations that can adapt to the different weather conditions and seasons.

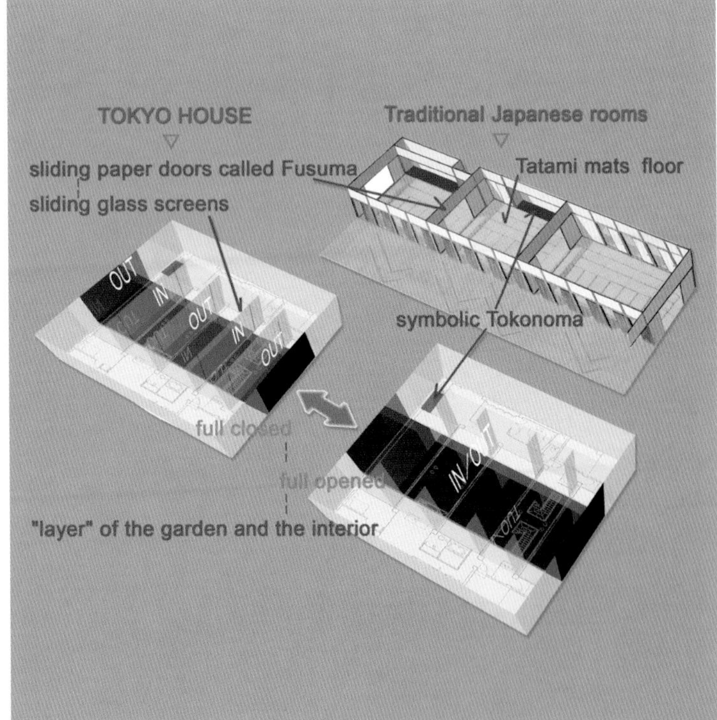

0934

On a snowy evening, reflections from the snow between the rooms will make ceilings glow a pale gold color. I thought that the solution for the commission *A Place to Live* was to provide a place for creativity and discoveries.

0935

On a sunny morning with soft breezes blowing, a completely open space with no distinctions between inside and outside is a pleasant space to enjoy. On a rainy afternoon, the wet stones of the walls fill with light, emulating the surface of a lake.

0936

The walls facing the garden have wave-like patterns in amber colored granite and the wave-like surface has its intended effect when it catches the light. Three types of section shapes were combined. The surface angles were digitally calculated by simulating the light that hits the walls during the summer and winter and checking the reflections produced.

Photo at left: A complete elevation of the wall is laid on the floor to check continuous smoothness of the waved granites. Photo at right: A curved granite before polishing.

0937

The black granite of the *tokonoma* alcove in the Japanese room ripples like the surface of a body of water. This rippling effect was digitally reproduced as the interference generated between the concentric waves of two adjacent circles.

0938

The *tokonoma* is a space found in traditional Japanese rooms. About the size of one *tatami* mat, it has a symbolic function and a history that is said to go back about 600 years. It is normally raised slightly above the level of the *tatami* mats and floored with planks of expensive, carefully selected, and beautifully grained wood. It is forbidden to step on the *tokonoma* floor.

Photo, top right: Pouring water to confirm undulation, in manufacturing stage. Photos at bottom: Every guest wants to touch the surface of *tokonoma*, thinking of it as a surface of water.

0939

The wash stands on the second floor jut out into the void. As you are washing your face, you can see the first floor through the water in the basins. According to one of the second floor residents, this is an interesting experience every morning. When seen from below, drops of water appear to be floating overhead.

0940

The walls around the site are painted with layers of six wave-like patterns in four colors. This was facilitated by a new specially developed Environmental Color Program, forming part of the Induction Design series. The colors must be in harmony with the environment, while also asserting their independence.

Latz + Partner/ Planer BDLA, OAi Lux

Ampertshausen 6
85402 Kranzberg, Germany
P.: (+49) 81-66-67-85-0
www.latzundpartner.de

0941

Recycling
Longevity and recycling of materials are cornerstones of sustainability. The technical solutions to processing rubble, remains, and waste have generated a new aesthetic.

In the Duisburg Nord Landscape Park, concrete, soils, and surface materials were recovered from demolition waste. Recycled sand and chips became robust surfaces which could be vegetated. Even entire elevated catwalks and staircases were reused.

© Atelier 17 · Christa Panick

0942

Water
Water has always been the main attraction of parks. Shortages and high costs demand sensible approaches, such as, for example near-natural cleansing and oxygenation systems. In Duisburg, the concrete bed of the former sewer was transformed into a clean water system with flora and fauna. On its way to the new canal, water from roofs and hard surfaces is cleansed in biotopes located in former cooling ponds, and aerated by wind powered circulation systems.

© Michael Latz

0943

Metamorphosis
Often times design is not the new, dominant, and defining idea, but rather a metamorphosis of the existing. That is to say, the existing conditions are redefined by the reinterpretation of existing layers of information, or the addition of new ones. From the Landscape Park Duisburg Nord we learned that industrial ruins, scrap, or debris can be fascinating structures when changed into the layers of a landscape. The perception of manufacturing waste shifts, in part, from a rational neutrality toward a semantic quality, thanks to new ways of looking at things.

© Michael Latz

© Markus Tollhopf

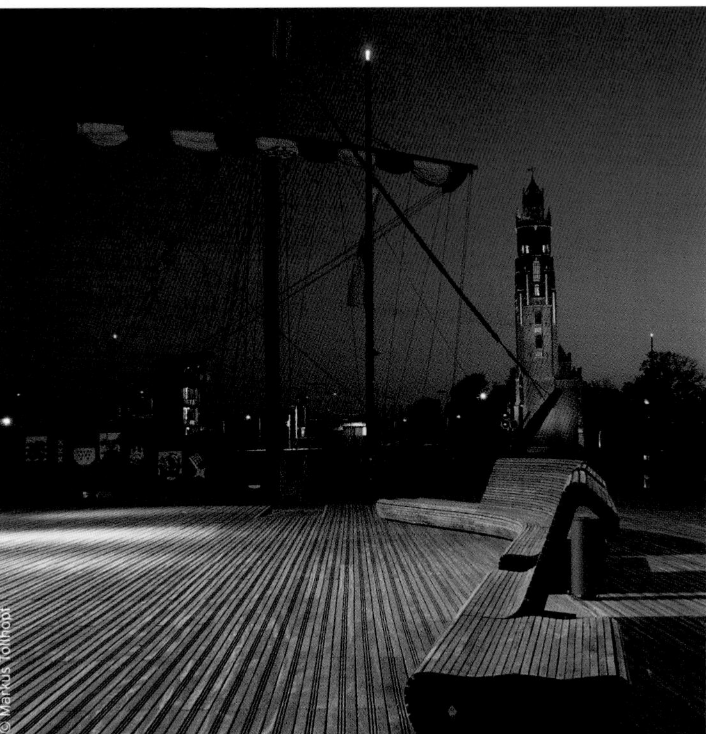
© Markus Tollhopf

0944

Spatial relationships

The aesthetic quality of open spaces often does not only depend on their own introvertive design, but on the connections and relations developed with respect to their context, on the effect that elements of distance have on the space.

In Bremerhaven, a square was situated within the main axis of the town, opening up the perspective and extending the harbor's influence far into the city.

0945

Plants

In landscape architecture, plants can define both form and character. The plant expresses both art and nature. We can choose from an endless wealth of patterns and forms of appearance from the history of garden culture. On the Kirchberg, the structure of the Central Park is created by contrasting plantings and by varying maintenance regimes.

© Michael Latz

© Michael Latz

0946

Materials

Timelessness is a goal of detailing and realizing a project. As open spaces do not develop their idealized state until later, materials must primarily be durable rather than simply exquisite, and show regional expression.

In the Central Park on the Kirchberg in Luxembourg, the walls are constructed of light-colored sandstone from local origin. The tarmac surfaces contain material of the same color.

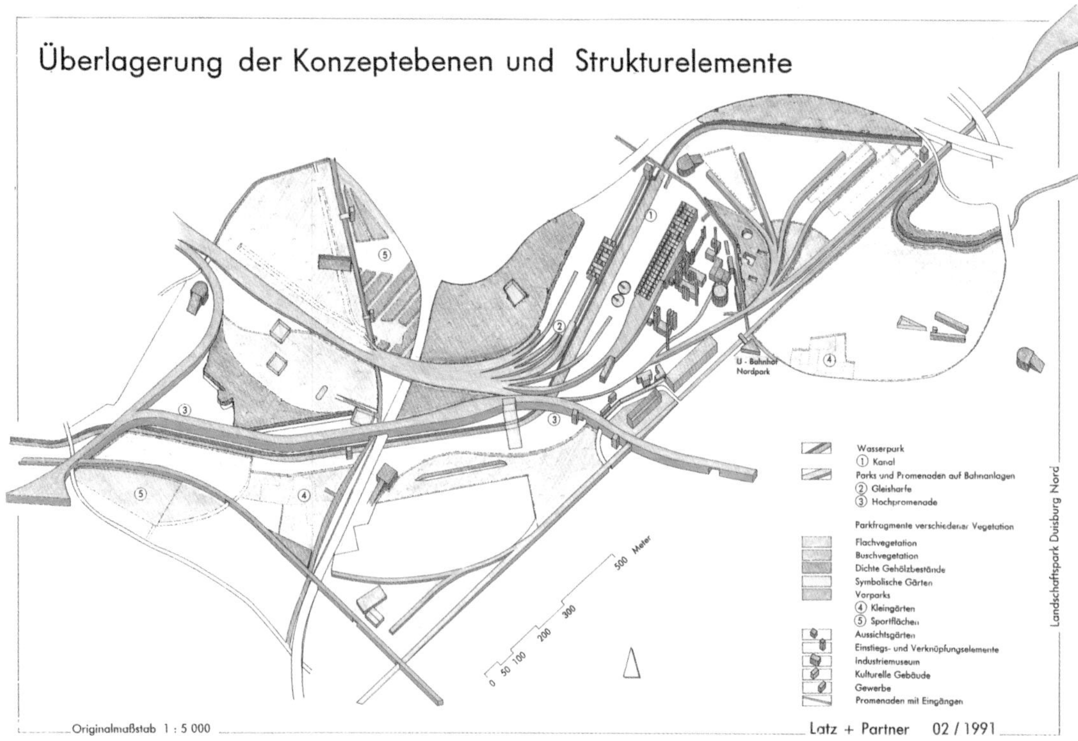

◄0947

Vision concentrated in abstraction
Design can be understood as invention, as an abstract idea that provides the means to define spaces, communication, and layers of information. The structure remains open to further interpretation. In Duisburg, the conceptual design shows individual systems that operate independently and connect only at certain points. The top layer is the railway park, the bottom layer the water park. Other systems are the promenades and the single clumps of vegetation.

0948►

Vision concentrated in the object
Distilled to an icon, objects symbolize spatial and temporal vision. Spiral and turbine-like figures direct the air flow. It directs the mist produced by high-pressure nozzles to form a compact pillow of fog. Being exclusively built with irregularly broken slabs of Jura marble, these figures became the symbol of garden festivals.

0949
Use
The use of a site is not fully defined at the outset of the process, but is an invention of the visitors and changes periodically. Seen in this way, use is a decisive part of public participation. Just opened, Place Square in Brussels, is a hard plaza amidst the densely built Ixelles quarter, and has been adopted by residents.

0950
Participation
Public participation is understood to be part of the design development. As such, it presumes a democratic process that continually evolves in terms of its local and temporal scope. Becoming part of the design process can accelerate innovation. For an entire decade, dozens of clubs and hundreds of individuals invested their time in the Landscape Park Duisburg Nord. While driven by self-interest, all participants took the bigger picture on board, thereby significantly contributing to the overall concept.

URBANUS Architecture & Design

Shenzhen office:
Building E-6, 2nd Floor, OCT LOFT
Nanshan District
Shenzhen 518053, China
P.: (+86) 755-8609-6345
www.urbanus.com.cn

Beijing office:
801/819, Ruichen International Centre
13, Nongzhanguan South Road
Chao Yang District
Beijing 100125, China
P.: (+86) 10-8403-3551

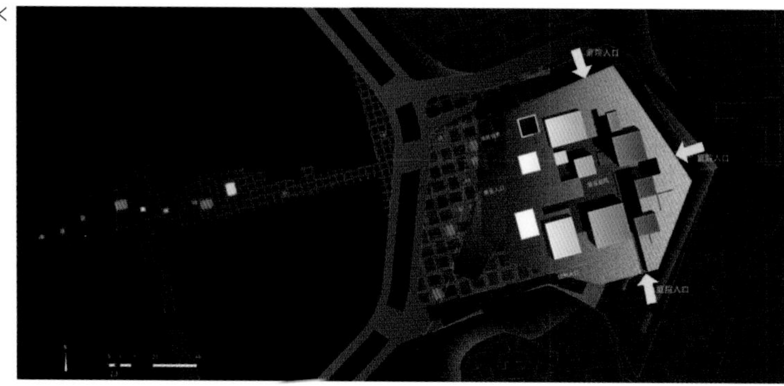

0951

The urban and cultural implications of Dafen Village have long been considered as a strange mix of pop art, bad taste, and commercialism. A typical art museum would be considered out of place in the context of Dafen's peculiar urban culture. The question is whether it can be a breeding ground for contemporary art and also take on the more challenging role of blending with the surrounding urban fabric in terms of spatial connections, art activities, and everyday life. Our strategy for the Dafen Art Museum is to create a hybridized mix of different programs, including art museums, oil painting galleries, shops, commercial spaces, rental workshops, and studios, all under one roof.

0952

The design shows how we changed an old laundry on the main road, between a Spanish-style OCT Hotel and the Hexiangning Gallery, into The OCT Art&Design Gallery.

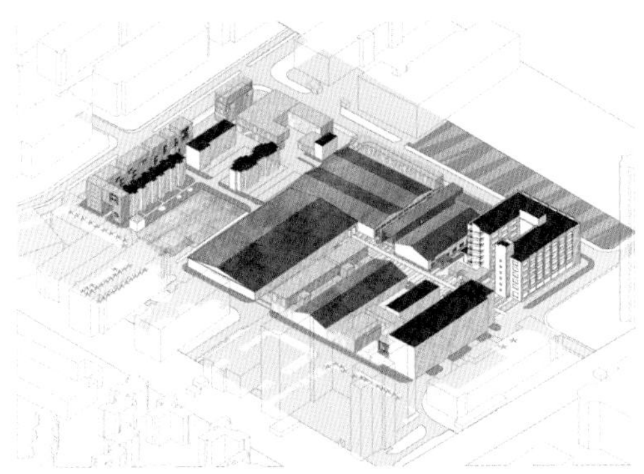

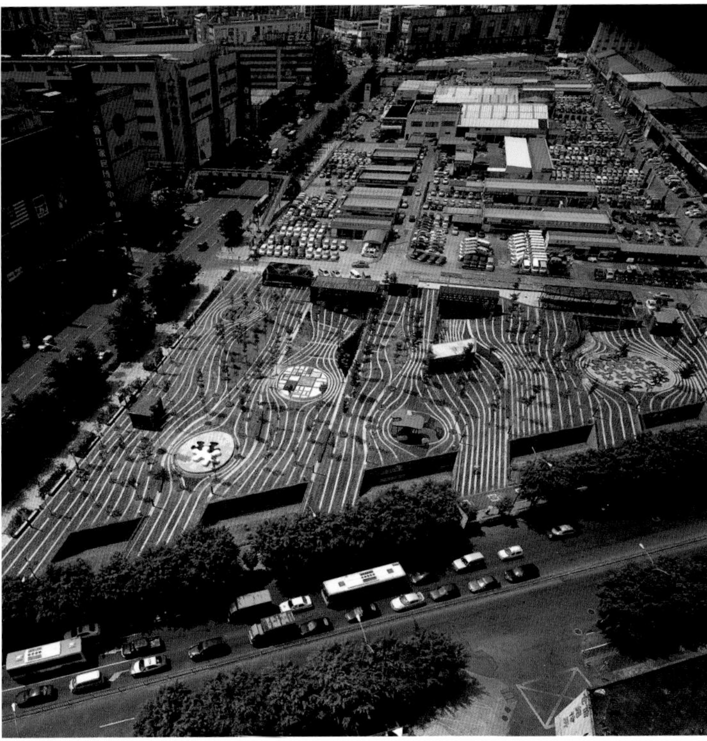

0953

The site contains ten factories, warehouses, and dormitory buildings all built in the early 1980s. The empty lots among these buildings are to be gradually filled up with galleries, bookshops, cafés, bars, art studios, and design shops, along with lofts and dormitories. These new additions fill the gaps and set up new relationships with existing buildings by sprawling, wrapping, and penetrating the existing fabric.

0954

The project returns to fundamental ideas in Chinese living as expressed by the saying "hills outside hills, and gardens inside gardens," an idea referring to a continuous and occasionally repeating rhythm of space and form found in many traditional villages and mountainous landscapes. The relationship between nature and building is blurred in an attempt to create a new kind of urban village.

0955

Inspired by the natural texture of the earth, the whole surface of Sungang Central Plaza is covered with one coherent skin of undulating strips, which resembles the water tides flowing up and down. While shedding the existing underground parking lot, this free-form skin also helps to connect two adjacent lots interrupted by traffic. The linear paving pattern also suggests a strong sense of dynamic urban activities. Along with the flow of the strips, oases of flower islands are randomly arranged to create pleasant and intimate urban enclaves contrasting with the chaotic surrounding urban environment.

0956▲

Traditional *tulou* units are evenly laid out along its perimeter, like modern slab-style dormitory buildings, but with greater opportunities for social interaction. Although this housing type is very suitable for low-income housing, simply copying the form and style of the *tulou* would not be a good solution for the design. However, by learning from the *tulou*, one can help preserve community spirit among low-income families.

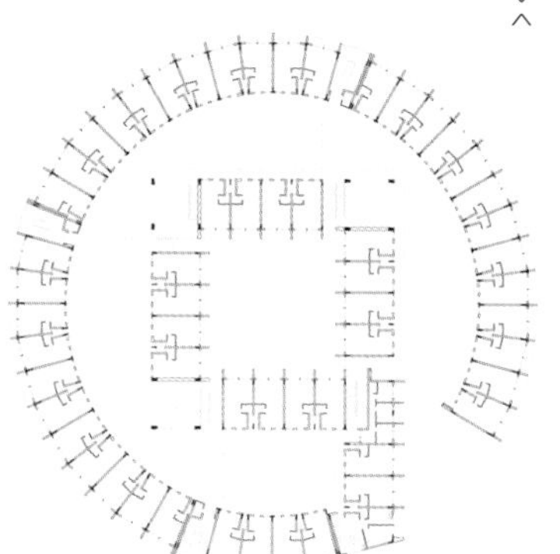

0957▼

The project is built within a 1.3-sq-mile (3.4-sq-km) logistics park. Located at the southeast corner of the container field, the Merchants Maritime and Logistics ltd tower will see construction work in the next ten years. Dust blown by the marine wind continually permeates the area, and large-scale factory buildings, piled-up containers, sling carts, and fast-running cargo trucks all indicate that this is a place for industrial processes. Within this context, the design aims to build the project as an oasis in the desert.

0958▼

A long and narrow site occupies a whole block stretching some 1,000 feet (305 m) along Shennan Avenue, in the city center area. The architect aimed to design a series of continuous buildings along the street, and transform four individual buildings into a unified series of masses that can be identified even from a fast-moving car. Hotel, office, business, apartment, and shopping space are all integrated within the undulating, folding façade. In addition, this belt helps conceal the dirty and chaotic urbanism of a village amid the city to the south.

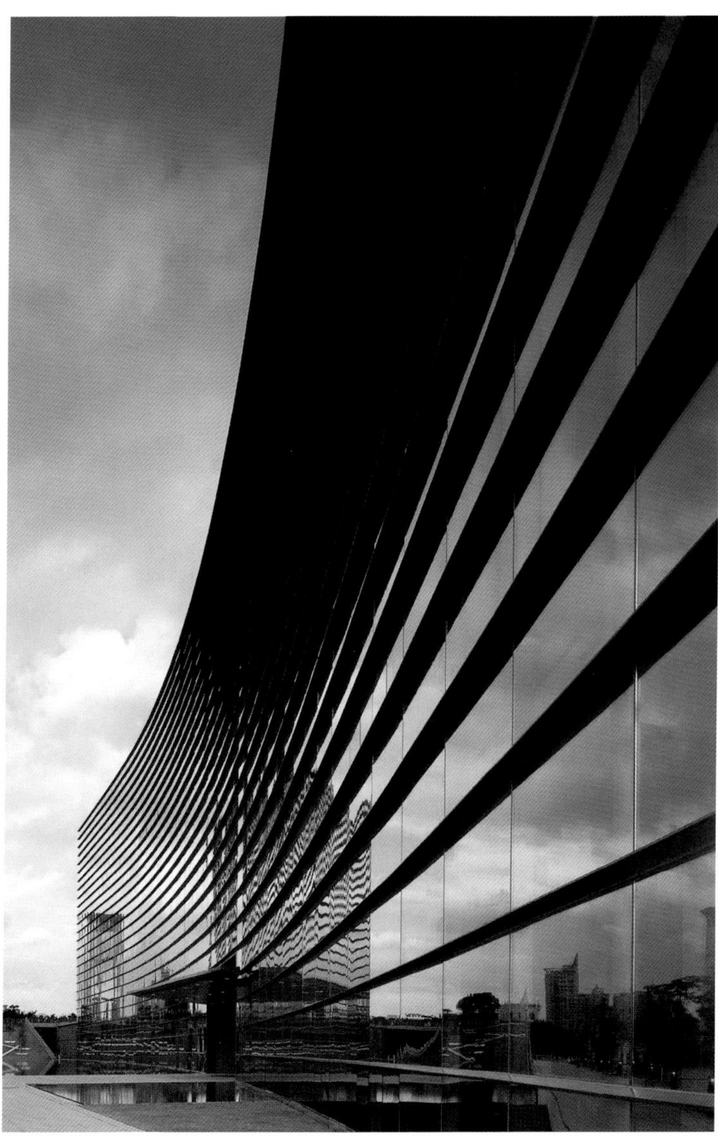

0959

In contrast to the rigid, closed, and pompous attitude typical of government buildings, this design for the Shenzhen Planning Bureau stresses openness, transparency, and modesty. As a means of achieving openness, an intimate connection between the building and the ground is emphasized so as to make the entrance of the building an unconscious extension of the surrounding environment. The transparency of the building's image is not only materialized by the widespread application of glass, but also by interlocked parts in a transparent spatial arrangement.

0960

The project around Vanke Experience Center is to create a three-story exhibition space to show the latest impressive, innovative product designs from the research group, as well as to provide a place to communicate and share the experience of the products with users. Vanke wants an encouraging, inspiring, and stimulating space within the existing hollowed lobby.

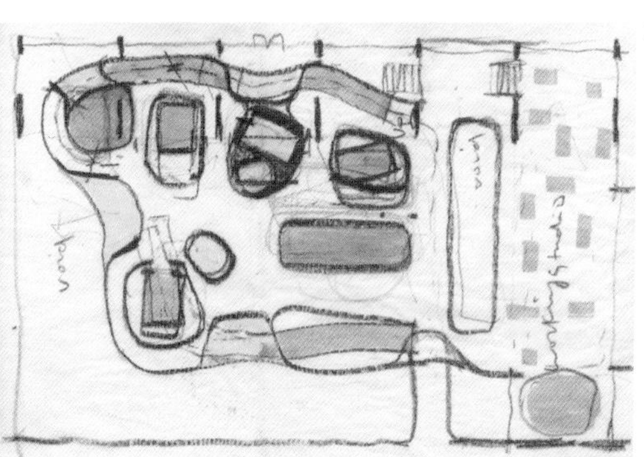

X-Architects

105, Bldg-47, DHCC
Dubai, United Arab Emirates
P.: (+971) 4-429-8309
www.xarchitects.com

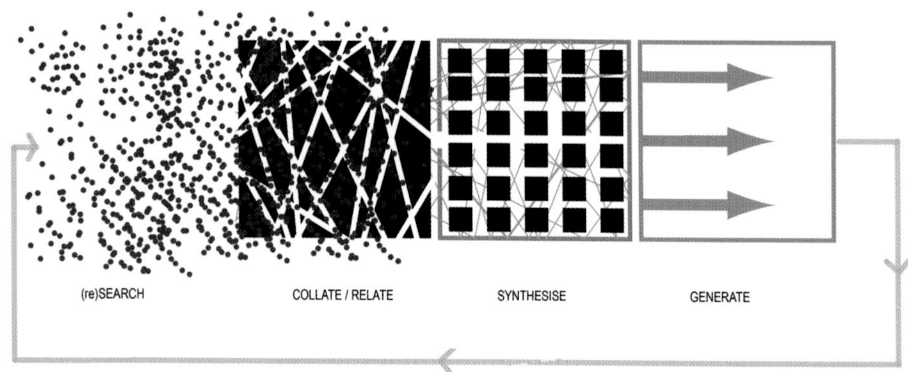

0961▼

Tectonic simplicity
Capturing a complex programmatic and spatial experience in a simplified and readable tectonic design is the biggest challenge faced by architects. This single family residence uses minimal, strategically located planar geometries to define and delineate spaces.

0962▲

Ideogram
Generating ideas and exploiting their potential are the two main components of creative design. Our design *modus operandi* is to first search—unrestrictedly—for ideas, inspirations, and insights into the matter at hand, then look for relations and dependencies between them, which can be filtered and synthesized. This cyclical process clarifies the design issues at every stage and helps to generate mature strategies.

0963

Interoperability
The essence of interoperability is generating a spatial fluidity that encourages a lifestyle with equal emphasis on interior and exterior activity. The generously sized outer decks on the house boat enable the interior to flow outside and vice versa.

0964

Spatial layering
Nested forms provide a rich experiential discovery in which the transitions between the different layers are a highlight of the programmatic and landscape elements. Layering can also be used as a tool in arid weather locations in order to create shading and protect inner volumes.

0965

Cross programming
Collaborative design has opened the doors of architecture to encompass a variety of design arenas. The house boat is one such example; here, architectural sensibilities were injected into a nautical theme to create a seafaring home.

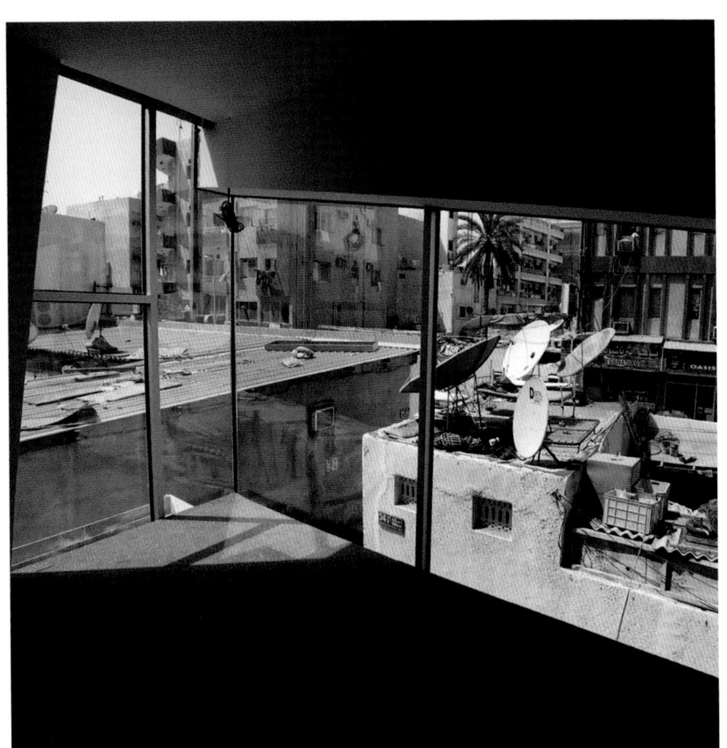

0966

Urban relationships
Infill sites set an interesting challenge for architects to respond to changed urban settings. This showroom project responds to its surroundings by strategically placing faceted openings that capture the most vibrant elements in its urban context.

0967

Contextual response
The exterior façade system of the showroom utilizes a new understanding of spatial and surface geometry. Individual panels, based on the programmatic and urban scenarios, clad the building mass while also maintaining an overall coherence.

0968

Materiality
The façade of the building is not only a protection, but also a public exhibit; it is the first interactive part of the building. This sales center uses perforated skin as a branding tool by skillfully repeating the client's logo. Changes in internal and external lighting provide subtle changes to the building's character and animate the façade.

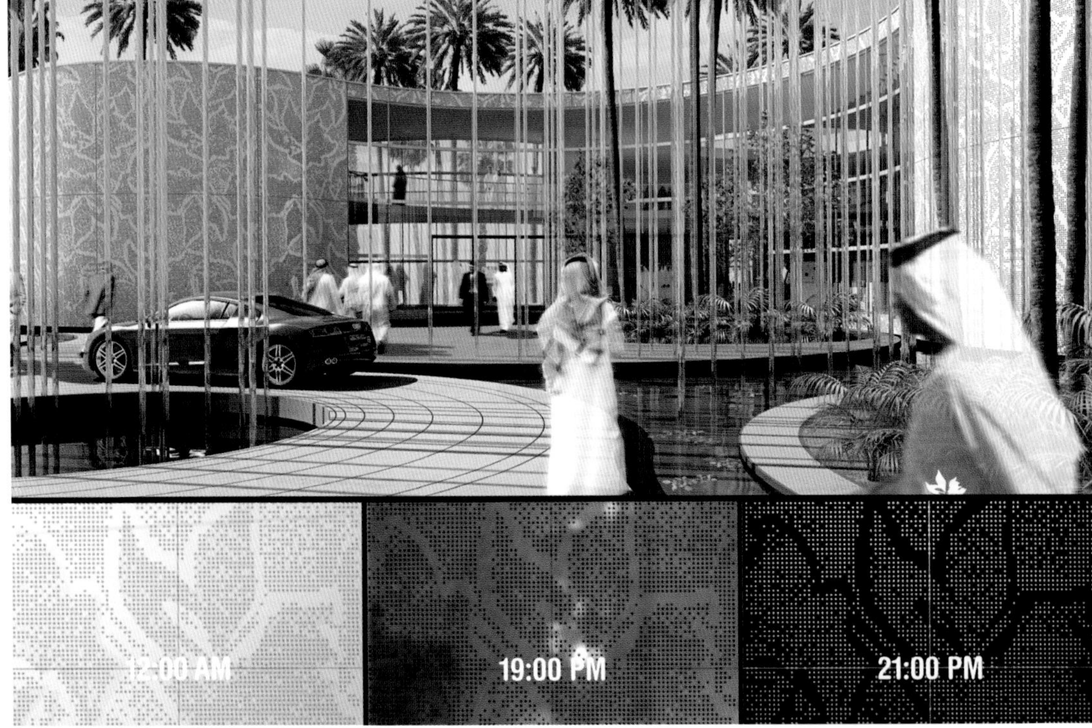

0969

(Re)active living

The design of the architectural typologies in this urban creation is determined by the search for solutions, focusing both on resource-saving principles and on creating a pleasant environment for social interaction. The solutions are climatically active on all scales of the building block, dwelling and façade. The pedestrian permeability enables inhabitants to benefit both physically and visually from the proximity to the landscape.

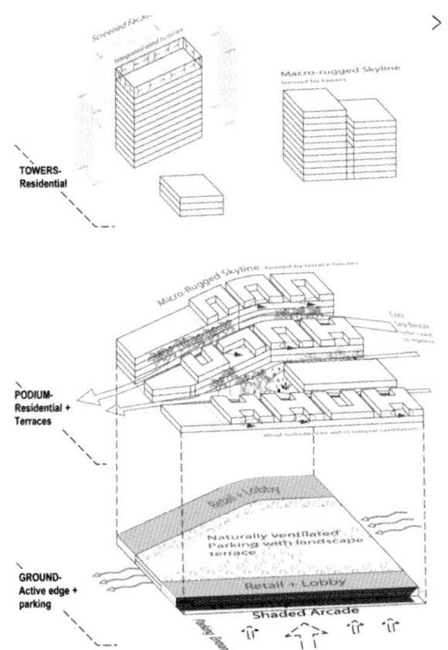

0970

Climatic response

Designing outdoor spaces for a hot climate requires careful planning to ensure that they are properly utilized throughout the year. This urban design employs shading structures that double as solar collectors, providing up to 80% shading in exterior public spaces.

oslund. and. assoc. landscape architects

115 Washington Ave. N Suite 200
Minneapolis, MN 55401, USA
P.: (+1) 612-359-9144
www.oaala.com

0971

Panoramic views are afforded on the journey up the mound.

© Michael Mingo

0972

The Gold Medal Park creates a foreground for the Guthrie Theater while responding to the surrounding context of the Mississippi river valley.

© Michael Mingo

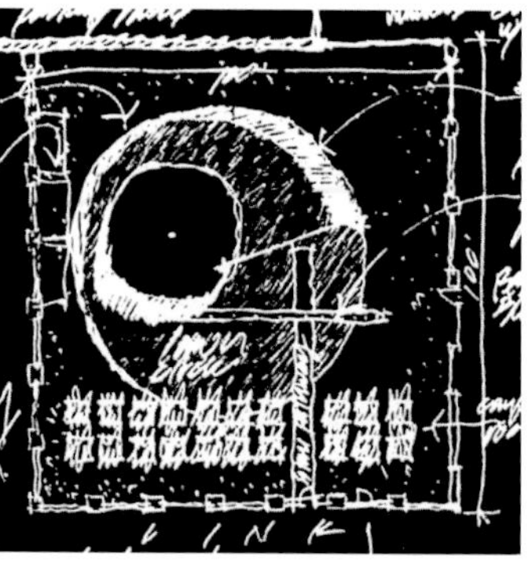

0973

Patent Garden: simple, balanced, and beautiful.

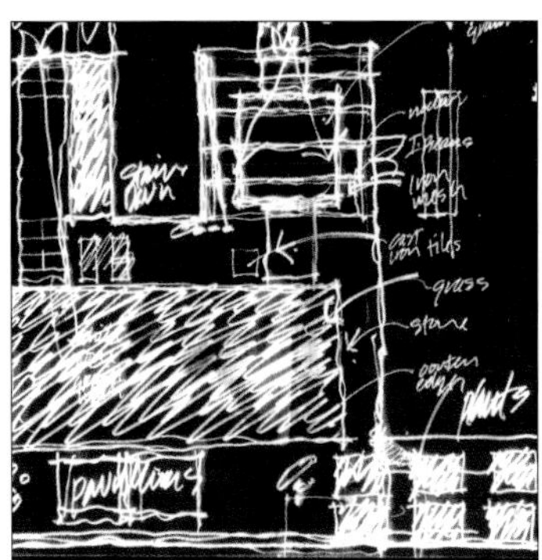

0974

Floating planes define the elements of the garden with the major space defined by a floating grass field.

0975

Native mounds found along the river valley, and its surrounding drainage patterns, inspire the diagrams.

© George Heinrich

0976

The idea of a wild rice garden grounds itself in the topography, becoming a display laboratory for the new science building.

0977

Science on display.

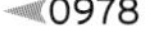0978

At Medtronic Patent Garden, the Corten wall embraces and holds the space providing its backdrop.

0979

Benches utilized as light fixtures dance throughout the park.

0980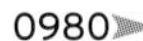

The garden coexists with the interior spaces of the living units creating both a physical and visual symbiotic relationship.

UNStudio

© Miranda Koopman

Stadhouderskade 113
1073 Amsterdam, The Netherlands
P.: (+31) 20-570-2040
www.unstudio.com

0981

You can always renew, reinvent, and rediscover things about buildings. New production techniques and materials are constantly evolving and leading to design innovations. But we also find inspiration in new uses, effects, and concepts.

© Christian Richters

0982

Innovation exists! You just have to accept that today, innovation is impossible on your own. Real, significant innovation occurs when several people simultaneously have the same idea and move in the same direction. Experiment by working with others, including other architects. What do you have to lose?

© Christian Richters

0983

Thank God that architecture is not art. Architects suffer less from self-imposed restrictions and instructions than artists. Of course architects labor under the same yoke as anyone else. The architect faces the client and engages with questions of utility, economy, and construction. The fact that the architectural search for form is invested with so many questions and demands makes it easy.

© Christian Richters

© Christian Richters

0984

The good thing about producing a building is that people continue interacting with it for a long time, much more so than with a new film or novel. The product of architecture can at least be partly understood as an endless live performance. The project transforms, becomes abstracted, concentrated and expanded, diverse and ever more scaleless. The true nature of architecture is found in the interaction between the architect, the project, and the public.

0985

Thank God that architecture is art. Or is at least halfway art, tracing movement patterns and user groups, and the various virtual and infrastructural ways in which we distribute ourselves across the globe. Yet what does it all mean? These numbers tell us too little about the motives triggering these patterns, or about the effects of these structures and constellations. We end up sculpting the statistics, painting with information in bold, brutal brushstrokes or refined minimalist gestures, just like any old artist.

© Christian Richters

0986

More often than not Architects are disciplined and relatively humble. Being closely related to engineers, the traits of perseverance and patience run deep in the architectural personality. If you allow your true self to come forward, you will discover a surprisingly accommodating, even faintly servile side to yourself that finds pleasure in servicing the infinitely more complex character of the client.

© Christian Richters

© Christian Richters

0987

The practice of architecture occupies a privileged position in the roving, capitalist-driven contemporary world of work. You can be an architect on your own, with a small atelier, with a huge factory-type design studio, or operate within a network. You can be good, bad, or mediocre. However you choose to exercise your profession, you are sustained by your training and your unique expertise, which still comes down to a combination of ancient ways of thinking and modern material knowledge.

0988

We can go to the core of our understanding of time and space, and discover processes that, in themselves, discover proliferation instead of atrophy as a paradigm for architecture.

© Christian Richters

© Michael Moran

0989

Don't be shy! When all is said and done architecture does take up a lot of space, so the least you can do is say something. Make a statement, put across an idea. It is the construction manager's role to be the silent hero; the architect's to be Donald Duck, the desperate chatterer full of bright ideas.

0990

It's over; you may never have to do another building or another project again. In the present day "the building" is a rarity. In seventeen years we realized only three houses and two museums; the other projects that made it into reality were all hybrids, complex packages of needs and desires relating to urban life, transportation, and mixed program uses. But that does not mean you have to disappear as an architect. Few people have been trained to cultivate the encompassing imagining powers that architects possess. In the complex situations that characterize today's densely populated, increasingly urbanized sites, which are increasingly striated by infrastructural connections and hubs, those imagining skills are vital.

Pezo von Ellrichshausen Arquitectos

Lo Pequen 502
4070376 Concepcion, Chile
P.: (+56) 41-221-0281
www.pezo.cl

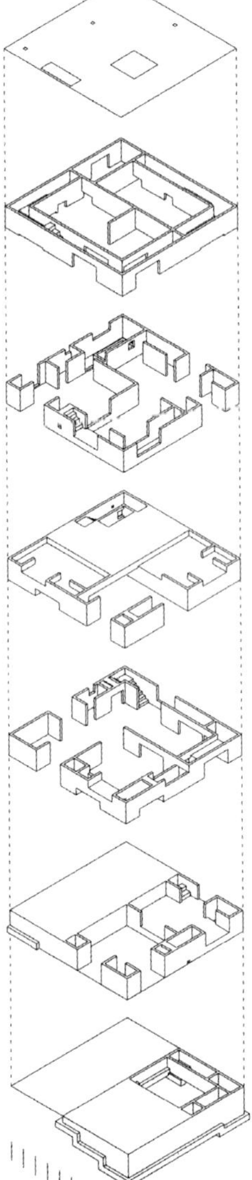

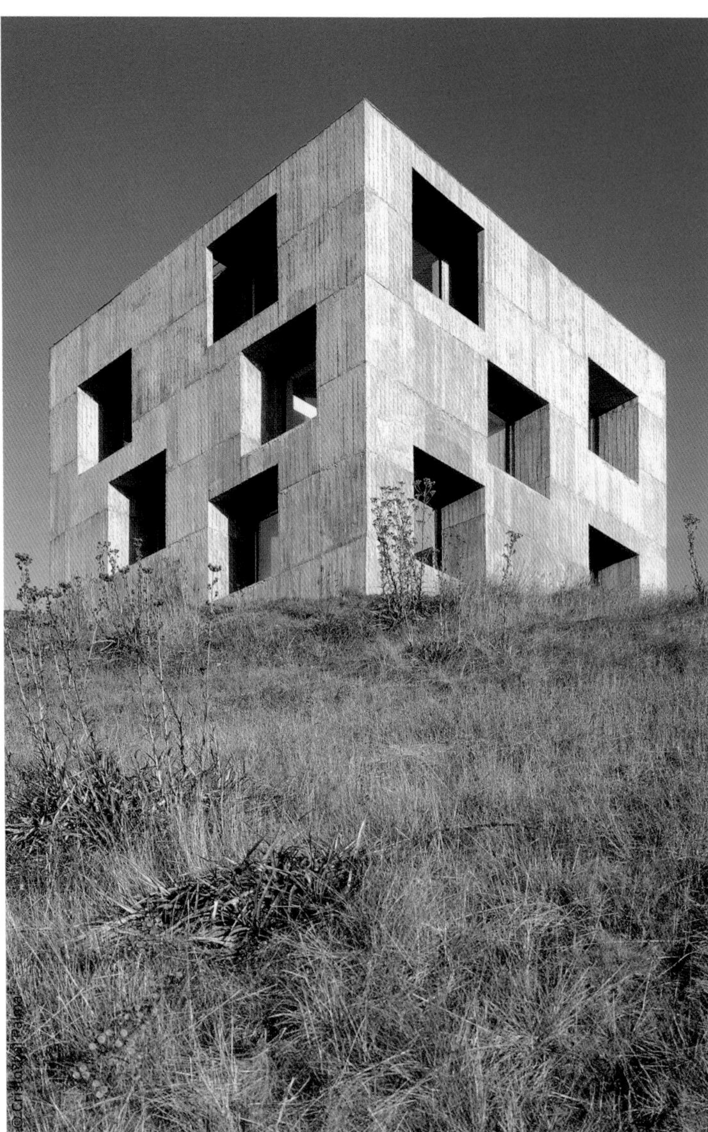

◄0991

The entire dwelling is constructed from hand-mixed cement and natural wood formwork using just one small cement mixer and four wheelbarrows. The house is arranged in horizontal layers, matching the mix emptying levels, measured with a half board panel.

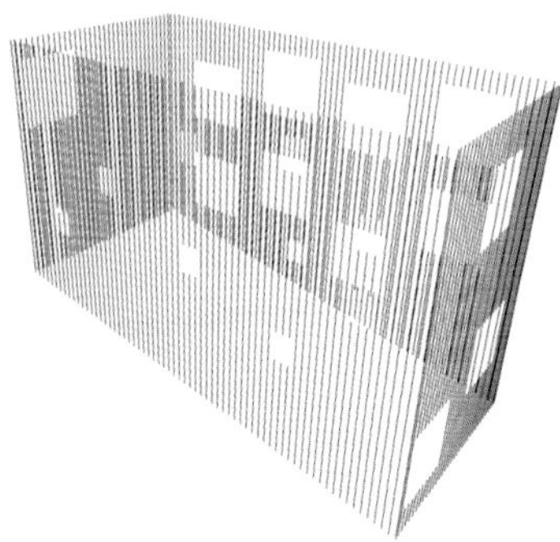

0992▲

The external surface of Casa Rivo is covered by a layer of natural pine cladding and vertical joint covers, finished in the black carbon oil that is traditionally used in local rural constructions.

0993

Once the main body of the work was finished, we reutilized all the formwork wood to clad the interior walls and make sliding panels, which alternately cover the perimeter of the service area, and protect the windows when the house is empty. The furniture and domestic equipment can be stored within the perimeter space, freeing the interior for a variety of activities.

0994

The service areas, the vertical transit spiral, and the various storage spaces confine the oppressive lateral distances of the site. Longitudinally, the two largest rooms occupy the ends on different levels. The rear is devoted to the social spaces, which are connected to the ground. Toward the front, is the area for gatherings that are more family-orientated and informal.

0995

As well as occupying the residual deltas left by the tilted walls, the vertical structure is faceted with slight diagonal deviations that do everything possible to avoid overlooking the closest neighbors and to make the most of the space in the two small, fallow garden spaces.

0996

The labyrinth-like irregular structure, together with the variations in the size and proximity between the rooms, contains nine open-air courtyards. These are like nine clearings that help to organize the density of the floor plan.

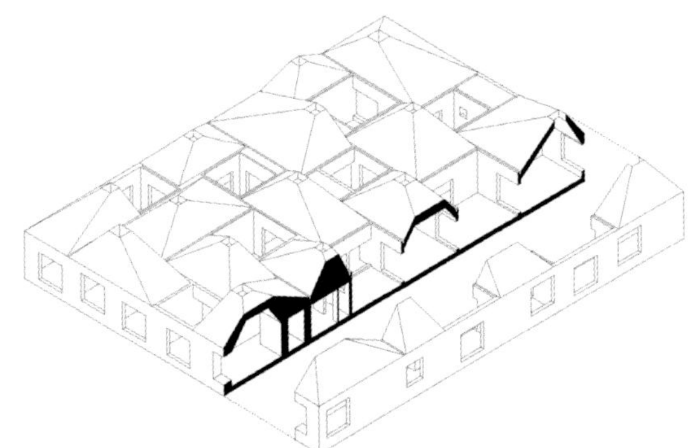

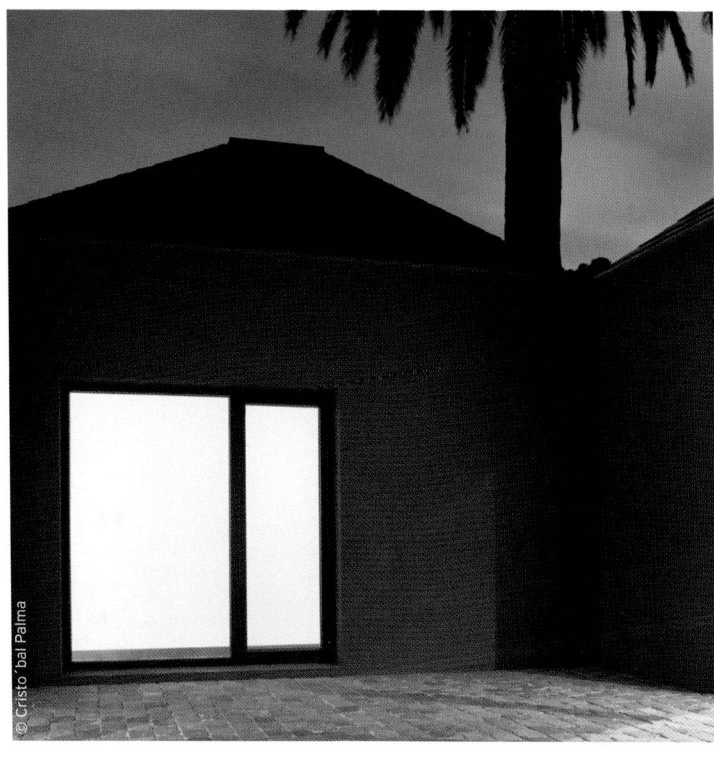

© Cristo´bal Palma

0997

The floor is on one level. Spaciousness of some was achieved by raising the roof to double the height, preventing courtyard shading. To enable this, the roofs, which always descend down to the courtyards, were tilted, shading only the walls. The roofs were also dissected at the top, allowing natural lighting to enter the space in accordance with the different programmatic needs.

0998

The weight of a tiled skin—that somehow evokes the old timber mansion—falls from these fourteen truncated prisms. The only way of removing the joints from its ridges was by using small metal parts to keep with the industrial and traditional character of its surface.

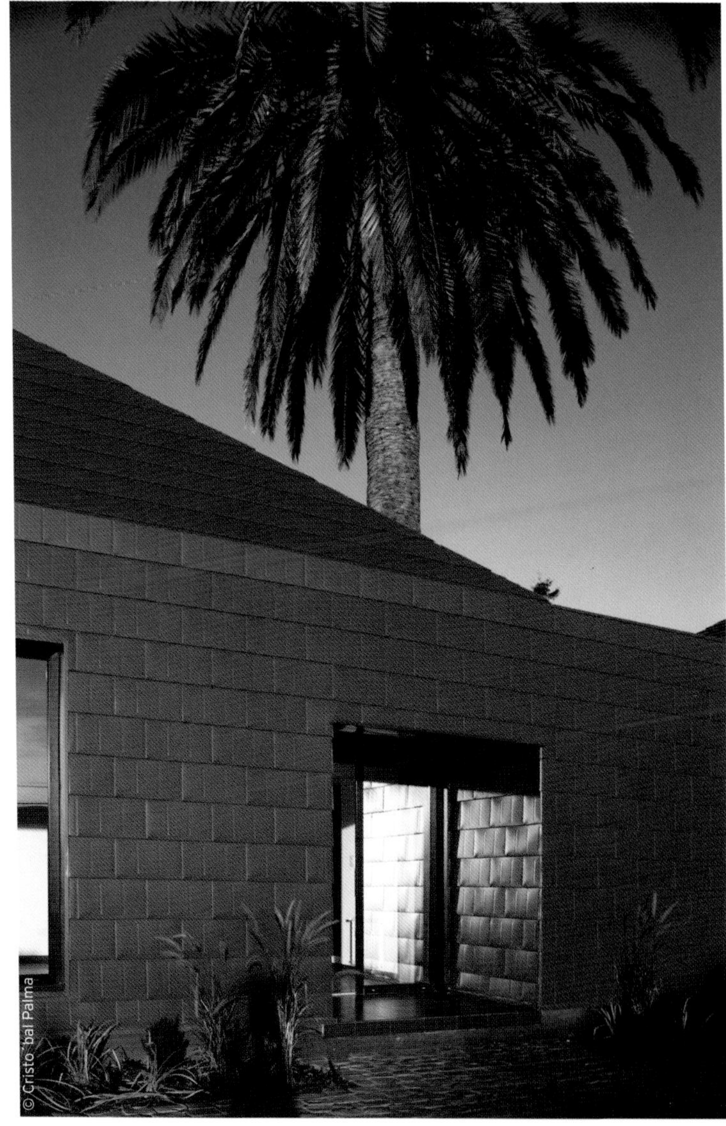

© Cristo´bal Palma

0999

The skin is a vertical continuous texture accompanying the falling rain. It has a bronze hue that changes with the varying natural lighting and is hardly broken by the clean cut frameless windows, smooth to the exterior lead fittings.

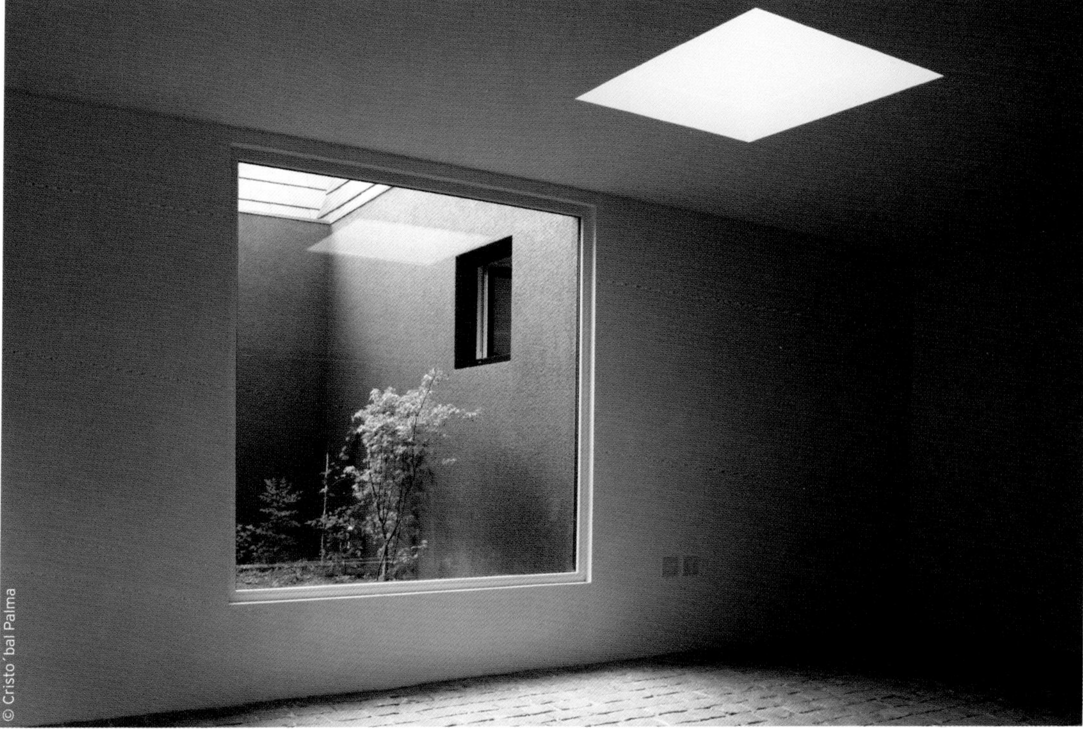

1000

In the exterior spaces, there are no other visually appealing elements. The program of Casa Parr is therefore arranged horizontally, running deeply into the tree-filled gardens, taking on a rather profound introspection with an invisible exterior presence.